MW00338095

WHY
BHARAT
MATTERS

WHY BHARAT MATTERS

S. JAISHANKAR

RUPA

Published by
Rupa Publications India Pvt. Ltd 2024
7/16, Ansari Road, Daryaganj
New Delhi 110002

Sales centres:
Bengaluru Chennai Hyderabad
Jaipur Kathmandu Kolkata
Mumbai Prayagraj

Copyright © S. Jaishankar 2024

The views and opinions expressed in this book are the author's own and
the facts are as reported by him which have been verified to the extent possible,
and the publishers are not in any way liable for the same.

All rights reserved.
No part of this publication may be reproduced, transmitted,
or stored in a retrieval system, in any form or by any means,
electronic, mechanical, photocopying, recording or otherwise,
without the prior permission of the publisher.

P-ISBN: 978-93-5702-760-1
E-ISBN: 978-93-5702-640-6

Fifth impression 2024

10 9 8 7 6 5

The moral right of the author has been asserted.

Printed in India

This book is sold subject to the condition that it shall not,
by way of trade or otherwise, be lent, resold, hired out, or otherwise
circulated, without the publisher's prior consent, in any form of binding
or cover other than that in which it is published.

CONTENTS

LIST OF ABBREVIATIONS

AI	Artificial Intelligence
APEC	Asia-Pacific Economic Cooperation
ARF	ASEAN Regional Forum
ASEAN	Association of South-East Asian Nations
AU	African Union
BJP	Bharatiya Janata Party
BIMSTEC	Bay of Bengal Initiative for Multi-Sectoral Technical and Economic Cooperation
BRI	Belt and Road Initiative
BRICS	Brazil, Russia, India, China, South Africa
CARICOM	Caribbean Community
CDRI	Coalition for Disaster Resilient Infrastructure
CELAC	Community of Latin American and Caribbean States
CEPA	Comprehensive Economic Partnership Agreement
CET	Critical and Emerging Technologies
CM	Chief Minister
CPEC	China–Pakistan Economic Corridor
CTC	Counter-Terrorism Committee
EAM	External Affairs Minister
ECTA	Economic Cooperation and Trade Agreement
EU	European Union
FDI	Foreign Direct Investment
FIPIC	Forum for India–Pacific Islands Cooperation
FTA	Free Trade Agreement
GCC	Gulf Cooperation Council
GDP	Gross Domestic Product
HADR	Humanitarian Assistance and Disaster Relief
I2U2	India, Israel, the United Arab Emirates, the United States of America

IAFS	India-Africa Forum Summit
IBSA	India, Brazil, South Africa
ICWF	Indian Community Welfare Fund
IFF	Identification Friend or Foe
IGN	Intergovernmental Negotiations
IMEC	India–Middle East–Europe Economic Corridor
IPMDA	Indo-Pacific Partnership for Maritime Domain Awareness
IOC	Indian Ocean Commission
IPOI	Indo-Pacific Oceans Initiative
IORA	Indian Ocean Rim Association
IPEF	Indo-Pacific Economic Framework
ISA	International Solar Alliance
IT	Information Technology
IUU	Illegal, Unreported and Unregulated
LIFE	Lifestyle for Environment
LAC	Line of Actual Control
LDC	Least Developed Country
LWE	Left Wing Extremism
MMPA	Migration and Mobility Partnership Agreement
NSG	Nuclear Suppliers Group
ODA	Official Development Assistance
O-RAN	Open Radio Access Networks
OSOWOG	One Sun One World One Grid
PIF	Pacific Islands Forum
PLA	People's Liberation Army
PLI	Production-Linked Incentive
PoK	Pakistan-Occupied Kashmir
PPE	Personal Protective Equipment
PRAGATI	Pro-Active Governance and Timely Implementation
PRC	People's Republic of China
PM	Prime Minister
RCEP	Regional Comprehensive Economic Partnership
RIC	Russia-India-China
SAARC	South Asian Association for Regional Cooperation
SAGAR	Security and Growth for All in the Region

SCO	Shanghai Cooperation Organization
SCRI	Supply Chain Resilience Initiative
SDG	Sustainable Development Goals
SME	Small and Medium Enterprise
SOP	Standard Operating Procedure
SPICE	Smart, Precise Impact, Cost-Effective
SR	Special Representative
UAE	United Arab Emirates
UK	United Kingdom
UNCLOS	United Nations Convention on the Law of the Sea
UNFCCC	United Nations Framework Convention on Climate Change
UNGA	United Nations General Assembly
UN	United Nations
UNSC	United Nations Security Council
US	United States of America
USSR	Union of Soviet Socialist Republics
WHO	World Health Organization
WTO	World Trade Organization

PREFACE

For the last decade, I have had not just a ringside view of foreign policymaking, but the privilege to participate in the process as well. As External Affairs Minister (EAM) and previously as Foreign Secretary and Ambassador to the US, the analysis, debates and strategizing of this period are exercises in which I have been deeply involved. It is not my intention to pen my memoirs, certainly not while still in the midst of discharging responsibilities. But because this has been a deeply transformational era, it is also imperative that an objective explanation of the changes is provided to the public. The analytical world appears to be tangled in its own pre-conceptions and struggling to grasp developments that do not fit its mould. The political arena has become exceptionally polemical, with some parties articulating positions that go against their own grain. The burden of communicating, in that sense, falls on the actual participants. With an earlier experience of presenting my thoughts, there was a natural inclination to take up this challenge. This is the thought process behind this book.

My own background as a diplomat well into a fifth decade biases me in favour of presenting a clinical picture of the global landscape, its challenges and complications as well as of the implications for India and a suggested course of action. This is what I have done for a living all these years. It is not that we avoid personalities and relationships or underplay their importance. On the contrary, so much of diplomacy is about chemistry and credibility that the human factor is always central to an accurate judgement. But what usually happens is that a vast number of objective and subjective elements are distilled into an integrated picture, which acquires a relatively dispassionate character.

In this particular endeavour, I contemplated a world that is struggling with economic disruptions, the Covid pandemic, the Ukraine conflict, an exploding West Asia (Middle East) and sharpening great power competition, and sought to assess India's prospects in ascending the global hierarchy in such volatile conditions. That exercise brought home to me how much we have progressed in the preceding years and how differently we are now seen as compared to the era before 2014. India has today moved out of the defensive non-aligned posture, engaging multiple nations on a range of issues with equal confidence. It is also a greater contributor to solutions, regional or global. This marks its emergence as *vishwa mitra*, a partner of the world that is making a greater difference with each passing year. The New Delhi G20 Summit not only affirmed our ability to shape the global agenda but also underlined that other nations value their relationship with us as well.

The problem with a purely detached examination is that it is unable to convey the full flavour of this transformation. Moreover, it could suggest that there was an inevitability about it, thereby neglecting the power of ideas and the importance of leadership. A truly accurate understanding of the journey we have been through and the possibilities that await us requires a personalized picture as well. Some of it involves the granular aspects of the diplomatic process, but much emanates from the personal views and thoughts of Prime Minister (PM) Narendra Modi. So, after some hesitation, I decided to prefix this book with a preface that would give the reader a glimpse of how policies were formulated and decisions taken.

My personal acquaintance with Narendra Modi began in 2011, when I was Ambassador in China and he was the Chief Minister (CM) of Gujarat. While awaiting his visit, I was struck by the meticulousness of preparations and his interest to assess China's progress in different fields. It was apparent to me even then that he envisaged developments in both India and China in terms of civilizational resurgence. What also stood out was his request for a political briefing since he did not wish to deviate from what were national positions while abroad. Terrorism and sovereignty understandably were the focus, given the agenda of our ties.

It was also my first exposure to a working style that emphasized comprehensive briefings and constant feedback. My cumulative impression was one of strong nationalism, great purposefulness and deep attention to detail. His openness to the ideas and experiences of others was also manifest. Those few days spent together allowed me to express my own thoughts on comparative modernization in Asia and gauge his own views. He was clearly impressed by the economic and technology advancements of Japan but also by their social cohesion and cultural pride. I also have a recollection of him speaking well about the leadership quality of Lee Kuan Yew. It was no surprise that he made it a point to attend his funeral later on in 2015. Occasionally, I have reflected on this first encounter because there were pointers there about his strong views on terrorism, his forthright manner of putting across national concerns and his focus on socio-economic advancement. It also gave me a glimpse of a thinking that, after 2014, would drive the endeavour towards cultural rebalancing.

The second contact was an indirect one, around the time of the 2014 general election. It was widely speculated even ahead of the counting that there could be a change of guard. As Ambassador in Washington, D.C., it was my duty to plan for all contingencies. Discreet preparations were accordingly made for an early phone conversation between President Barack Obama and the Indian PM-designate. In this particular case, there was more than just logistical and protocol issues to worry about. Addressing the overhang from the past was clearly a significant concern. In the event, this was effectively finessed. But the episode does bring out PM Modi's instinct to put national interest ahead and take a strategic approach towards a potentially important partner.

Any account of this period must necessarily include a reference to the Madison Square Garden event in 2014. This is not so much because of the event in itself but because it began a trend in diaspora connection and public projection that continues to this day. In my first meeting with PM Modi, the idea came up in the context of the impact of the diaspora and shaping India's image abroad. I was essentially told that the gathering must be organized in New York in such a manner that its reverberations would first reach Washington, D.C., and then be a message across the world. Since that experience, this has emerged as a signature aspect of Modi diplomacy that has travelled successfully across nations and continents. Leaders of the democratic world are obviously enthralled and often keen to participate. From Denmark and Japan to Africa and Australia, this is seen akin to a political rock concert.

For the diaspora, it has been a motivation and recognition at the same time. And not least, this has emerged as a high-profile platform to share the 'India Story' with the world, constantly refreshing it with updates. This concern for the diaspora itself emerges from a combination of factors. It expresses appreciation for their continued contribution to India's welfare. At the same time, enthusing them does encourage efforts to make their society of domicile more interested in India. But there is also the deeper issue of preparing Indians for the era of a global workplace. This requires facilitating their mobility, enhancing their ease of living abroad, addressing specific concerns of students, professionals, etc., and, most important, standing by them at times of distress. In line with actions in other domains, here too, declarations have been backed by delivery. The PM has taken a particular interest in the establishment of online portals, welfare funds and response systems for such contingencies.

There is a lot that is personal about diplomacy, particularly at the leadership level. One of the visible achievements of PM Modi has been the ability to establish the right chemistry with his international peers. It could vary from Western leaders to Gulf rulers, from democratic politicians to those less cyclical, and from those proximate to India to others from a very different ethos. There is no set formula, but one can see that many relationships emerged from exchange of experiences and respect for achievements. Like any competitive domain, those who are doing well, be it in popularity rating, source of ideas or governance delivery, tend to naturally attract the interest and admiration of others. But it could also be something more personal or cultural. For example, PM Modi's discipline of fasting was a major talking point during his 2014 visit to the US, and even afterwards. It elicited a lot of curiosity about the underlying outlook as well. Similarly, his propagation of yoga and his own practice of it was often a subject of conversation with fellow leaders. And this extended from food habits and traditional medicine to culture, heritage and history, to the extent that as these encounters left their impressions, India too ended up occupying greater mind-space.

Then, there was the influence of ideas and thoughts that PM Modi often articulated on contemporary issues. The United Nations (UN) Climate Change Conference (COP21) in Paris in 2015 was such an occasion, where he surprised many with his fervent advocacy of solar energy. In fact, some Western leaders came to meet him expecting that they would have to argue for climate action. They ended up finding India a few steps ahead of their own beliefs. It is interesting that many of the big thoughts of the last decade in this domain have come personally from PM Modi, including at the Glasgow COP26 in 2021.

Another aspect of relevance is how much Modi's focus on technology has contributed to forging connections across the world. Initially, it began with global interest in how his 2014 campaign was shaped by its application. But soon enough, it extended to governance practices and policy drivers. The manner in which digital delivery worked for social welfare or Covid management was certainly noted internationally. Leakages, I was often reminded, is not a uniquely Indian problem. As we made moves in various scientific fields, from semiconductors and renewables to drones and aircraft technology, a tech-friendly PM contributed to the perception of India as a trusted collaborator.

There are some issues that could be put in the category of core beliefs. Standing up to terrorism would certainly rank high among them. After my initial exposure to that in Beijing in 2011, whenever the occasion warranted, it was made abundantly clear that we would not allow cross-border terrorism to be normalized under any circumstances. When Uri happened in 2016, there was little doubt among us internally that we would respond in a

fitting manner. I was not in government during Balakot in 2019
but can only say that it was very much in keeping with character.
At the UN, we have consequently pushed strongly for sanctioning
of terrorists. And when others have sought to block it for some
political objective, there has been no hesitation in calling them
out publicly. As a member of the UN Security Council (UNSC) in
October 2022, we organized a meeting of the Counter Terrorism
Committee (CTC) in Mumbai at one of the venues of the 26/11
terror attack. India has also been a strong votary of initiatives like
'No Money for Terror'. From a foreign policy perspective, it is, of
course, always advantageous to be functioning with clear objectives
and firm instructions. This was also the case when it came to
engaging the world on the Article 370 issue. A nationalist outlook
will naturally produce a nationalist diplomacy, and it is something
that the world will need to get used to.

Economic priorities at home will always be a powerful driver
of policies abroad. Enabling the flow of resources and absorbing
best practices have acquired even greater priority in recent years.
In many ways, PM Modi has led from the front by engaging
entrepreneurs, visiting technology centres and seeking to promote
innovation and skills. In all of this, employment creation and
talent promotion remain his focus. His travels abroad often feature
visits to institutions and activities that are relevant to our national
flagship programmes. One can sense a strong determination to
accelerate India's growth and build further its comprehensive
national power. On occasion, it can mean going against orthodox
thinking and global mantras. A relevant case was that of joining
the Regional Comprehensive Economic Partnership (RCEP) in
2019. Despite considerable pressure, PM Modi took the courageous
call to not accede. Since then, that decision has been more than
amply validated by geopolitical developments. There have been
other trade and economic negotiations that have each presented
their dilemmas. Our positions have been guided by clear-eyed
calculation and sound gut instincts about social consequences.

Yet, it would be a gross mistake to project the Modi government
in protectionist terms. On the contrary, rarely in our history have

more strenuous efforts been made to attract global capital and technology. Where our partners have offered reasonable terms and met our national interests, bargains have been struck often at remarkable speed. There is a much sounder appreciation of the complexity of the global economy, especially of its intricate supply chains. And the internationalism of outlook has been demonstrated convincingly, whether it is the Vaccine Maitri, first responder operations or expanded development partnerships.

If India's diplomacy appears more nimble and creative now, much of the credit should go to a leader who has consciously striven to make it more contemporary and responsive. The whole 'Neighbourhood First' thinking developed from the 2014 swearing-in ceremony and his personal experiences. This idea of a non-reciprocal and generous policy took time for a bureaucracy to absorb, but it did finally get through. The Security and Growth for All in the Region (SAGAR) outlook was an effort to break long-standing silos even within the foreign ministry. When it came to the Gulf, there were decades of lazy assumptions in India about their lack of interest that had to be overcome. With Israel and Palestine, we have ended practising a hyphenation that we resented when applied to us. Moreover, India also made a distinction between its position on the need for a Palestinian state and its clear-cut condemnation of terrorism. The focus on opening new embassies in Africa and engaging more deeply was putting into practice what had been preached for long. As for the Pacific, till 2014, it was really beyond our horizons. The aggregate of all these changes, when stitched together with a cohesive global analysis, presents a very different picture.

While implementing policy is a daily chore, there are decisions taken from time to time that represent inflection points in the rise of a nation. India naturally has been subjected to its own set of tests and challenges on this score. And it has been the decisions taken under difficult circumstances that have become the hallmark of difference. A significant one was the decision even in the midst of the Covid lockdown to mobilize and deploy forces on a large scale in the border areas with China. Tens of thousands of troops with accompanying equipment were rapidly airlifted in a decisive step. This was in response to Chinese military movements that violated our long-standing agreements. Not just that, thereafter, fashioning a diplomatic posture to convey the abnormality in our ties in a sustained manner was no small matter.

Then, there was the establishment of the Quad and its steady growth, both in protocol terms and agenda. This, too, was taken forward despite strong pressures to desist. I have already made a reference to the call taken in Bangkok to not join the RCEP. When it came to oil purchases from Russia, India was being publicly pressurized by those who had softened the consequences for themselves. Each of this was decided by putting the interests of India first.

There were also occasions that involved larger concerns of a regional or global nature. One was to take the call to supply vaccines to the Global South even when vaccination was ongoing in India. Another was the scale and speed with which India responded to Sri Lanka's pressing economic needs. Interestingly, when the I2U2 and India–Middle East–Europe Economic Corridor (IMEC) initiatives were tabled, we surprised our other partners by the swiftness of our response, precisely because our analysis of the region anticipated their coming.

An early exhortation within the Modi government was to get the world to change its thinking about India. This meant building and demonstrating capabilities across a wide spectrum. It required us to be involved in key global debates and be perceived more as part of the solution than the problem. Another expectation was that India would assume greater responsibilities and make stronger contributions. From our side, we strove for better understanding of the various dimensions of transformation of our society. Our endeavour was also to establish India as a more credible and trusted partner. Each of these factors became an input into the influence game that characterizes international relations. Bringing them all together means creating a different narrative, one that captures the progress while articulating the future. This is very much central to the projection of the message of a New India.

The diplomacy of a major country is very arduous, even more so when it is a rising power. Leadership and conceptual clarity may make it easier to be executed. But arriving at a comprehensive vision and refreshing that regularly is no easy task. If our international profile has become sharper in the last decade, this is the outcome of a series of policies, decisions and activities. Visions and even goals need strategizing to be realized on the ground. This means interactions, investments and messaging in a focussed and sustained manner. What the public sees is an elegant swan; underneath, there is furious paddling.

The most noticeable feature of PM Modi's work style is the ability to constantly integrate the big picture and the smallest of details. He could be as immersed in briefings about chip wars or energy futures as in handling of evacuation operations or in the value of a best practice. Every visit, every speech and every engagement has a meaning; they end up as one part of a larger mosaic. Some of what is debated and decided responds to the demand of events. But the more persistent thread is of determinedly charting a strategic course and adjusting that to the unpredictability of our times. It would probably surprise many to learn how much time and effort has gone into that larger exercise over the last decade. The unfolding may look natural and often spontaneous, but the reality is actually one of continuous planning and implementation.

The 'what' and the 'how' of Modi's foreign policy is there for all to see. The 'why' is a more complex proposition, one that is perhaps sensed intuitively by the public. Much of it flows from a strongly ingrained belief in India's capability to contribute to a better world. It resides in a self-perception of a well-wisher to the world, for whom the international community is a family, clearly a more confident posture than in the past. But that itself is only a facet of a deeper commitment to national rejuvenation and the resurgence of a civilization. At home, they obviously take the form of building capabilities, undertaking reform and enhancing the quality of governance. Abroad, this is expressed in terms of a greater ability to influence the global agenda. This outlook is able to meld progressive thinking and embrace of technology comfortably with the traditions and authenticity of India. And it sees no contradiction in espousing internationalism abroad while articulating nationalism at home. This is an India determined to play on the big stage, even change the stage itself where necessary to advance its interests. Its motivational power at home is paralleled by a desire to promote understanding beyond its borders.

This book is a collection of 11 essays, all of them interconnected and some even overlapping. They range from an analysis of the global landscape to an identification of India's opportunities. There is the big picture but also the real practicalities that make up the world. Key relationships are addressed in detail but the entire global framework is presented as well. Some forays take us into the past, others into the future. All together, they seek to explain a decade of change.

India's quest to ascend the global hierarchy is an endless journey. But as we take stock of the progress made and anticipate the challenges ahead, it is certainly reassuring that this is propelled by such deep national commitment and confidence. Whether drawing strength from its heritage and culture or approaching challenges with the optimism of democracy and technology, this is certainly a New India, indeed an India that is able to define its own interests, articulate its own positions, find its own solutions and advance its own model. In short, this is an India that is more Bharat.

1.

PRESENTING A WORLD VIEW

Calculations, Culture and Clarity

Three years ago, in my earlier book *The India Way: Strategies for an Uncertain World,* I had urged that 'this is a time for us to engage America, manage China, cultivate Europe, reassure Russia, bring Japan into play, draw neighbours in, extend the neighbourhood, and expand traditional constituencies of support'.[1] In the period that has passed, much of this has advanced but, obviously, not equally on all fronts. Some have progressed smoothly; others have been more complicated than expected. In the meantime, the world itself has witnessed deeper transformation. The challenges of a global order in transition have been magnified by the back-to-back impact of the Covid pandemic, the Ukraine conflict and the fighting in West Asia.

There is no question that this has now become a much tougher world. For India specifically, the going has been far from easy. Many of the larger concerns have impacted it directly. The changed posture of China on the border, in particular, is a major factor in its strategic calculus. But a determined leadership and a supportive society are helping it to navigate this turbulent era. Rising powers seek stability most of all; India must plan to rise amidst serious unpredictability.

International relations for the last quarter of the century have been dominated by five phenomena: globalization, rebalancing,

---

[1]S. Jaishankar, *The India Way: Strategies for an Uncertain World,* HarperCollins India, 2020.

multipolarity, impact of technology and the games that nations have always played. Globalization, the most fundamental of them, will only intensify, even though its earlier model of creating dependencies has come under growing challenge. It has led to rebalancing the relative weight of players in the world order. That initially unfolded economically, but its political and cultural facets are now making themselves felt. As it proceeds, rebalancing, in turn, will create multipolarity. A new lot of more consequential powers will separate out, joining those dominant since 1945. This is still work in progress, one could even say in the early stages. Much will increasingly depend on how and with what agenda combinations of states come together.

Technology, too, has become more of a game-changer than in the past. Its ability to impact the daily routine is much deeper, as indeed the capability to weaponize our normal activities, needs and resources. In fact, the pace has reached a point where we are compelled to think in terms of 'techades'. And then there are the perennial games that nations play, expressed through competitive politics between individual countries or, sometimes, groupings. Each of these phenomena is a key factor in the fashioning of contemporary Indian foreign policy, individually as much as cumulatively. Today, India has to not just prepare for a re-globalization that corrects economic and technology concentrations but also use that opportunity to strengthen comprehensive national power.

Given that there is at least as much change as there is continuity in world politics, it is obvious that our approach cannot be overly reliant on muscle memory. Certainly, the structural framework and previous experiences have a critical bearing. But, at the same time, the processes described above that are continually shaping our current existence need to be given full recognition. There are important shifts in power between and within states that are also relevant to the overall calculation. Much of that centres on the US, whose dominance is clearly not what it was in the past. That it has changed is indisputable; what it leads to will be still very much a matter of debate. And recent events have demonstrated that neither its capabilities nor its influence should be underestimated. Reading its new posture right is a challenge in itself, especially when it exercises influence in a more off-shore manner. How invested it is in various regions is a natural question, one juxtaposed against the growing presence of other nations, especially China.

Political polarization within societies is also a factor that the diplomacy of many states needs to take into account. Domestic changes, in the US as much as China, are compelling some countries to recalibrate their posture accordingly. As geopolitical arenas go, a world long used to thinking of West Asia and Europe as the central theatres of competition is increasingly looking at the Indo-Pacific instead. Even distant countries are, therefore, compelled to come up with their respective Indo-Pacific approaches. The Ukraine conflict and its energy consequences, significant as they may be, are unlikely to dilute this development.

Each of these trends also had their own resonance on Indian foreign policy. Handling this volatility effectively has required both intensive strategizing and tactical fine-tuning. Our domestic policies not only ensured recovery from the pandemic but also, thereafter, became the basis for Covid diplomacy. In regard to Ukraine, a political posture took into account not only the imperatives of energy and food security but the broader dynamics of Eurasia as well. On China, a robust deployment on the border was accompanied by conscious constraints on cooperation. With Quad partners, we were one of the few nations who made the transition smoothly between successive administrations so different from each other. But there were also important political calls taken at the right time, including the upgradation of the Quad, creating the I2U2 and devising the IMEC.

The exercise of engaging in multiple directions and constantly balancing competitive relationships was also tested in this period. Having invested so much in intensifying cooperation with Europe, harmonizing that with maintaining traditional ties with Russia was not easy. As the North–South divide deepened, undertaking the Voice of the Global South Summit at the commencement of the G20 presidency was a timely move. And when multipolarity continued to unfold, the broadening of India's engagement sought to keep pace.

The factors that drive the choices of nations have also undergone a profound change in the last few years. Earlier, the established way to measure the advancement of power was to use more orthodox military and economic metrics. Our assessment of opportunities was also more predicated on partnerships between nations. Recent events have, however, introduced many more parameters to evaluate security and calculate gains. And our outlook, be it directly economic or more broadly national security, must adjust accordingly. De-risking the global economy is now a principal preoccupation. For market economies and democratic polities, this focusses on establishing more resilient and reliable supply chains. In the digital domain, we see a parallel emphasis on the importance of trust and transparency. A more decentralized world economy is increasingly perceived as the most viable solution to current anxieties. Such sentiments against economic concentration are only likely to intensify as tech wars gather greater momentum. We must also accept that interdependence, in itself, cannot always be an assured basis for international peace and security. Re-globalization in an open-ended techade will call for trusted collaborations of a kind that will be a new experience for all of us.

SAGA OF A RISING POWER

It is this scenario that confronts India and the world as they both contemplate and calculate. We are heading into volatility and upheaval, where mitigation and navigation go side by side. In fact, the transformation that we long speculated about is now actually upon us. Externally, India is discovering the merits of converging with like-minded nations, even while maintaining its distinct identity. Its domestic journey enables it to offer new terms of engagement to a growing range of partners. As the most populous nation and currently the fifth largest economy, its salience is underlined by the manner in which it conducted the G20 presidency. The interaction between a changing India and a more dynamic world is clearly novel for both of them. In that situation, the quality of its leadership will make the difference. I have sought to capture the various happenings of a world under exceptional stress and present them as trends against which we assess India's prospects. Like my previous effort, this too is intended to contribute to an ongoing debate in an argumentative society.

Major nations that make an impact on the world do so after a defining event. It could be a conflict, a revolution or a major economic shift. Underlying all of them are both a jump in capacities and the character traits of a new player at that level. In India's case, its early diplomacy was eventually constrained by the capability factor. It may have shown up in national security and political challenges, but was actually a cumulative outcome of limited progress in socio-economic and technological fields. But somewhere, there was also the inadequate projection of a great civilization. India's progress has been more staggered than others in its peer group. Today, all these variables are coming together into play as India advances across multiple fronts in a self-supportive manner. Politics, economics, demography, culture and ideas make a potent combination. These deep changes across broad domains are contributing to the creation of the New India.

The last decade has witnessed an expansion of India's space and a rise in its international profile. The *mandala* of its diplomacy has taken a clear form, even as the Neighbourhood First policy struck roots and the extended neighbourhoods advanced in all directions. The global footprint is widening too, visible as much in Africa and Latin America as in the Pacific and the Caribbean. Multiple engagements simultaneously with major power centres have also intensified, though not always without challenges. The Vaccine Maitri strongly reaffirmed credentials as a champion of the South, just as first responder operations highlighted our international commitment. Operations like Kaveri, Ganga, Devi Shakti and Ajay underline that Indians abroad could count on their government during times of difficulty. And a decade that began with the advocacy of yoga is appropriately seeing the espousal of *Sri Anna* (millets). The journey will continue but this is a time to take stock and assess what difference we have made. And that exercise will surely bring out why we matter more to the world.

At the end of the day, foreign policy is very much about clinically assessing the global landscape and calculating one's prospects. Only if the larger picture is accurately read can the risks and benefits of any course of action be assessed. But no nation plans or acts in a vacuum. It must have a vision for itself, an architecture in mind and objectives to attain. For both practical and cultural reasons, these may not always be spelt out explicitly. But by analysing the world, describing processes and suggesting solutions, their outlines can nevertheless be discerned. To that extent, this is also a volume to be read between the lines.

India's G20 presidency is also instructive in offering insights about how to navigate current world politics. By relentlessly shining the spotlight on the concerns of the Global South, we were able to ensure that the G20 returned to its basic mandate of promoting international growth and development. Defining priorities in that regard and devising collective solutions were also objectives that were attained to considerable measure. Faced with the parallel challenges of East–West polarization and North–South divide, each was utilized to mitigate the other problem. A firm diplomatic posture that included some new practices on interim outcomes encouraged consensus to be reached when it really mattered. Taking the initiative to enable the permanent membership of the African Union (AU) was notable in itself and helpful in strengthening the larger narrative.

A takeaway from the G20 Summit in Delhi was the demonstration that the more ambitious the agenda, the harder it would be for others to play spoilsport. Equally, by nurturing crucial relationships over a period of time, all the participants developed stakes in India's success. Whether it was the manner in which diplomacy was conducted, culture and heritage projected or popular participation was encouraged, the G20 presidency was very much an exercise in the India way.

As a practitioner long associated with our diplomacy, there are two responsibilities that I seek to discharge through this book. One is to share the thinking of a rising power with a world that has become increasingly aware of that happening. The other is to communicate the necessity of accurately understanding global developments to our own people. Only then can our nation fully appreciate the opportunities and challenges that lie before it. These twin exercises are, however, united in their cultural underpinnings. After all, this foundation influences our approach to the world as a family, as it does the pluralistic and consultative nature of our society. They shape our political ethos too, just as they promote our democratic choices. The manner in which debates are conducted, decisions reached and positions articulated, all have their own cultural signature. But above all, they bring out the values and ethics that are at the core of our collective personality.

Sagas of nations, while developed to grip the imagination of their peoples, are a distillate of wisdom, beliefs and habits. For those whose cultures and traditions came under pressure in difficult periods of history, they are also a crucial motivator. The really great tales offer insights that help to spread influence beyond boundaries and to help propagate messages. It is, therefore, tempting to draw from them lessons that can be applied to the contemporary world. Especially in times of turbulence, episodes and outcomes can provide guidance, offer parallels and strengthen self-belief. Indeed, because epics serve as an instructive way to view the happenings of any period, they remain eternally relevant.

Of India's two major epics, the Ramayana and the Mahabharata, it is the latter that is normally associated with statecraft and diplomacy. There are many reasons for this perception, among them the storyline itself. But even that arises from the fact that these two sagas are set in different eras, each with their own behavioural expectations. The Ramayana, which is the earlier one, has purity of thought and nobility of conduct as its central message. In contrast, the Mahabharata is much more a chronicle of human frailty and pursuance of ambition. In today's terminology, we would see one as a quest for the observance of rules and norms, while assessing the other as an exercise in realpolitik. Since the international order cannot be built on unrestrained competition, the quest to establish and uphold standards has always been relevant. This is perhaps even more relevant today in a world that is so much in ferment. The Ramayana could be studied from that perspective, highlighting both the merits and challenges of building a rules-based order.

The ethical dimensions of the Ramayana are exceptionally strong as compared to not only the Mahabharata but even to the epics of other cultures. Its grassroots understanding is one of a clear-cut battle of good against evil. This is why it is celebrated through festivals and fables across much of Asia. But even within this template, there are complexities, dilemmas and compulsions that hold lessons for a student of strategy. How goodwill is leveraged, commitments are made, coalitions are built and choices exercised are all graphically illustrated by the narrative. In most cases, the decisions appear obvious, yet, the crucial events have a backstory without which our understanding is not complete.

In essence, the Ramayana is a saga of a divine force that assumes human incarnation, Rama, to cleanse the world of evil. In that process, he sets the norms for personal conduct and promotes good governance. For that reason, we may see his rule as the epitome of a rules-based order, known as 'Ram Rajya'. The narrative, as it unfolds, is understandably much more complicated than only these propositions. It begins with building strengths and acquiring capabilities that give Lord Rama, the chief protagonist, his formidable reputation. While subject to various tests, he is able to handle them with a dexterity that prepares him for the final challenge. His relationship with his half-brother Lakshmana is particularly close, though he also commands the affection of his two other siblings, Bharata and Shatrughna. The tale is one of political intrigue, as Rama's stepmother Kaikeyi invokes one of the two boons given by his father Dasaratha to insist on Rama's exile at the very time when he is to be crowned. The abduction, during his forest exile, of his wife Sita by the demon-king Ravana is the key event on which subsequent developments are centred.

As Rama prepares a campaign to rescue her, a number of stratagems emerge, all of which have found their way into folklore. The 10-day battle in which Rama is ultimately successful is not without its moments of anxiety. The role of Hanuman as his devotee, emissary, resource person and adviser is particularly noteworthy. But whether it is the importance of reliable friends, the challenges of creating coalitions, the dangers of open-ended commitments, the perils of strategic complacency, the value of effective diplomacy or the need for informationized warfare, there is much that today's world can learn from this era.

Most of all, the story of Lord Rama is an account of a rising power that is able to harmonize its particular interests with a commitment to doing global good. The tests that he is subjected to encourage strategic creativity. Many of the decision points are those of principle, and the choices are, consequently, less ambiguous. But there are also occasions of self-interest, where the justification for an action stems from a particular need. Lord Rama's intervention in the battle between the monkey-kings Vali and Sugriva, explained at length later, is a case in point. It is not without its ethical aspects; it is just that the understanding of ethics is different from its orthodox assumptions.

Life is rarely a black-and-white choice, and appreciating the complexities of decision-making is an essential part of grasping international relations. A major rising power, however, needs more than just an accurate landscape analysis and the ability to act on it. It must, first of all, be confident of its own values and beliefs and base its policies on those convictions. These will draw from the totality of its culture, heritage and traditions. That is why India can only rise when it is truly Bharat.

❋

2.

FOREIGN POLICY AND YOU

Making a Difference in Your Daily Life

India may matter to the world and vice versa. But that does not mean we Indians should not watch out for ourselves. From that national perspective, what is a 'good' foreign policy? Perhaps we over-complicate the answer by confusing sensible pursuit of interests with complicated formulations. So, it is important to look beyond the terminology and validate it through gut answers.

A 'good' foreign policy must work for you personally. Your everyday needs from the world must be better met. Since we are a collective as a country, our national security must be ensured. As that is done, the pursuit of our aspirations must be facilitated. Foreign policy, being the link to the outside, should enable us to draw what we seek. It could be technology, capital, best practices or work opportunities. And obviously, we would all like to be strong, look good and feel appreciated.

In the final analysis, good foreign policy must read global trends well and anticipate what portends for our nation and our people. When the unexpected happens, it must respond nimbly and effectively. At the same time, it must message our intentions and project our image positively. Any effort that ensures these goals has a lot going for it. It does not necessarily need to sound nice; it must simply pass the smell test.

Put yourself in the shoes of an Indian student who happened to be in Ukraine on 24 February 2022. Focussed on educational prospects, you are now caught in the middle of a serious conflict. It is not just you and thousands more of your fellow nationals, there are millions of Ukrainians who are trying to get out of the country at the same time. Internal travel is dangerous and complicated. The borders are even more so due to overcrowding and congestion. In the conflict-impacted cities, there is even fear regarding the physical danger of stepping out in the open due to shelling and air strikes.

This is when you really look to your government for support and extrication. And indeed, this is when its entire foreign policy apparatus swings into action as it did through Operation Ganga. It did so by facilitating transport, including trains and buses. It intervened at the highest levels in Russia and Ukraine to ensure ceasing of fire for safe passage. It engaged the border authorities to enable border crossing. And in extreme cases, such as in the city of Sumy, its representatives even traversed conflict zones to ensure the necessary logistics for your safety. Once you were out of Ukraine, it worked with neighbouring governments in Romania, Poland, Hungary and Slovakia to establish transit camps, utilize air fields and organize the flights required for a return home. Reflect for a moment on the efforts, interventions and relationships at various levels, starting from the very top, that were involved to make all of this happen.

Revisit then Kabul on 15 August 2021. Imagine that, for whatever reason, you found yourself stranded when the Taliban suddenly took over the city. Apart from navigating a city now controlled by Taliban checkpoints, you could well ask how difficult going home could be. Well, a great effort had to be made by the Indian government. It was as challenging as combining access to a secured American airbase that was on edge, surrounded by desperate Afghans and suspicious Taliban; using Tajik rear support for quick response; accessing Iranian airspace at short notice; and quietly utilizing Gulf facilitation! Some others were beneficiaries of seats in flights run by the United States of America (US), the United Kingdom (UK), the United Arab Emirates (UAE) and France that were delicately negotiated. This might seem like exceptionally complicated logistics. But it was more than that: behind it were years of relationships that really delivered at a time of need. Equally important is that this represented the efficacy of a flexible and pragmatic Indian policy of multiple engagements.

The Operation Devi Shakti flights from Kabul may have been extraordinarily stressful, but they were still manageable at short notice. In terms of numbers involved, India's response to the demands generated by the Covid pandemic was much bigger. The Vande Bharat Mission, which brought back millions of Indians from multiple countries by air, sea and land, is perhaps the largest recorded evacuation exercise in history. The movement of people was only the tip of the iceberg. Driving it was a complex and intricate set of activities that included organizing, gathering, testing, housing and even feeding those waiting to be repatriated.

Starting first at Wuhan and then moving on to Italy and beyond, this involved an intensive engagement with local, provincial and national authorities. And it covered everybody, from tourists and students to professionals and workers, even pilgrims, fishermen and seafarers. It was not limited to Indians coming back. Many staying abroad, in the Gulf, for instance, were given support directly or by interceding with local governments. Here, too, the results of cultivation by political leaders and diplomats paid off.

A more recent example was that of the Indian community caught up in armed civil strife in Sudan in April 2023. Tensions may have been steadily building up over the past year, but nevertheless, expatriates are usually reluctant to leave until the worst case actually happens. In this instance, when it suddenly did, it put almost 4,000 Indian nationals in jeopardy. Overnight, the Indian response mobilized by setting up the command centre at home for what came to be named as Operation Kaveri. At the same time, Indian aircraft were positioned in Saudi Arabia for short-notice flights, while Indian naval vessels were sent to the Red Sea. The extrication process was again incredibly complicated because our nationals were dispersed in small numbers across a vast area. In the civil war situation, law and order broke down completely and even basic necessities became difficult to access. The Indian Embassy worked under the most challenging circumstances, including the occupation of its premises by a warring party. The solution was to evacuate as safely, inconspicuously and rapidly as possible, three objectives that often collided especially in the face of personal and political pressures.

Yet, it was an operation that delivered fully because it was a combination of a committed official presence on the ground, adept diplomacy with neighbours and enablers and a detailed SOP that had been honed over years. Our diplomats and military personnel performed outstandingly, often taking high personal risks. We saw partners like the Saudis, the British and the Egyptians go out of their way to help as well. If there is a common thread among these stressful experiences, it is that of larger dangers that impact individual lives. And that is, in fact, a predicament all through human history.

When a sage first took Rama and Lakshmana to cleanse his hermitage of evil demons, little did they realize what that encounter presaged for their lives. It was their first brush with the forces of darkness, whose full powers they were far from grasping. Indeed, the very Maricha whom Lord Rama first neutralized came back in the form of a golden deer to deceive him in his later exile. Years later, in the initial phase of his banishment, he again pledged to protect the sages of Sharabhanga, perhaps unknowing of where this was to lead him.

There are so many instances of the future being decided by the juxtaposition of complicated events, be that the fate of the monkey-king Vali or the eagle-king Jatayu. A few like Maricha sense it but are still powerless to halt the course of destiny. In fact, the triggering event of King Dasaratha's boons is an example of an unintended decision leading to unanticipated consequences. This is also illustrated by the fact that Ravana does not even imagine the ultimate results of his abduction of Queen Sita.

In our modern world, we, too, live with uncertainties and turbulence. No amount of anticipation can prepare us fully. Yet, we must always assess, plan and be ready to respond. A sensible government, which has the welfare of its citizens at the centre of its thinking, will naturally put in place rules, regulations, mechanisms and practices for unforeseen contingencies. It would also constantly refine them based on experiences. That is exactly what has changed in the last decade, and if we look back, it is visible how much of a difference that has made to our common citizens.

DEALING WITH A GLOBALIZED EXISTENCE

A parallel example in public health during the same period is equally instructive. When the first wave of Covid hit India in 2020, we scrambled across the world to procure personal protective equipment (PPE), masks and ventilators and did so in a seller's market as the demand far exceeded supply. Ingredients for the pharmaceutical industry with escalating requirements were also greatly sought after. Even the inputs for vaccines came from tens of companies spread out in multiple nations, and they were subject to the primacy of local demands. Commerce by itself was not adequate in such circumstances; contacts were needed for effective access and regulatory approvals. The second wave in 2021 saw a similar spike in demand for oxygen and specialized medicines from abroad. Locating, negotiating and contracting supplies became the priority of Indian diplomacy. And it really bent its back to deliver. These examples may be the products of extraordinary situations, but they do illustrate what is an undeniable reality. And it is that our daily life is increasingly influenced by what happens elsewhere, be they problems or solutions.

So, the next time you are watching a foreign visit, hearing a discussion on an important relationship or reading a debate about interests abroad, take it very seriously. Remember that this may have a direct bearing on your well-being. Foreign policy matters not just in distress situations. It could literally determine your security, your job, the quality of your life and, as we discovered recently, even your health. It shapes what you hold dear: pride, values, reputation and image. For all these reasons and more, it is important that you take a greater interest in the world and understand what that could mean for your prospects.

Let us explore what foreign policy could mean for you personally. If you are an Indian student, it may be the ease of getting a visa, the ability to travel during times of Covid and perhaps employment after studies. If you are a businessperson, it could help you get access to foreign markets, receive information on regulations and practices, and, where circumstances demand, obtain assistance to solve problems. For professionals and workers, this may be visible in ensuring fair employment contracts, a stronger sense of protection and welfare measures in times of difficulties. For a stranded tourist, a sympathetic embassy provides much-needed succour and support and, in more threatening circumstances, even evacuation.

But you do not have to be abroad to need foreign policy; it matters at home just as much. When it comes to security, external or internal, diplomacy could be a preventive measure, a mitigator or a problem solver. It can help raise awareness of a shared threat just as it can find partners against common dangers. So, if you are a soldier guarding our frontiers or a policeman grappling with terrorism, a good foreign policy makes your life a little easier. And then there is the economy, with its search for investment, technology and best practices, which can be enabled only by foreign policy.

In each of these sectors, foreign relationships can accelerate India's progress. Cumulatively, what they do is expand employment and improve your quality of life. Whether it is the price of cooking oil that is imported or a smartphone produced collaboratively, a larger policy decision has just made some difference to your purse. Indeed, if there were any doubts at all on that score, the pressures and responses coming in the wake of the Ukraine conflict have set it to rest.

But also reflect for a moment how much the big issues of our times, pandemic, terrorism and climate change, impact your very existence. Ask yourself whether we should not have a greater say in the search for solutions. It also matters to all of us what other nations think of India, our culture and our way of life. After all, the G20 presidency offers a unique chance to make the world more conversant with India and our own people more ready to explore opportunities abroad. Should we not then shape our image and influence the narrative? At the same time, the challenge is to do so without opening a way for external forces to interfere in our national debates and development. These are but a sample of how, in an increasingly connected world, the attitude, perceptions and interests of others are so relevant. If they have to be managed and leveraged, then it is all the more necessary for a sharper realization at home that foreign policy really matters.

DIPLOMACY AND NATIONAL SECURITY

For all societies, security ranks foremost in their priorities. The reason is obvious: it affects the very nature of our collective. This has a territorial aspect as well as that of safety, law and order and well-being. They are often connected because together, they determine the national spirit and existence. India faces more than its fair share of external challenges, in part because many of our boundaries have not been fully settled. The resulting contestations are obviously a call on both determination and resources. We saw that earlier with Pakistan and more recently with China. But they demand equally that energies be focussed on ensuring optimal positions, on the ground as much as in negotiations. Given the serious repercussions of such differences, it is also very relevant to ensuring peace and tranquillity, if not more.

Diplomacy is a natural partner of defence. Most of the time, it is the first line; on occasion, it is also the back-up. After all, most military situations do end up at the conference table! Indeed, the achievements of foreign policy in stabilizing the neighbourhood are very much the basis for progress and development at home.

With the world being what it is, self-interest and convergence cannot be fully counted upon to forecast the behaviour of others, including neighbours. Neither their ambitions and emotions nor their risk-taking propensity are always predictable. Few would have anticipated the sharpness of the downturn that India's relations with China have taken in the last three years. Any prudent polity, therefore, backs its posture with capabilities and deterrence.

A big responsibility of Indian diplomacy is to create the widest set of options for such contingencies. This could mean acquisition of defence equipment and other supportive measures; securing understanding for our policies and actions from the international community; and, for that matter, in mitigating or resolving more fraught situations. Let us look at how all of that has worked in the last few years.

A notable achievement of the Modi government was to conclude and implement the Land Boundary Agreement with Bangladesh in 2015. In conjunction with the resolution of maritime differences, this has had a positive impact on the security situation in the East. More than that, it has opened up possibilities for economic cooperation and connectivity for the entire sub-region. The beneficiaries are not just India and Bangladesh with respect to trade and travel or Nepal and Bhutan for the same but the northeastern states of India as well, and that also to a very significant degree.

A very different challenge is being faced on our western boundary vis-à-vis Pakistan. On that front, the initial goal of diplomacy was to expose and de-legitimize Pakistan's cross-border terrorism. When counter-actions were required, as in Uri in 2016 and Balakot in 2019, effective diplomacy ensured global understanding of India's actions.

As far as China is concerned, the diplomatic negotiations that are going on in parallel to the military stand-off since May 2020 illustrate that foreign and defence policies are really joined at the hip. Here, too, the value of global support and appreciation is self-evident. The leveraging of a multipolar world has been particularly visible in terms of weapons and technologies needed by our defence forces. That a Rafale aircraft acquisition from France can take place in the same timeframe as that of an MH-60 helicopter or P-8 aircraft from the US, the S-400 missile system from Russia and SPICE bombs from Israel speaks volumes of our nimbleness. These are typically accompanied by military exercises and policy exchanges that bring about greater strategic comfort. In short, diplomacy supports, empowers and facilitates the national security effort.

Some of this happens on the domestic side as well, even if it is less obvious. Peace at home has often been troubled by insurgent groups operating from the neighbourhood. Adept diplomacy, however, has effectively discouraged neighbours from providing shelter or support. From time to time, it has taken a little more than that to achieve results. That, too, has been persuasively justified.

Separatism, violence and fundamentalism have also been propagated from destinations afar, misusing the protections of free speech. Canada and the UK have both witnessed such happenings. These also require vigorous and continuous countering, since some see preaching violence against others not to be in discordance with democratic rights. Where arguments and persuasion yield little result, firmer diplomatic measures may also be required. Our overall posture does radiate the message that India will no longer be a punching bag in the politics of others.

Arguments must be met with reason, but polemics clearly demand a more vehement reply. Extremism and other challenges to governance that find encouragement from sympathizers, whether in the name of civil society or identity, need a robust response as well. A world of borderless politics also generates its own set of concerns that supplement traditions of influence operations. There are powerful forces with their distinct agenda that encourage the overriding of democratic choices. Their intolerance of anything different is manifested in attempts to delegitimize other points of view. Established newspapers giving UN-sanctioned figures access to their opinion page or eminent broadcasters doing political hatchet jobs are indicative of both a mindset and an objective. That there are many effective tools in play, including the power of technology and influence of civil society organizations, makes this challenge formidable. When it comes to politics, the battle of narratives is a perennial exercise. India has to patiently make the case that its pursuit of national interest is very much in tune with its advocacy of global good. A large part of the answers lies in the world of argumentation and in the effectiveness of communication. Diplomacy, thus, has a responsibility as both the shield and sword of a polity.

Recent global debates about India have implications for our security. As a federal polity of such extraordinary diversity, the quest to nurture the union should be most appreciated in our context. Yet, what we find is that efforts to strengthen national unity, sovereignty and integrity are often undermined by misrepresenting facts. Surprisingly, improvements in governance, applications of technology and progress on long-festering issues can be depicted as detrimental to freedom. Even prominent institutions indulge in disinformation in pursuit of a cause. History can be airbrushed and unfavourable events conveniently ignored. In our quest, we have discovered that political votebanks are a reality strongly beyond our shores as well. Robustly defending the nation against such undermining is a commitment that must be recognized.

If this was just a debate, perhaps that would matter less. But it is a harsh reality at work. Some of it may be ideological, but there is also the competitive nature of international relations. Bluntly put, there have always been interests that militate against a strong and united India. In the past, they exploited every faultline that our society provided: religion, language, ethnicity and social strata. Today, in a different garb and with new arguments, they are even more active than before. Perhaps, more of us need to ask ourselves why separatism in India finds regular support in quarters abroad. For that matter, how terrorism directed at us is consistently underplayed or even rationalized. Indeed, why some foreign forums lend themselves so readily to the denigration of our record and achievements. The task of foreign policy, when confronted with such calculations and stratagems, is to push back strongly even while advancing our own narrative.

ACCELERATING NATIONAL DEVELOPMENT

Since the drive for prosperity is a constant endeavour for all societies, it is natural that policymaking is also devoted to this goal. The most obvious expression of that is the promotion of trade and investments. Markets do not always work by themselves; in reality, pretty much everybody utilizes encouragement and facilitation. Those with historical handicaps have an even stronger reason to do so. We are still playing catch-up on industrialization, technology acquisition and competitiveness and will continue to do so for some time.

Just building capabilities at home, however, may not be adequate. Securing business abroad needs information, networking and access. There is a virtuous cycle at work here, whereby greater trade and economic activity strengthens skills, capabilities and employment at home. And that, in turn, constantly updates and tests our mettle. In many ways, foreign policy is an exercise in competitiveness and its economic facets a reflection in a particular domain.

In the last few years, India achieved ambitious export goals that would have been considered unrealistic till just recently. Now, this is not just a substantial increase in aspiration but one realized as the world economy is still recovering from the Covid pandemic. The basis for this confidence is a range of reforms in manufacturing, labour, finance, skills and trade facilitation. Added to that is a steady improvement in the ease of doing business. Foreign commercial policy is being tasked to obtain access to markets and lower trade barriers. This can be done in an orthodox way but hastened through negotiated understandings, including free-trade agreements (FTAs) and global supply chains. That may be an objective in itself; its larger significance for employment and prosperity are obvious.

Increasingly, foreign policy contributes to the creation of new capacities at home. In Asia, all modernizing economies have single-mindedly focussed their external interactions on obtaining capital, technology and best practices from abroad. Japan was the pioneer in this regard during the Meiji era, and China, after Deng

Xiaoping, was the most successful in terms of scale. In the last few years, India, too, has embraced this mindset. We have notable examples of benefits to people from endeavours at the enterprise level or in national projects. It may be information technology (IT) or auto manufacturing, food production or food processing, metros or bullet train, space capabilities or nuclear energy: the fruits of foreign collaboration are there for all to see.

Newer challenges like green growth and climate action have started to open up more possibilities. Our partners have expanded from the older industrialized economies to more innovative ones. All this happens because of our ability to identify, engage, negotiate and leverage opportunities of interest abroad across many domains. The most effective foreign policy is the one that focusses and delivers on development.

The resources and opportunities provided by external collaborations speed up the natural growth of the domestic economy. Valuable as they are, they do not, however, substitute the continuous nurturing of deep strengths at home. As we have discovered through experience, confusion on that score can have damaging consequences.

Three decades ago, India embarked on much needed reforms and opened up its economy. The benefits of doing so are undisputed. However, in the name of efficiency and modernity, easy options were taken at the expense of our small and medium enterprises (SMEs). Instead of building effective domestic supply chains, we opted for integration and value addition that were more profitable and less painstaking. Infrastructure projects were given out to others without any effort to absorb learnings for our own industry. The pursuit of short-term gains made us lose ambition and, with that, a sense of strategy. As a result, economic growth did not witness the commensurate scaling up of skills, strengths and capacities.

In the last decade, we have awoken to the realization that mantras about globalization, if mindlessly applied, can cause real damage. Not just that, if economic choices are divorced from a strategic context, it could lead the country down a very dangerous path. The real debate is not whether we should be an open or a protected economy. It is whether we are an employment-centric and capability-driven one or just a profit-obsessed society content to be a market. Along with vulnerabilities, a dependent mindset has also been rationalized, which masquerades as globalized thinking. India's destiny is bigger than to be just a part of the future of others. Real growth is not only about GDP increase; it is equally about infrastructure, supply chains, skills, finance and socio-economic progress. When we sacrifice the latter for the former, our long-term prospects are imperilled. We could slide into strategic lock-ins without even being aware. Foreign policy is surely an instrument to advance our strategic course; it is equally an insurance that our big picture is the right one.

In an era of more interdependence and interpenetration, it is also expected that all nations will seek to expand their zones of deep influence beyond their national boundaries. In the past, trade, finance, military activities and migration were some of the means to do so. Nowadays, the role of connectivity and socio-economic collaboration has become more salient. This is an important realization for a nation like India, whose reach was constrained by Partition. As we grow in different dimensions, strategic sense dictates that our prosperity serves as a larger incentive for the entire region. Realizing this, the Modi government has significantly expanded connectivity and collaborative initiatives with neighbours. Its results are evident in new road and rail connections, waterways, port access and transit rights, power grids and fuel flows, and especially in the movement of people.

South Asia is undergoing a real transformation by encouraging win-win outcomes and buy-ins by partners. The Neighbourhood First outlook addresses this challenge in the immediate vicinity, just as parallel policies do in the extended neighbourhood. India's support to neighbours during the Covid period also reflected this very thinking.

Interdependence, however, has its own downside and can be leveraged unfairly when global norms are cast aside. Exposure to competitive polities, therefore, needs constant monitoring. We cannot always assume that all others will play by the rules. For that reason, as an interpreter of the world, diplomacy is also voice of caution. It informs a society of the risks and pitfalls even as it explains opportunities. Doing so in a systemic and organized manner is part of formulating strategy. By its very nature, foreign policy develops a comprehensive outlook and can guide other sectors. It could be trade and technology, or education and tourism. Current times, in particular, require a holistic approach to relationships.

ACCESSING A GLOBAL WORKPLACE

India may be blessed with an enormous human capital. But among the shortcomings is the inability to utilize that advantage to the fullest. Like many other aspects of life, that, too, is changing. National campaigns launched after 2014 are addressing a vast range of socio-economic challenges, ranging from gender discrimination and health to education, skills and employment. In this period, virtually every domain has seen a change due to progressive policymaking. Infrastructure growth, manufacturing expansion, smart cities and labour codes are among the notable examples. Our definition of basic necessities has changed to include access to water, power, housing and health. This has consequences not just for our national ambitions but also for global society.

At a time when demographic constraints are impacting the developed world, there is a real prospect of Indians gaining significantly in the global workplace. Till now, that has been self-driven, with policymakers largely agnostic on this happening. However, a conscious effort at bringing our human capital into play on the world stage can create a different set of outcomes.

Employment prospects of Indian students studying in the US, Canada, Australia and Europe are now prominent in our agenda. Migration and mobility partnerships have been done with Portugal, UK, Australia, France, Germany and Italy, even as other European nations are starting to follow suit. In fact, in the period of Covid-induced uncertainties, the educational interests of students have become a subject of focus.

In terms of skills, we strive to ensure that Indian talent is treated in a non-discriminatory manner in the US, Canada, Oceania and Europe. Where they already reside, community welfare and cultural concerns, too, are a subject of our attention. The largest numbers with the greatest need are, of course, in the Gulf. Their well-being is of utmost priority, and that has been fully reflected in decision-making. The liberal usage of the Indian Community Welfare Fund (ICWF) speaks of a stronger sense of responsibility towards them, as do programmes for job training and creating facilities for those in distress. The agreement on rights of domestic workers signed with Kuwait is one illustration of our commitment to ensuring a better workplace abroad. Endeavours to get back social security payments made abroad is another. Indeed, making it easier to get visas has become much more central to our diplomatic efforts.

This mindset, in fact, goes back further up the chain, starting from how much easier it is now to get passports at home. By expanding the application centres four-fold and simplifying the verification process, the ability to travel and work abroad has undergone a sea change. Today, new prospects are opening up for Indian skills as a result of negotiated agreements, be it with Japan, Europe, the Gulf or Russia. Foreign policy is helping to make the world much more accessible to the average Indian. And they set out far more confidently than before, knowing that we have their back in times of difficulty. The Vande Bharat Mission, which brought back millions of Indians during the Covid waves, was as much a statement of capability as of commitment towards our workers and students, seafarers and tourists.

Those who have forayed into the world recently may have grown in numbers. But let us not forget that contemporary migrants join historically established communities to create the largest diaspora in the world. It is natural that their welfare and interest is connected deeply with foreign policy. As India's global standing has gone up, they too have reaped the benefits of association. This is quite apart from the undoubted achievements that they can legitimately boast of in their lands of domicile. In a more globalized world, they inevitably emerged as a more effective bridge to India. At the same time, a confident India has also taken pride in their successes and not shied away from a visible relationship.

In some ways, the Indian diaspora is quite unique because, in contrast with those of other societies, its mobility was not driven by turmoil at home. On the contrary, its bonding with Mother India has grown emotionally stronger with the advent to power of a more authentic representative. The 2014 event at Madison Square Garden marks a new era in diaspora connectivity. Its role has acquired greater value at both ends of the chain. For foreign policy, this may mean some additional responsibilities but surely provides greater sources of support. As a result, initiatives pertaining to the diaspora have expanded so as to strengthen its bonding with India.

Sensible foreign policies obviously have to address bread and butter issues. However, there are bigger questions to consider as well, especially for large nations. Three contemporary examples of urgent global concerns are pandemics, terrorism and climate change. No country can really afford to be oblivious or indifferent to such challenges. Smaller states are impacted; larger ones even more so. For a nation like India, quite apart from their direct consequences, there is also the need to shape the direction of global debate. This, therefore, becomes as much an exercise of responsibility as of influence.

An examination of the recent record on these matters offers some learnings. India has been a major factor in global deliberations regarding the countering of terrorism. If the awareness of those threats is more or the tolerance is less, our efforts have made no small difference. On climate change, India not only helped forge a consensus in Paris in 2015 but, in contrast to many others, has stayed true to its commitments. In Glasgow in 2021, these were taken to an even higher level. The International Solar Alliance (ISA) and the Coalition for Disaster Resilient

Infrastructure (CDRI) are two notable examples of its leadership in climate action. On the pandemic, its supply of medicines and vaccines and deployment of teams abroad spoke volumes about its internationalism.

In the decade that has passed, the new energy in India's endeavours is evident, notably in PM Modi's own engagements. Indian diplomacy has changed profoundly, be it in terms of bilateral visits, collective summits, development partnerships or opening of embassies. Indian citizens of every category are more assured that their concerns are addressed and interests advanced.

The benefits at home of a more proactive approach abroad are equally visible. On the global stage, India's greater relevance is being demonstrated in a variety of ways. Some of it was evident in the conversations and agenda, especially on terrorism, black money, etc. It was also visible, in outcomes and initiatives, notably in Paris and Glasgow on climate change. Our willingness to step forward in disaster-relief situations and to meet the Covid challenge has also been appreciated by the international community. Our national persona, be it on democracy, innovation, yoga, millets or Ayurveda, has gained recognition. We have, in the last few years, steadily built up the image of a first responder, pharmacy of the world, a reservoir of talent, climate action leader, development partner and cultural powerhouse.

When 10 ASEAN or five Central Asian leaders (virtually) attend our Republic Day, 27 European ones engage us together in a meeting or 41 African leaders come to India for a summit, clearly something has changed for the better. This is the India that took on the presidency of the G20 at a time when the world was, and continues to be, sharply polarized. It used this occasion to not only validate an approach of engaging multiple partners but also speaking up for the Global South.

A stronger and more capable India, one truer to its roots and culture, is a key factor in the larger rebalancing that characterizes our contemporary world. At a time when there are many more power centres, our place in a multipolar order is clearly more assured. In an era that is more globalized, our talents, capabilities and contribution have a growing value for the rest of the world. As we celebrate 75 years of independence, there is good cause for Bharat to be confident about its prospects. But to be so, it is equally important to be fully aware of the opportunities and challenges that the world currently presents. And surely, that will happen once we appreciate that foreign policy really matters to us.

3.

THE STATE OF THE WORLD

Understanding the Landscape

When PM Modi declared in Samarkand in September 2022 that *this is not an era of war*, the statement resonated across the world. It did so naturally because of its immediate context. But the message also captured the interdependence of our world that has now made conflict very dangerous for everybody. In a sense, it was a caution as well to others who may be contemplating their own options. The fact that such a pronouncement had to be made at all is a reflection on the fragility of the current global order. That it was in transition was already well recognized. But that this process could take the forms we are witnessing today was anticipated by very few.

In 2020, when I wrote *The India Way*, the world already appeared uncertain and unpredictable. Little did we know at that time that we hadn't seen anything yet. In the years that have passed, we have been traumatized by the Covid pandemic, impacted by the Ukraine conflict, grappling with a new level of violence in West Asia, afflicted by frequent climate events and subjected to serious economic stress. They have aggravated both an East–West polarization and a North–South divide. If there is continuity with my earlier endeavour, it is in the underlying phenomenon of how nation states, still the key concept of international relations, struggle with the problems of globalization. This applies as well to the main takeaway: that the world matters for each one of us as never before. As we consider that, the question confronting every Indian is about what our value, weight and prospects are in the contemporary era. We do so not knowing what even the immediate future holds because the pace of technological, economic and social change has accelerated so much. This is no longer an issue of more variables; we are really moving into uncharted territory. Naturally, at such a moment, it is worth reflecting on how our forebears dealt with the uncertainties of their era. And in that context, analogies from the past certainly offer some guidance.

The two figures most popularly associated with diplomacy in Indian traditions are unquestionably Hanuman in the Ramayana and Sri Krishna in the Mahabharata. One is perceived as an exemplary embodiment of service, who performs his duties undaunted by any obstacles. The other is regarded more as a strategist and counsellor, a source of wisdom in difficult moments. Each has his criticality in the given context, and Hanuman is at his best when confronted with uncertainty and tough odds. The process of a nation's rise is not unlike the arduous campaigns which embedded both of them so deeply in our consciousness. In fact, it is more than a campaign; it is an endless exercise of expanding prospects. And like Hanuman, it requires true believers and problem solvers who are at it 24x7.

As Lord Rama's emissary to Lanka, Hanuman's cleverness in gaining critical intelligence about an adversary, and even access to the confined queen Sita, were crucial developments. In addition, he used his mistreatment by the *rakshasas*, who set his tail on fire, to do them immeasurable damage by burning the city. But he also developed key insights about Ravana, his temperament and his advisers. Equally vital is his judgement of Ravana's brother Vibheeshana, who alone stood up for him when he was brought before the court. It is Hanuman's certification of his integrity that encouraged Rama later to welcome Vibheeshana after his defection from Ravana. Typically, people tend to think of diplomacy just as mediation. But in reality, there is so much more to it, including the ability to read competitors, allies and the landscape correctly.

Hanuman is also noted for his persistence, a quality he demonstrated when his fellow monkeys were inclined to give up on their search for Queen Sita. His ability to improvise and solve problems is equally in evidence when he lifts an entire mountain in order to bring back a single life-saving plant. At the end of the war, he is sent on a delicate mission to inform Bharata of the outcome and to assess whether he would really welcome Lord Rama's return to Ayodhya. Each of these attributes are today the prized quality of a successful diplomat.

A different illustration of the complexities inherent in diplomacy is provided by the monkey-prince Angada. He, too, was sent by Rama to Ravana's court in Lanka and cleverly played to his strengths. In his case, that specifically was his leg, which could not be moved once firmly planted on the ground. By making it a challenge, he embarrassed those who tried unsuccessfully to shift his limb. Finally, he humiliated Ravana when the latter tried to reach out for it and dropped his crown that Angada then picked up and threw it back to Lord Rama. As an envoy, he not only resists blandishments proffered by Ravana but improvises to make his points effectively. Denied a seat that is due to him, he is said to have made a chair for himself by elongating his tail and placing himself on par with the demon-king before him. After all, mind games are a key element of diplomacy.

A very different kind of skill was displayed by his mother Tara, the wife of the monkey-king Vali, who was earlier killed by Lord Rama. In the cases of Hanuman and Angada, they were dealing with Ravana, a haughty and irreconcilable adversary. Their mission was to both obtain information and leave psychological scars that would affect the morale of the other side. In the case of Tara, she was confronted with the anger of her current king Sugriva's allies Rama and Lakshmana. Sugriva had failed to deliver on his promise to locate Sita once he ascended the throne after Vali. It was then that Tara was sent to parley with Lakshmana as he approached Kishkinda, twanging his bowstring to signal his aggressive intentions. Her tactics were astute, and she initially appeased Lakshmana by admitting to Sugriva's fickleness. Having done so, she underlined his devotion to

Rama and embroidered reality by highlighting the search for Sita set into motion just then. Even if it meant taking some liberty with details, her effort at defusing a conflict between the brothers and the *vanaras* (monkeys) was successful. If Tara stands out, it is also because she is an exception to the self-absorption that characterizes her kith and kin.

The three cases may be different from each other in objectives and approaches. But what brings them together is a shared understanding of the larger task that confronts them. They have to grasp the enormity of the threat and actively contribute to the search for solutions. There is both a sensitivity required in respect of the larger environment as well as an awareness of their own predicament. Strategic choices have to be advanced but in a tactically astute manner. Honouring of commitments and upholding of principles are essential, but even these need to be optimized. The complex dynamic between the landscape and the game plan is always a perennial issue in diplomacy. Getting them both right is the prerequisite for success.

TOWARDS AN UNCERTAIN, INSECURE FUTURE

Pondering over the complexities of our own times, we might want to start by reflecting on how a pandemic that first engulfed a distant Chinese city then went on to completely take over our lives for more than two years. Or how and why an ongoing conflict in Europe, an entire continent away, is now affecting our daily life and its costs. And for that matter, the implications that climate events are having on the many processes that we take for granted. Or it could be a different kind of trauma, were any of us to be caught up in an act of terrorism or distantly inspired violence. In some cases, as we saw with students trapped in Ukraine or travellers stranded during Covid, stresses might happen when we are out of our country. But in others, be it Covid, conflict, terrorism or natural disasters, such developments can come right to our doorstep, sometimes even inside our homes. In the age of globalization, there is no escape from the world.

That does not mean that we need to be apprehensive about global developments or defensive in our approach. The flipside of the very interdependence is that the same world is also full of possibilities. If we brought back 7 million plus Indians during Covid through the Vande Bharat Mission, it reminds us that the India of today utilizes the global workplace extensively. It is equally due to the fact that our talents and skills are now an intrinsic element of global innovation, manufacturing and services. This is also reflective of how many Indians travel for personal or professional purposes. Indeed, these very issues are now central to the priorities of Indian diplomacy. We strive to ensure better access to our talent, stronger protection for our workers, greater opportunities for our students and fairer markets for our businesses.

But the world is not simply about mobility and migration. It is as much about partnerships, compacts and understandings that serve all parties well. In fact, a deeper engagement could lead to accelerating our national development, exploring more markets, procuring resources, improving our quality of life, expanding employment and, not least, shaping crucial global issues that determine the future of our planet.

To accurately assess what the world means to us, we must first of all appreciate that the globalized era in which we live is very much a double-edged existence. It is hard to separate the vulnerabilities from the dependence or the risks from the benefits. The very mobility that brought Covid to our homes was otherwise such an enormous source of livelihood for so many. The supply chains, which created disruption when they did not function, were a veritable boon when they actually did. Their complexity may be now hard to describe, as indeed their salience to critical aspects of our life. But the Covid era showed us how much we were all dependent on the cross-border flows of goods and services.

Not surprisingly, India was both a contributor and beneficiary in that regard. We sent out shipments of vaccines to almost a hundred nations. But we received ingredients from many of them as well. Nations in the Gulf were critically dependent on Indian exports for their daily consumption. And that continued without interruption because there was a deep understanding of this requirement. This paid off during the medical oxygen crisis in 2021, when the same countries cited it to make shipments to us.

Indeed, if there is one big lesson for the globalized economy from the Covid experience, it is that of more capabilities and options. The 'just-in-time' approach with its concentration in a limited geography showed how vulnerable the world could be in a crisis. De-risking the world economy now requires a 'just-in-case' outlook with more diversified production. Where India is concerned, this could mean another chance to board the bus of manufacturing that we had missed a few times before. And this is exactly what the 'ease-of-doing-business' approach and the offer of 'production-linked incentives' are intended to ensure.

The last few years have also encouraged us all to become more digitalized. We, in India, have a record that is generating widespread respect for good reasons. The scale of our digital delivery, whether it is in food, finance, health, pension or social benefits, is very much the talk of the world. Here, too, the visible efficiency of that transformation has been accompanied by corresponding risks of data privacy and data security. Where our data resides and who harvests it matter increasingly. The political sociology of such residency or processing is no longer irrelevant.

As a result, trust and transparency have become important guiding factors in digital decision-making. This is even more relevant as we enter a world increasingly driven by artificial intelligence (AI). The potential of critical and emerging technologies (CET) also poses its own set of issues. Whether it is for climate change or strategic concerns, countries have shifted towards greener and cleaner sources of energy and mobility. The resources, technologies and production associated with them have their own concentrations and consequential vulnerabilities. As a result, nations have made CET a priority for both their national capabilities as well as their collaborative endeavours.

Beyond the intricacies of supply chains and the vulnerabilities of data harvesting, there are larger changes underway in international affairs. These emanate from the weaponization of a broad range of services and activities that were regarded till now as essentially benign. In recent times, we saw how trade, connectivity, debt, resources and even tourism became points of political pressure. The Ukraine conflict has dramatically widened the scope and intensity of such leveraging. The scale of financial measures, technology controls, service restrictions and seizure of assets has been truly breathtaking.

At the same time, it is also an undeniable fact that global rules, regimes and practices have been gamed for national advantage for decades. In that scenario, the world of comparative advantage had no chance against 'unrestricted economics'. The complacency of the previous era has ended decisively, and each line of questioning now is producing deeply uncomfortable realizations. Sharpening great power competition is inevitably enhancing stress factors across multiple domains. And they will not cease simply because vested interests and political correctness wish to cover them up. The challenge for many nations, including India, is whether they can be converted into opportunities.

At one level, today's uncertainties induce greater caution about international exposure, whether we consider it from the perspective of implementing strategy or mitigating vulnerabilities. India happens to have concerns on both scores. But beyond a point, that cannot be fully hedged against, since the very nature of our existence now is very globalized. For each nation, especially the major ones, a set of answers has to be found that optimize risks and benefits.

This has led to a revival of interest in strategic autonomy, now redefined as ensuring national capabilities in core and sensitive areas. This process of adjusting towards a different basis of global interaction has naturally generated its own outlook. In our own domestic discourse, we know this as *atmanirbhar* Bharat, that is, self-reliant India. The digital domain has seen its own variation of similar compulsions. Events in 2020 sharpened awareness in India of an exposure that had been built up over decades. The clean app approach and the embrace of concepts like 'trusted providers' and 'trusted geographies' are a resulting outcome.

It is a paradox in many ways that while we speak of the advancements of technology and promise of science, world politics is actually moving 'back to the future'. Some of this arises from the expectations placed on globalization proving to be over-optimistic. This is not to suggest that the underlying economic interdependence is not well-founded. But widening differences among and within societies and creation of new global equations have meant that counter forces of globalization have been set into motion. Once challenges began to be articulated, the globalization model was not easy to defend precisely because its benefits were so heavily skewed.

Political expressions of globalization have also created their own backlash. When self-appointed custodians of correctness sit in judgement over democratically elected representatives, they cannot expect to be unchallenged, especially when they have such visible stakes in the preferred outcomes. To add to that, some countries are advancing aspects of their own model as an example abroad. Cumulatively, this has led to a situation where political and social identities have resurfaced strongly, creating inherent tensions with the nature of economic flows. Because there are so many moving parts, these predicaments are not easy to resolve.

Consequently, different nations are struggling to find the right balance, though the reasons in each case may be different. Some seek to address regime security, others to protect their technology leads or way of life, and still more who would like to limit exposure and build capabilities for themselves. These new forms of competition are likely to be among the fundamental characteristics of the politics of our era. Our globalized world is likely to be fractured in some respects and even selectively disengaged in areas of particular contention. These are some of the inevitabilities for which India needs to plan intelligently.

REFRESHING ANALYSIS AND POLICY

Such examples may reflect more recent trends, but we cannot forget that old-fashioned national rivalry also continues to be very much at play. Especially after 2008, the world has seen a sharper re-balancing and the steady emergence of multipolarity. The shifting terms of the US engagement with it in the last decade is a key dimension. The ending of a 'forever war' in Afghanistan only heralded different ways of ensuring American security and furthering US interests. But the manner in which it did may have signalled weakness of a kind that was not intended. That, too, is going through a process of correction.

The rise of China is an equally profound happening, one whose global consequences are becoming more apparent. That so much of it is taking place outside established constructs is clearly conceptually challenging for both policymakers and analysts. Far from being a zero-sum game, these developments have also opened up space for other players, some essentially regional and others with greater potential. Clearly, the world perceives India to be in the latter category. As all of this is unfolding, the Ukraine conflict has reminded us of the importance of Russia while underlining the strategic mobilization of Europe. If this matrix already looks complicated, then the volatility is further compounded by the impact on the developing world of a range of economic challenges. Throw in a whole lot of pre-existing and neglected problems. As a result, the world as a whole is staring at a far more uncertain and insecure future.

Such a prospect clearly calls for greater diplomatic energies and political creativity. It is even more necessary now to harmonize the pursuit of national interest with a responsibility for collective good. For a nation like India, where such a large segment of its population is so vulnerable, it means, first of all, to mitigate the impact of key negative trends. In doing so, we not only stand up for our own welfare but speak up on behalf of the Global South as well. Indeed, a domestic outlook that so strongly advocates inclusive growth has a natural inclination to display a similar approach abroad. At the same time, we also have an obvious interest along with the rest of the Global South in cooling down overheated global politics. This is obviously not going to happen overnight, yet, we must persevere.

Beyond the immediate compulsions, there are also the structural challenges of the current world order that confront us. Most of those emanate from the outcomes of the Second World War and the fashioning of international architecture in 1945. But they are also underpinned by a few centuries of Western domination, whose intellectual and cultural facets still remain prominent. The oldest trick in the diplomatic book is to freeze the moment to your advantage. This is reflected in cherry-picking events and outcomes and portraying them as the 'normal' or in creating mechanisms and concepts that are presented as immutable. That, in fact, is what some countries have done so successfully for the last eight decades. Pursuing reform in the multilateral domain and ensuring that global decision-making reflects democratic reality is, therefore, a quest of no small importance.

Allowing the past to influence thinking is, however, not a predicament that can solely be attributed to others. Sometimes, it is an assumption that we maintain ourselves because a particular experience continues to resonate. Thus, even six decades later, the 1962 war with China stirs suspicion of that country in the public mind. Similarly, our hesitations concerning the West derive from the memories of the 1947, 1965 and 1971 conflicts. This applies even on the positive side of the ledger. The 1991 economic reforms, for example, were impactful enough that the need to build on it was not given priority till recently. Such complacency contributed, till a decade ago, to impassivity towards strengthening manufacturing and developing technologies as well as improving our social indices.

At this stage of its rise, India must have the courage to revisit its past and draw the right lessons from abroad as much as from home. Sometimes, this is misinterpreted as political distancing when it is, in fact, an objective audit. It is not only dangerous to remain a prisoner of our experiences but, even more, to romanticize them. We now have the ability to shape the landscape more significantly and must use that more often. It is already expressed in new concepts like the Indo-Pacific, mechanisms like the Quad or the I2U2 and initiatives like the ISA. The China challenge can only be countered by reversing past neglect of the border infrastructure and maintaining deployments and, indeed, by utilizing the possibilities that global dynamics can offer. On the economic front, we have to be judicious in picking the FTAs and frameworks that truly serve our interests. The need to refresh both analysis and policy will only increase in a turbulent world.

CONTINUITY AND CHANGE

For any polity, national security has an undeniable primacy. Indians are much more conscious of this than most since it has been challenged so often in the last 75 years. In fact, when we evaluate the merits of leadership, it is largely perceived as a mix of addressing crises and ensuring delivery. A lot of our foreign policy is devoted to preparing for, obviating, mitigating and reacting to security threats. Clearly, a time has come that we must decisively address longstanding vulnerabilities that a competitive world regularly exploits. It may have been a political surprise in August 2019 that the Article 370 issue was firmly settled. But the fact is that mainstreaming Jammu & Kashmir was long overdue, and only vested interests were standing in the way.

We need to equally apply ourselves to the hard task of securing our borders effectively, including through promotion of Vibrant Villages Programme. At the same time, as the world penetrates into our daily existence more prominently, we must develop awareness and responses to the problems posed by the 'normal'. These are dangers emanating from the routine, be it digital, financial, ideological or even mobility-related. Just as international economics is grappling with the challenges of new practices, national security, too, must address more contemporary dangers.

A foreign policy that impinges so many aspects of our life understandably has deeper personal implications on our safety, welfare, prospects and opportunities. It has transactional and collaborative connotations, especially in the economic and technology domains. There are, of course, threads of continuity that run parallel to the compulsions of change. As always, foreign policy is a constant exercise of building power and exercising influence, whether for national or collective purpose. It can be a competition of ideas, values or culture that combine to set forth a vision of our future. Each of these facets, old and new, co-exist with others perhaps much more dynamically in an era of interdependence and interpenetration. International relations are played out in more domains and with greater integration than before. But precisely because it impacts us so profoundly, each one of us today has an obligation to take interest in the games that nations play.

While we overcome constraints, hurdles, habits and black swans, it is particularly necessary for the young generation to appreciate how the world looks at India now. Indeed, many of the very problems of the last few years have earned us credit for coming through in the manner in which we did. The combination of changes in India's political standing, economic weight, technological capabilities, cultural influence and the successes of the diaspora is moving the nation into a higher orbit. Admittedly, there is much more work to be done. But nevertheless, we see a growing recognition in the world that India is at last getting its act together. Some observers have actually said that PM Modi has succeeded in shaking up India in a manner that could not have been foreseen.

Equally, there is a realization that the big issues of our times cannot be solved without India's contribution or participation. This is a moment when India can reset the terms of its engagement with the world. It is also a juncture at which we should be prepared to take up greater responsibilities. The G20 presidency offered an important opportunity to demonstrate that to the world. By tabling new ideas, shaping the agenda, ensuring a consensus, fashioning action plans and promoting G20 enlargement, India certainly made the most of it.

For those who are starting off in life, I can only say that they have every reason to be more confident. India today has determination, vision as well as the perseverance to enhance its global standing. Those more experienced and part of our journey for the last 75 years will appreciate the transformation underway and value the outcomes that it has generated. But all of them would certainly share the conviction that today, even as the world enters a new era of turbulence, we matter more. And with the right leadership, we can definitely weather the storms and make the most of our opportunities. The confidence with which we will accomplish all this is one of the defining characteristics of Bharat.

4.

BACK TO THE FUTURE

As National Security Balances Globalization

Till 2014, like the rest of the world, much of India too was lulled by the soothing sounds of globalization. First came Brexit and its challenge to the European experiment. Soon thereafter was the election of Donald Trump and the articulation of *America First.* A China–US tussle, which was supposedly only tactical, became truly serious with the passage of time. Each episode enhanced the realization of the vulnerabilities that economic and technology concentrations had created. Then came the Covid pandemic, which thoroughly exposed the hollowing out of so many economies in the name of global efficiency. A new consensus began to emerge on the importance of resilient and reliable supply chains, as also on digital trust and transparency. A legacy issue, meanwhile, ground to an abrupt end with the hasty exit of American troops from Afghanistan. This was followed by the Ukraine conflict whose global impact confirmed how deeply integrated we all now are. And not least, the West Asia tinder box saw our worst fears realized with a new level of conflagration.

So, we have the revival of all the negatives of global politics that were thought only recently as anachronistic. Did we really not see it coming? Were we in denial? Perhaps some combination of both, enhanced by strong vested interests, their ability to lull the international community and a human propensity to hope for the best. All that globalization optimists were convinced was behind us has now returned with a bang. World politics is struggling with the intense interdependence of technology, finance, trade and resources coexisting with the overwhelming compulsions of security, sovereignty, privacy and values. The former pulls us towards developing closer linkages, while the latter cautions us about its vulnerable consequences. Navigating these contradictions will surely challenge all our creativity because the tensions of the present now collide with the prospects of the future. From its messy outcomes could emerge a different architecture of international cooperation, one that is more sensitive to values and interests as much as to employment and culture.

It was not as if the twenty-first century began particularly well. Almost at its very start, the 9/11 attacks in New York shaped its global direction. Their consequences then consumed the world for the next two decades. Much of what unfolded could hardly have been anticipated then, including how the preoccupations of one power could help open up the pathway for another. Soon thereafter, an unnecessary conflict in Iraq led to even more unpredictable outcomes. On the economic front, a world that was recovering from an Asian financial crisis slid into a global one within a decade.

The entry of China into the World Trade Organization (WTO) in 2001 heralded a model of globalization that was to have profound political and social repercussions in many societies. Quite a few found themselves unable to compete for reasons of scale, nature of the model, or against such massive subsidies. The resulting hollowing out obviously created its own politics in due course.

As these long trends unfolded, different regions and countries grappled with their individual challenges and opportunities. Greater sensitivity to employment, protection of technologies and safeguarding of data in a digital world were notable concerns. In a more connected existence, their domestic churnings also began to be reflected more strongly on the global stage.

By the time we reached the end of the second decade, it was clear that the very fundamentals of the world order were shifting. Trend lines indicated a movement towards greater turbulence and big power contestation, challenging assumptions with which we were comfortable. What no one expected was that an already troubled world would get a 'once in a century' shock in the form of a pandemic. When we add the consequences of Afghanistan and Ukraine, the future looks even more open-ended. It is certainly a new world out there, quite definitely not a brave one.

SHARPENING GREAT POWER COMPETITION

Prominent among the postulates that have shaped our thinking is the centrality of the US to the current international system. It is evident, however, that the two 'forever wars' in Afghanistan and Iraq have greatly affected that polity. That one was marked by conceptual confusion and the other was altogether avoidable is beside the point. The rationale of both conflicts may continue to be debated by those still interested. But what is done is done, and the US has come out much worse.

There was also a parallel economic pressure growing in this very period, one paradoxically created by the US on itself. The globalization model that many Americans advocated for so fervently has had a corrosive impact on its own strengths and capabilities. The last and obviously weakest justification for its continuation is that of the importance of the dependencies that it has already created. But the implications for American manufacturing prowess and technology leads were visible enough to be expressed, first as a political backlash and, thereafter, as a national security challenge. The Trump presidency certainly marked a turning point, but many of the debates matured further during the Biden Administration to emerge as a systemic posture. The net outcome of these developments is a strategic evolution of the US that is reflected in a changing stance abroad and different terms of engagement that it now offers to the world.

This is not a situation that has emerged overnight. On the contrary, rhetoric notwithstanding, we have seen a growing caution in US power projection since 2008. In tandem, there have been persistent efforts to address its overextension. In fact, there is a consistency in this regard over three Administrations that it may not readily admit to. Whether it is footprint, extent of involvement or the nature of activities, we are witnessing a very different America. And this America is moving towards greater realism, both about itself and the world, as it seeks to achieve global objectives in a more cost-effective manner. It could assume a broader posture as an off-shore balancer in more regions in a way that protects its influence without expanding its risks. This has different aspects, key among them a striving for a better balance between its domestic revival and its external obligations.

There is a sharper recognition, too, of an emerging multipolarity and growing strategic autonomy that characterizes the current era. This impels a quest for new options, even while consolidating old relationships. There is also not only an acute consciousness of the challenges to its position but a realization that these have made much headway. The real question is the ability of the US to reassess and reinvent itself. What this means to the world is a new kind of diplomacy, one more in tune with an awareness of its limitations and, consequently, of the value of greater and more contemporary partnerships.

Even as all of this happens, the world also witnesses the rise of China. Indeed, this correlation between the fortunes of the two nations is difficult to dispute. The emergence of a power at a global level is a unique happening in any circumstance. That this is a 'different' kind of polity, both ideologically and culturally, enhances the sense of change. The Union of Soviet Socialist Republics (USSR) may have borne some similarities, but it never had the salience to the global economy that China has today. We are, therefore, contemplating scenarios very different from the post-1945 situation.

The consequences of China's growing capabilities are particularly significant because of the extrapolation of its domestic seamlessness to the world outside. As a result, whether it is connectivity, technology or trade, there is now an ongoing debate on the changed nature of power and influence. Separately, we have also seen a sharpening of tensions on territorial issues across the breadth of Asia. Agreements and understandings of yesteryears now seem to have developed question marks. India had its own experiences, especially in 2020, with regard to the border situation.

Time will, of course, provide more answers. But what is evident is that establishing a multipolar Asia as a foundation of a multipolar world is now more urgent than before. Obviously, much of this will happen in the backdrop of intensified great power competition, and understanding how that could unfold is, therefore, vital. Here too, the Ramayana has some instructive insights.

Among the backstories of the Ramayana is the competition between two sages, one who can be regarded as an entrenched power and the other as a rising one. Their rivalry originated in an attempt by King Kaushika to forcibly seize Sage Vasistha's particularly productive cow. In the fight that followed, all his sons and his entire army were destroyed. Kaushika then acquired formidable weapons through penance but was again unsuccessful in his attacks on Vasistha. He then intensified his prayers and steadily moved up the ranks of the sages. But in the process, he discovered that rising was not such an easy task, especially to the summit level. Moreover, his besetting weakness was a tendency to lose his temper and expend his powers on the immediate provocation. And those happened to be many, some deriving from his enmity towards Vasistha, but others being distractions deliberately put in his way. Not content with being recognized by Lord Brahma as a 'rajarishi', he ultimately pushed himself to attain the highest status of 'brahmarishi'. But even then, Kaushika was not satisfied until he heard this recognition from the lips of Vasistha himself.

This tale of the two sages has some resemblance to developments in current world affairs. Rising powers are constantly pushing themselves, with the established one as the standard to be matched. Some may be driven by memories of humiliation, even if others are more at peace with themselves. In this process of reordering, only gaining the respect of competitors is not always enough. There is equally a deep desire to be formally acknowledged as an equal. The fire inside, which drives such a quest, can encourage a mentality of winning at any cost. And that, today, is understandably the biggest challenge to the establishment of a rules-based order. Not to forget, entrenched powers such as Sage Vasistha have a deeper influence that cannot be easily overcome.

If there is another trait that has carried on uninterrupted in history, it is that of political suspicion. Much as they may deny, even the closest of partners watch each other for contrary signs. It is a moot question whether the absence of her own son Bharata on the day of Rama's coronation added to Queen Kaikeyi's anxieties about his (and her) future. Certainly, these thoughts would have been magnified by her evil help Manthara, who had instigated her to make unreasonable demands by invoking the two boons given by King Dasaratha. This, incidentally, is also a telling example of how a smaller player with their own agenda can take advantage of the insecurities of a larger one. We can see that happening in our own neighbourhood.

But personalities aside, the hard realities that underpin international relations are those of competition and benefits. For all the talk of globalization and common good, nations still calculate unsentimentally what is to their particular advantage. The world may be changing but, in some respects, the more it does, the more it remains the same.

BEYOND WESTPHALIAN POLITICS

While it is natural to visualize the developments pertaining to the US and China in a related manner, it would nevertheless be an oversimplification to see them as a zero-sum game. To begin with, both of them are aspects of a larger rebalancing that is taking place in the world. Certainly, they have impacted each other and there are causal connections. American retrenchment has provided greater space to Chinese influence, given that it extends across so many domains. As much of the world put the colonial period behind, new centres of economic activities inevitably came into being. Of course, the pace and quality of this transformation was shaped by political choices, especially of the US.

China may have been a particular beneficiary of the geopolitics of the last century. But the fact remains that the shortfalls on the American account today cannot be readily filled by the growth of China's capabilities. Some of that reflects from the sheer spread of the US and its extensive grip on the international order. But there is also the crucial difference in the very nature of the two polities.

The US has prided itself on its universalism and consciously promoted these traits. China, in contrast, considers itself singular and its globalization is not readily converted into universalization. Each will play to its strengths. In an interesting way, the two will be a study in contrasts. One will make the most of its openness and diversity while building on its unique ability to attract global talent; the other has developed formidable strengths by leveraging the world, even while developing autonomous capabilities through extraordinary fusion. Paradoxically, a challenge that awaits them both is to ensure that these very qualities are not exploited by the other.

What is relevant for our purpose is the lessening convergence in their respective world views. And what that will lead to is a period of uncertainty, limitations and frictions in world affairs. This will be most evident on global connects like supply chains and data flows as well as challenges like maritime security, pandemics and terrorism. After all, we have a situation where not just the distribution of power has undergone a change, but along with it the characteristics of those who will now wield greater influence. Quite apart from their ability to work together or not, how they view enlightened self-interest and how much that would propel them to contribute to safeguarding the global commons are the questions that await answers.

It is not just eastwards in the Indo-Pacific that India is witnessing a radically different situation. Towards the West, the politics of our proximate region is also undergoing a transformation with the American exit from Afghanistan. Diplomats in the UN may have articulated the concerns of the international community in terms of terrorism and radicalization, treatment of women and minorities, freedom to travel and inclusive governance. But strategists with an understanding of the region would also be forced to recognize how open-ended its prospects have become. The balance of values, ideologies and interests are being carefully weighed by all relevant parties.

Just beyond, another change in the making arises from the transition in American Administrations and the negotiations on Iran's nuclear programme and regional influence. Where that finds a landing point is of no small consequence. Paradoxically, West Asia has witnessed simultaneously a radical departure from past political battle lines as well as their intensification. The optimism of the Abraham Accords has been countered by the terrorist attacks on Israel. The resulting balance, however transitory, is still far from clear. What can be safely asserted is that this time around, the very underpinnings of West Asian politics are being transformed.

Quite autonomously, Western liberal politics is also increasingly at odds with regime comfort in some nations. It has triggered reappraisals that are enhanced by evolving global dynamics. On its part, the Abraham Accords are noteworthy not only for their departure from entrenched positions but for the promise that they hold, especially on economic and connectivity issues. The I2U2, a new grouping, contains the kernel of ideas that could suggest a greater Indian involvement. And that need not be the only game in town. Saudi Arabia's greater focus on Asia also offers openings for India. This includes the IMEC initiative with possibilities of cooperation in connectivity, logistics and energy. Building on a tradition of contacts between India and Europe that went through Arabia, it represents a 'return of history'. In the final analysis, the balance between entrenched politics and emerging economics will determine the region's relevance to the world beyond.

Insofar as Europe is concerned, even before the Ukraine shock, it had started emerging out of its fortress mentality. One sign of that was how gradually it had become more alive to its interests on a global scale. The adoption of policies by the European Union (EU) on the Indo-Pacific and on connectivity was a telling indication. However, the enormity of the Ukraine crisis obviously radically transformed the security outlook of individual states, as also of the collective. It fast-forwarded strategic globalism, as Europe itself chose to define the impact and responses in that framework. The challenge nevertheless remains that a continent, which fervently believed in 'change through trade' and was supremely clinical about its interests, now seeks the world's support and understanding. That it has cushioned itself from some of the sharper pains while advocating hard options for those much poorer makes this exercise much more difficult. This was most evident in regard to energy imports from Russia, though it also extends to other aspects of commerce.

Even if the smoke clears somewhat, what would be of great interest to India are Europe's changed relationships across the Atlantic and towards the Urals. Both are likely to encourage a re-evaluation of its Asian engagement. The big imponderables are the future of a German posture so assiduously built over two decades and how much others will seek to take advantage of its ongoing dilemma. Where Asia is concerned, European positions will necessarily be different from the US because it is no longer defending global supremacy. At the same time, risk awareness has certainly grown in recent years. In many ways, the outcomes will be a compromise between pressing compulsions and medium-term calculations.

It is, however, the premier power of our times that is the bellwether of change. Influential Americans have argued that a less globally dominant US cannot afford the economically generous stance of the past. Their reservations are no longer restricted to just free trade agreements but also extend to the nature of global supply chains. As a result, more innovative endeavours are made to intensify economic engagements abroad that are sensitive to the realities at home. An example is the Indo-Pacific Economic Framework (IPEF), which commenced on the sidelines of the 2022 Quad Summit in Tokyo and has progressed by the time of the 2023 Asia-Pacific Economic Cooperation (APEC) meeting.

It is not only that the US is looking to realize opportunities differently. The strategy that it fashioned in respect of the Ukraine conflict has also been instructive in highlighting the vulnerabilities of our era. Indeed, the entire game has become one of which party is able to better leverage its hold on the other. A key question is the American ability to address multiple major challenges simultaneously. And of course, that is precisely what distinguishes the dominant power of our times from others. American awareness of strategic competition is greater, and is combined with domestic compulsions to build and protect better. The aggregate of these developments, some long in the making and others more immediate, are truly transformational.

What we are currently experiencing is also being shaped by concerns that go beyond the orthodox belief in Westphalian politics. Admittedly, the Cold War saw systemic competition with the goal of asserting superiority of a set of values over another. But this was balanced by the strong sovereignty sensitivities of a post-colonial order. Along the way, a broad compromise was struck where internal affairs were respected, while making exceptions in a few egregious cases. Even that was heavily tempered by strategic considerations; all departures from the supposed norm were not treated equally.

When it came to economics, transactionalism was much greater and societies were treated like black boxes. At a macro level, economic choices were not personal; it was just business. What was happening inside the box was not supposed to be our concern. But as globalization steadily promoted greater interpenetration of societies, this could no longer be dismissed with the same degree of complacency. We were letting in players into our lives who may believe, think and act very differently. It was no longer just a question of importing their products; in fact, they were now operating in our territory as well. And while this maybe physical in some respects, a digital age ensures that AI ranks foremost among our concerns.

Such an exposure naturally raised concerns about transparency and trust. It understandably bothers us if the restraints and firewalls that are our norm are not theirs. Not just that, the behavioural shifts in world affairs started to impact the global structure itself. In more sanguine times, we focussed mainly on efficiencies and competitiveness. However, as market shares and interdependence began to get strategically leveraged, the extent of our exposure also emerged as a national security concern. Such volumes did exist earlier; it was just that they were not manipulated in the same manner so prolifically before. There is no question that we have now slipped into a different culture of diplomacy, one with less inhibitions and greater coercion. Among the key developments of the last decade has been the weaponizing of the routine. It could be trade, tourism, connectivity or finance. As a result, everything needs to be hedged against now. Such anxieties have also fed into supply-chain concerns. The age of political agnosticism has effectively come to a close.

Ironically, the turn of events in Afghanistan could be interpreted as going in the opposite direction. For many, the real problem there was how intrusive the foreign presence in that country had become with the goal of nation-building particularly coming under criticism. It is a moot question whether the foreign presence in Afghanistan after the 9/11 attacks could have limited itself without adverse consequences. But even that is probably entering a false debate. The true challenge was not the ambition of the goals but the understanding of the landscape. For two decades, the US struggled with the paradox that the very country that was fuelling the fighting against it was also the one critical for its logistics. The dilemma was so acute that even the presence of Osama bin Laden in Pakistan could not bring it to head. This should not take away from the dexterity with which those cards were played by the Pakistani military, leaving a generation of American military and political leaders with scrambled identification, friend or foe (IFF) systems!

Today, however, the world contemplates the opposite quandary. It desperately hopes that irrespective of developments within the

Afghan society, there would be no negative external implications. Some countries define that in terms of terrorism and radicalization. Others are more concerned at the possibility of refugee outflow or treatment of women. Whatever happens, the truth is that international relations continue to grapple unsatisfactorily with the problem of reconciling sharply divergent cultures in a more tightly integrated world.

THE ARRIVAL OF 'OTHERS'

Some of the frictional aspects of the current situation have spawned their own discourse on how best to advance interests. In an effort to correct the outcomes of a less strategic era, there has been a debate about the virtues and viability of de-coupling. Like most other concepts, it is sensible to avoid extreme interpretations.

The global economy is today far too interlinked for it to be nationally separated in a comprehensive way. No society can really afford to see that happen, which is why it will not. At the same time, there is open talk of strategic competition that cannot be wished away either. Competitors clearly are not going to trust each other beyond a point. Any two-way link, be it trade, resources, connectivity or pipelines, will normally be better leveraged by the harder state or the one smart enough to have anticipated it. The very openness that drives creativity and progress also becomes a vulnerability. The likely repercussions of such attitudes will be to encourage autonomy and safeguarding in selected areas and, at the same time, to try and develop redundancy and reliability wherever necessary in other domains. This also leads to a renewed focus on export controls and technology sharing. Chips and semiconductors are an obvious example. There will be sociopolitical consequences as well, as different nations will adjust their procedures and practices as per a less trusting ethos. From academia to business, from research to travel, the world will see this impact in the coming decade. On top of it all, the political economy and orthodox security will continue to play out.

Who will gain and who will lose when the external environment is less favourable is an interesting proposition. How power differentials assert themselves is no less significant. We have already seen that some players have misread the strategic culture of others, leading to unintended results. A world that is more united in some respects but struggling deeper in others will surely be a novel experience.

The response of states is naturally conditioned by changed circumstances and surroundings. It is, therefore, all the more important that we appreciate the structural changes underway. The reality is that the loosening in the architecture created by the limitations of the US and the rise of China has opened up space for others. We may have two major powers, obviously not quite at the same level. But even this does not translate into traditional bipolarity. There are now many more players whose growth is autonomous and whose weight is increasing. To varying degrees, they will exploit gaps, just as they will take advantage of competition. Some of that will be constrained by their biases, affinities and interests. But as a broad pattern, they will be tempted to make the most of the ambivalence of those more distant. The diversity of alliance interests could be a contributory factor.

We must also appreciate that alliances themselves are a product of a set of circumstances. Copying the broad and durable network created by the US is near impossible. No other power has the capacity to even attempt a serious replication. But changing times produce different models and the unceasing process of establishing a global hierarchy will surely find unique expressions. Economic integration and dependency may now become more determining factors in the emergence of a new order. The possibility of alternatives should not be discounted.

A broader spread of power among nations with less structural rigidity is exactly what defines the arrival of 'others' on the world stage. This category may itself be a spectrum, with some having a longer history of power projection and some a more immediate relevance. Again, a few could aspire to be leading powers one day, while some may be simply protecting the leads of the past. Moreover, a globalized world no longer requires all-round development of power to make a nation stand out in competition. If some facets are adequately developed, that in itself provides enough capability to make a difference. It could be military force, as in the past; natural or financial resources; a strategic location; a cutting-edge capability; or an effective platform. A combination of them makes a powerful case for greater influence.

The prominence of such powers is already expressing itself in greater regionalism. Whether in Africa, West Asia, the Gulf or Oceania, differences and disputes are being addressed in a more localized manner. In fact, the openings provided by the transformation underway are so significant that they can be leveraged even by smaller nations.

Few regions have displayed this more graphically than West Asia. Its stronger regionalization has been expressed in conflicts and tensions that are increasingly driven by resident players, both big and small. While the rest of the world continues to have significant stakes, their ability and inclination to intervene is clearly declining. Leveraging of natural resources has long been a tradition. To this has now been added the innovative applications of technology. Whether it is from Yemen or Gaza, we are witnessing how long-standing problems have acquired highly impactful contemporary forms. Much of this has also fed into regional competition, especially of middle powers.

Numerous players operating with greater agility and less constraints in an interdependent world make a compelling case for pragmatism. In certain senses, shared interests can help override ideological or systemic differences. Whether it is in domains of energy, connectivity or technology, those who have little else in common have come together for their individual gains. But here, too, there is a larger structural logic to what is unfolding in front of us. That the unilateralism of any single power is untenable as a standard operating principle is obvious by now. The 1990s are well behind us and cannot be reinvented even by the most powerful of those emerging.

At the same time, the problems of the world have also become so complicated that no bilateral relationship in itself is adequate to be a regular solution provider. Theoretically, there is good old multilateralism to which everyone always pays lip service. But its frailties and shortcomings are even more openly on display. It is not only anachronistic but functions at the lowest common denominator, that too with deep deference to vested interests. This then necessitates arrangements of convenience to assert themselves.

Such minilateralism is practised in different combinations on various issues. As it grows, a larger culture of plurilateralism has begun to emerge. In itself, this is not entirely new. Earlier, a regional explanation provided a basis for working together. So, we had the EU, ASEAN, SAARC, GCC, etc., where proximity was the foundational basis for shared activities. We also saw nations collaborating on specific issues like maritime security, counter-terrorism, export controls, non-proliferation and climate change. It could even be an effort to influence rebalancing and advance multipolarity. And it went beyond the compulsions of geography. BRICS is one case in point, where four continents were reflected in one membership.

The difference now is that such groupings can become broader in their agenda, while also more purposeful in their working. The Quad, in that sense, is a sign of such changing times. What makes this format more appealing is that it has much lower overhead costs. There are no treaties, obligations, establishments or even disciplines that come with better relationships. It would seem that frugality is also a virtue now in the area of diplomacy.

When it comes to multipolarity, it is essential that we do not judge this complicated world by a simple yardstick. The phenomenon itself expresses a range of credible powers, whose interplay influences the global outcome. But the fact is that nations have acquired such differential capabilities that they perform in an increasingly domain-specific manner. Consider how this appears from the perspective of a nation like India. Political multipolarity has an obvious set of players, among them the P-5 nations of the UNSC, collectives like the EU and ASEAN, and those individual states that are regionally important. Economic multipolarity, however, looks very different because it is a product of some other factors. India's most substantial trade accounts are the hubs of the EU, the US, China, the Gulf and ASEAN. The equation stacks up still more differently in the case of energy. The key partners on this score are Iraq, Saudi Arabia, Russia, UAE and the US. Viewed from the technology perspective, the answers would move much more in the direction of Western economies. When it comes to mobility and skills, the Gulf obviously has to be given its due weight, but it is the West that provides more value addition.

All of this is supplemented by a truly worldwide constituency when it comes to multilateral outcomes and global issues. Voting patterns of nations are often characterized by blocs and India's appeal is accordingly targeted. This complex picture underlines how much more layered foreign policy calculations have become in this day and age. A large nation and a rising power certainly cannot visualize its strategy in linear terms or with limited variables. And the beauty of our differentiated world is that everybody is pursuing their own matrix.

The commentary that accompanied the expansion of BRICS in South Africa in August 2023 merits some observations. Much of it suggested that the US specifically, and the West generally, were the elephants in the room. The truth, in fact, was very different. The outcomes were an intricate negotiation to find common ground among the powers that were actually there. Each one of them had their own reasons to chart an independent path and there were overlaps between them. The six invited states (Saudi Arabia, UAE, Iran, Egypt, Ethiopia and Argentina) all have strong and established relationships with India, as indeed with other BRICS members. Their own inclinations are very much towards multipolarity.

The occasion also saw a groundswell of pressure on the UNSC reform, which, therefore, led to a significant evolution in the collective BRICS position. That both current and potential members have a shared interest in promoting trade settlements in their national currencies was another point of convergence. The bottom line is that the international system is today headed in more independent and multiple directions. Viewing it exclusively through an anti-Western prism would be misleading.

A POST-COVID WORLD

As challenging as the long view is, nothing really prepared us for the enormity of the Covid pandemic. It was not the human toll that it took, which alone was mind-boggling. The disruption it caused to the routine was just beyond imagination. The reason for this was that the last time something similar took place, the world was not as tightly connected as we are today. The difference between the Spanish Flu and Covid is a statement about the evolution of global society. They influence our expectations of an effective response, as they do of the benefits of international cooperation. But the impact cannot be judged just in terms of problems or solutions; it is even more about mindset.

The implications for international relations are particularly far-reaching. The Covid experience has challenged the globalization model that had entrenched itself in the last three decades. The efficiency obsession has been balanced to a considerable degree by a hedging mentality, and the experience on the vaccine front has heightened awareness in the Global South about its interests.

This pandemic may be the most serious in living memory, but it should be seen as a recurring challenge and not a one-off. It demands cooperation on a scale that could not have been conceived of earlier. No national capacity, however large, proved to be adequate. And merely excess volumes from even the large capacities are not clearly enough to address global needs. A collective response, by itself, could fall short if it is just an aggregate of the present capabilities. What we will now have to conceptualize is re-engineering of the way the world works to respond to such cataclysmic events. The pandemic has certainly triggered debates on issues like supply chains, global governance, social responsibility and even ethics. It equally encourages an objective assessment of the contemporary world, so that we are better prepared for tomorrow.

As nations contemplate the world, there is no question that Covid has moved the needle in the direction of fears. This is reflected in national security acquiring a more expansive definition. In the past, defence, politics and intelligence drove calculations, with extrapolation into domains like resources, energy and technology. With some notable exceptions, their demands were balanced out by the requirements of global exchanges, economic efficiency and by social habits. These trends, in fact, became stronger as the globalization mantra took deeper root.

The pandemic, however, saw capabilities leveraged, commitments dishonoured, supply chains blocked, logistics disrupted and shortages created. When this applied to PPE, medicines and ventilators, we woke up to health security. Those who saw their essential supplies under threat now realized the value of food security. Where economies slowed down due to material disruptions, we now understood the need for manufacturing security. Call it buying nationally, middle-class concerns, dual circulation or self-reliance; its underlying message is not that different. The efficiency of others may have strengthened bottomlines in good times; they are now seen as too unreliable for difficult ones.

The nature of the Covid experience has also brought to fore concerns of transparency. Opacity can no longer be overlooked; it has real implications for the rest of the world. It was bad enough to be confronted with shortages and disruptions, worse that they could become pressure points. There are also worries that the financial distress caused by the pandemic could lead to new vulnerabilities. Consequently, strategic autonomy is now being debated as greater self-sufficiency, stronger partnerships and multiplicity of options, all of which are perceived as integral to risk mitigation. These can have geo-economic implications in the days ahead.

Behavioural aspects have also played their part. Stresses induced narrower definitions of self-interest and departures from collective endeavours. Few practised what they preached; some even stopped preaching altogether. Inadvertently, insights emerged on the interplay of culture, interests and values. Pluralistic societies remained more engaged with the world and solidarity was stronger between them. And those who saw the world also as a workplace, rather than just a marketplace, had a deeper interest in remaining connected.

Challenging as they may be, the essential realities of our times cannot be denied. Our globalization is deep and pervasive and will continue to shape activities and strategies. What Covid has brought out are some of the particular risks of its current incarnation. The task before us is to de-risk that, even while pursuing other objectives, including rapid economic recovery.

Every solution, however, also throws up new problems. The digital domain that is enabling so much delivery is raising issues of both privacy and security. That is even more so as AI gathers steam. Critical and emerging technologies are gaining in salience as revolutions in energy, mobility and communication unfold. Ensuring that newer supply chains do not enhance global vulnerabilities is of utmost importance. For India, this is the subject of engagement bilaterally with the US, trilaterally with Japan and Australia, and collectively with the Quad. The Trade and Technology Council initiative is a parallel exercise with the EU.

What is now clear is that the alarm bells set off by the Covid experience have brought into focus a larger challenge of ensuring trusted collaboration. The truth is that market economies and democratic societies offer a degree of reassurance that the international community recognizes as vital to the coming times. In line with this thinking is a growing realization that Free Trade Agreement (FTA) choices should not be divorced from strategic directions. Precisely because much that India has to build lies ahead of it, we have greater stakes in ensuring the requisite partnerships and accessing the necessary resources.

India is, however, in it not just for itself. For the Global South that has barely come to terms with Covid, the Ukraine conflict has added to their trauma. The 3F (food, fuel and fertilizer) insecurity has been aggravated by trade and tourism disruptions. Concerns have been intensified by the perceived insensitivity of the developed towards their predicament. As homilies on open markets are pronounced while shortages mount, many legitimately fear that their experiences of vaccine inequity will be repeated in other domains.

In this situation, India has to summon its rallying powers in addition to its production capacity. Even against some headwinds, we have championed the cause of the economic security of the South. Setting an example in that respect is itself a powerful message. We stood our ground against considerable odds when it came to Covid, refusing to sacrifice the interests of our citizens. Energy security is a different but not dissimilar fight and what we do has a resonance well beyond.

Let us, therefore, take stock of what we confront. As it is, a world order into its eighth decade had run its course and is ripe for change. This is driven both by the national prospects of major powers as well as the cumulative impact of greater rebalancing and multipolarity. To that is added the complexity of a more interdependent, tech-centric and borderless world, where the concepts of power and influence have acquired new meanings. And this mix now experiences a pandemic that exceeds any in living memory; a conflict that impacts the most complacent continent and beyond; a power vacuum in a sensitive region like Afghanistan and both departures and reaffirmations in a volatile one like West Asia. Some major players have heightened awareness of their predicament while others have made sharp assertions of power. This is really a new era of multiple strategic competitions. As a result, there is truly disorder under the heavens, and it will take all the fortitude and staying power of a civilizational polity like Bharat to tackle it effectively.

5.

A TRANSFORMATIONAL DECADE

Laying the Foundations of a Leading Power

In 2015, PM Narendra Modi publicly articulated India's quest to become a leading power one day. Some treated it as a statement of arrival when it was actually meant to be an expression of an aspiration. In the decade that has passed, it has also become clearer that this is now work in serious progress. While inaugurating the Bharat Mandapam in 2023, the same thinking was reiterated by the PM in a determination to emerge as the third-largest global economy. And a year before, in a departure from tradition, he made a public appeal to think and plan for an entire era, not just a term in office. This was characterized as *Amrit Kaal*, a quarter century with its goal as India's emergence as a developed nation.

Each of these assertions has a profound foreign-policy implication, especially because they are being voiced not merely as a broad ambition but with specific targets and goals for which India is now strategizing. The achievements of the last decade point to how steadily and systematically the foundations are being laid for a global footprint.

From his first day in office as the PM, Narendra Modi put his stamp on the nation's foreign policy. He demonstrated diplomatic imagination by inviting neighbouring leaders to his oath-taking ceremony in 2014, a step that orthodox thinking had not even contemplated. His US visit later that year served to bring on stage a new kind of public diplomacy. He infused greater energy into Indian endeavours, reaching out with an intensity and spread that was so different from his predecessors. In the time that has passed, PM Modi tabled fresh ideas and initiatives in various geographies and domains, ranging from energy and climate to counter-terrorism and connectivity. He has been active on key global issues, often directly shaping the outcomes.

This is not someone who is content with simply extrapolating on what he inherited. Instead, he has given foreign policy greater strategic clarity, stronger conceptual basis, heightened activity and better delivery. This was evident in the manner in which the immediate neighbourhood was approached and the extended one was engaged. It was also visible in the assessment of the global order and building stronger relationships with major power centres. There was then the planned cultivation of middle powers, of regions and sub-regions. This was paralleled by publicly upholding the interests of the Global South. The delivery of Indian projects there was radically improved, making them a visible symbol of a New India. First responder capabilities were effectively demonstrated, as was the ability to look after our citizens abroad when in distress. Fresh strategic concepts emerged, and so did new mechanisms and memberships.

The cumulative results were visible in India's higher global standing now. In other circumstances, it could well be called a transformational decade. But given the ambitious objectives set out, real changes have just begun. There is still a considerable road to traverse.

Nations and individuals come of age through demonstrations of strength. In the Ramayana, the relevant episode is the stringing of Shiva's bow by Rama when he goes to visit Janaka, the king of Mithila. This was a weapon of extraordinary capability that Shiva himself had given for safekeeping to Janaka's ancestor Devaratha, at a particular time when he could not trust himself to keep his emotions in check. Janaka had decided that he would allow only the person who could lift and string this bow to marry his daughter Sita. And it was this feat that not only ensured the marriage of Rama and Sita but announced the arrival of Rama into the world of warriors. This was immediately tested in a confrontation with Parasurama, a sage who obsessively fought the warrior community. Rama bested him by capturing and stringing Vishnu's bow made by Vishwakarma, the counterpart of Shiva's bow he had just strung, which had first come into the possession of Parasurama's grandfather. These were but the beginnings, and at every stage of his journey, Lord Rama overcame obstacles to realize his true potential.

Major tests do not come out of the blue. More often than not, they are preceded by earlier experiences of a significant nature. That is the natural evolution of people as it is of states. In Rama's case, this first happened when sages demanded his services to deal with demons that were ruining their sacrifices. Rama's father, Dasaratha, was naturally reluctant to expose him to such risks but finally consented with great hesitation. This attitude is also a systemic response in most countries when confronted with new threats.

In Rama's case, he first had to overcome the female demon Tataka in the Kamasrama forest. The next encounter in Siddhasrama was with more serious adversaries, the demons Maricha and Subahu. One was vanquished and the other reduced to ashes. Rama and Lakshmana then traversed the hermitage of Sage Gautama, where Rama was destined to revive the former's wife Ahalya who had been cursed earlier. It was only thereafter that the brothers proceeded to Mithila to perform the feat with Shiva's bow.

For a nation like India, it is to be expected that there will be rivers and mountains to cross as it moves towards becoming a leading power. Some of them could be direct challenges, others a product of larger circumstances. There could be recurring issues, as indeed Lord Rama was to experience with the demon Maricha. At the end of the day, the rising of a power is an exercise in perseverance, endurance and mental strength. If we are to look for a contemporary reflection of these events where India is concerned, this may be in building its infrastructure, upgrading its human resources, countering territorial challenges, developing deep strengths, exercising the nuclear option and improving the quality of governance. As it moves on to the next stage of its rise, India, too, needs to broaden its vistas, be more aware of competitors and strengthen its comprehensive national power.

THE NEW MANDALA

In any assessment, it is relatively easy to point to individual events and outcomes to demonstrate a sense of change. That may not be altogether without merit, but it cannot be the full story. Even inflection points are just that; they only serve to highlight a larger trend. Given the scale of what India is seeking to do over an extended period, it would be completely natural to expect that there would be a comprehensive approach to achieving its goals. And indeed, that is exactly what has emerged steadily over this period.

Some facets required an occasion to be unveiled, such as the enunciation of the SAGAR outlook during a prime ministerial visit to Mauritius in 2015. In other cases, the rationale followed the action such as the formalization of the Neighbourhood First policy some months after the 2014 swearing-in ceremony or, as was the case with ASEAN and beyond, additional layers had to be added for 'Look East' to become 'Act East'.

But there were also stark strategic decisions, such as the commitment to propagate the message of Indo-Pacific. Sometimes, particular events were devised to make a new move, such as the Forum for India–Pacific Islands Cooperation (FIPIC) summits. On occasion, certain circumstances brought out latent thinking, a good example being the Voice of Global South Summit in the aftermath of Covid and Ukraine. As we near the end of a decade, the overall strategy is obviously very much clearer than it was at the beginning. The dots have joined into lines, even forming concentric circles of interest.

What then is the *mandala* that captures India's thinking of the world today? At its core is obviously the immediate neighbourhood, the objects of attention at Modi's oath-taking ceremony in 2014. The approach here is to begin by recognizing that India occupies a unique position in the Subcontinent by virtue of its size, location and, increasingly, economic weight. It is obviously in India's interest that its immediate periphery be stable, secure and sensitive. Ensuring this in a competitive world will require us to underwrite the larger region and invest in the connectivity, cooperation and contacts that make for a more cohesive geography. There are challenges from both history, sociology and economics to overcome in this pursuit. While they need to be managed, the heart of the Neighbourhood First policy is for India to convince its immediate neighbours of the benefits of closer ties and then proceed to make that happen on the ground. This is essentially what we have seen unfold since 2014.

Today, we are looking at a distinctly different picture, where trans-border transmission grids, fuel pipelines, roads, railways and waterways, and smooth border crossing have become the hallmark of our times. All this is underpinned by the usage of each other's capabilities, be it in goods movement, ports or power generation. It has allowed the entire region to benefit through larger scale and greater efficiency. The real test of Neighbourhood First came in Sri Lanka's economic crisis and India's expeditious response has done much to enhance the credibility of its stance.

The second circle of priority is the extended neighbourhood. In every direction, the Modi government has, by now, laid out an intricate plan of engagement. In the case of ASEAN and Pacific nations, the upgradation of cooperation is expressed in domains like security, development and digital. As a result, the Act East Policy not only deepens India's presence in Southeast Asia but also positions it as a launching pad to the Pacific region and beyond.

Towards the Gulf, the 'Link West' approach has seen an unprecedented intensification of activities in a range of areas. Ties with the UAE, in particular, have helped to accelerate the pace of progress. Obviously, India only stands to benefit as others seek to compete. From the days when our vision of the Gulf was limited to energy and labour, this now extends to technology, education, innovation, investment and security. Even traditional areas like energy have witnessed broader Indian participation. Not least, the Gulf also serves as a bridgehead for greater involvement with Africa.

To the south, the SAGAR outlook brings together our maritime neighbours in an integrated manner. Some countries like Sri Lanka and the Maldives overlap with the Neighbourhood First policy. But others today note the stronger focus and larger resources that India is prepared to devote. Our development partnership with Mauritius has emerged as an exemplar in this context. The underlying maritime cooperation has also become the basis for an emerging security conclave that encourages more cooperative thinking.

To the north, Connect Central Asia Policy is the last piece of the puzzle which forges more systemic linkages with culturally comfortable partners. The agenda here is much more about connectivity, de-radicalization and development. For many of these states, India offers options that strengthen their overall positioning.

Clearly, how smoothly India advances in its multiple quests depends on the nature of its ties with major powers. In certain cases, Europe being one, constituent segments of a collective also need to be engaged individually. Many of them have the ability to facilitate this process; some have the ability to obstruct as well. It is naturally our endeavour to continually create an optimal mix. And this cannot be done by always staying the middle course or ducking the difficult problems. Obviously, there is a strong case for both prudence and perseverance. But there is an even more powerful one for understanding which relationship serves our interest best on which issues. As a result, contemporary diplomacy looks far from linear, often ending up in apparent zigzags. But the real test of its effectiveness is whether it puts India ahead in the competitive game. And such periodic assessments, therefore, assume importance in both policy validation and course correction, where required.

An essential part of preparing for a global footprint is to expand the breadth of interactions. The truth is that a very large number of nations have been engaged very perfunctorily by

India for many years now. Even today, there are countries that are receiving an Indian foreign minister for the first time in their history. Realizing this, our efforts in the last decade have been to find more efficient ways of conducting global diplomacy.

A vigorous participation in existing mechanisms and the invention of new ones helps to address this challenge. The Quad and FIPIC in the Indo-Pacific, the I2U2 in West Asia, and the India–Nordic Summit in Europe are relevant examples at the highest level. The IMEC is the latest in the list. Those with ASEAN, the EU, Africa and BRICS have, of course, continued apace. But these are now also supplemented at ministerial levels by formats with Central Europe, Caribbean and Central America. As with Europe and the rest of Asia, we can relate more purposefully to broader geographies like Africa and Latin America by dealing with sub-regions. The opening of new embassies, especially in Africa, is part of the same endeavour.

An important source of strength is the growth in investments, trade and projects of Indian businesses abroad. India is today among the top five economic partners of many countries of Africa and Latin America. The movement of our professionals is adding an additional layer to many relationships. Similarly, development projects supported through grants and soft loans across 78 nations of the Global South demonstrate capability as much as a solution to a local need. Quite apart from our national branding, it is the presence on the ground in so many manifestations that is imprinting India in the mind space of societies even far away.

The spatial *mandala* is accompanied by a conceptual one. Indian foreign policy today recognizes more explicitly the imperatives of national security in setting priorities and making choices. But security itself is perceived in much broader and deeper terms. AatmaNirbhar Bharat Abhiyan and Make in India are neither economic protectionism nor political slogans. They are, in fact, a quest to build deeper strengths and greater strategic autonomy that is required by a nation aspiring to be a leading power. Increasingly, economic security also cohabits with technological security.

The digital domain is its most visible expression, though obviously far from being the only one. India's goal is not of moving the needle in the direction of autarky but, instead, to create the capabilities that would make it a serious player at a global level. The demand for resilient and reliable supply chains are a chance that could be exploited with the right policies. Similarly, the knowledge economy is its big opportunity, and transparent and trusted data flows assign a value to India that must be fully appreciated. Participating more intensively in the global economy will not just require better preparations and the right outlook but also the appropriate human resources.

Investing in skilling them for contemporary times is now being paralleled by endeavours to promote Indian talent through start-ups and innovation. These are not just economic or even social initiatives but strategic steps laden with deep meaning for international relations. Let us not forget that one important driver of the transformed India–US relationship was the H1B visa flow. Addressing the rising aspirations of people at home and realizing ambitions abroad are but two sides of the same coin.

THE INDIA STORY

While the manner of engaging the world may be more considered, its effectiveness will really be judged by how the world views us now. It is, therefore, worthwhile to reflect on the changing external perceptions of India. Much of this centres on the nation's economic and technological progress. We were seen as the global back office for many years, but India has now surged well past that limited image. The knowledge economy has increasingly made us the crucial technology partner for many economies. The talk has now shifted to collaboration in complex fields like defence manufacturing and semiconductors. Our infrastructure improvements, coupled with making it easier to do business, have propelled us to become the largest destination for foreign direct investment (FDI). The Covid experience established us as the pharmacy of the world. That India handled the Covid well is widely recognized, but it is the economic bounce-back that is seen as the more consequential happening.

A lot of the India story discussed abroad revolves around improved governance. A digital delivery on such an enormous scale has been a particular source of fascination. Progress on the Sustainable Development Goals (SDG) front magnifies the sense of a society on the move. The mosaic is made up of many granules, from vaccines and health industry to 5G stack and space launches, or indeed, to educational branding or Make in India outcomes. The G20 presidency has also served to acquaint a wide cross-section of policymakers and influencers with infrastructure improvement and governance progress. This emphasis on delivery has led to more effective implementation of project commitments abroad. That great care is taken to synchronize budgeting is only proof again of how much diplomacy is an art of the detail. A successful diaspora certainly adds to this positive view.

There are also leadership factors and decision-making record in play. To begin with, a sharper strategic clarity has enabled India to prioritize and plan better. A relevant example is of Neighbourhood First and the seriousness with which it is implemented on the ground. Another is about overcoming hesitations of history with the US in particular and the West in general. Here, too, India has not let changes in Administration deflect it from pursuing its goals. At the same time, it has ensured that other balances are maintained to make this a smooth exercise.

Strategic clarity has also been accompanied by strategic communication. India's interests and intentions have been steadily messaged in appropriate forums and adjusted to changing circumstances. It could be about the Indo-Pacific, critical technologies, Covid-related needs or the Ukraine conflict. Partners are neither confused about our thinking nor doubtful of our intentions. A strongly independent stance has also helped India to effectively navigate a more multipolar and fractured world.

There is also a conscious endeavour to shape global issues, such as climate action, the pandemic, terrorism and digital infrastructure, and unleash the full power of ideas, be it in solar energy, disaster resilience, sustainable lifestyle, food security or even wellness. This has been backed up by projecting Indian traditions, history and culture more visibly on the global stage.

New India may be a message at home; it is equally an image abroad. It is not simply a more powerful and capable India that the world perceives; it is a more authentic and participative one, at ease as much with its nationalist spirit as with its international contributions.

The resulting interest in engaging India is today visible in many quarters. When it comes to matters of technology and economy, there is a growing perception of our relevance to the challenge of trusted manufacturing. This is all the more so since those processes have become so intensively data driven. One aspect of it is the reliability that emanates from our political and social characteristics. After all, it is evident that we are a political democracy, pluralistic society and market economy.

Increasingly, the misalignment of global demography and demand is making our human resources valuable for the international economy in a more tech-driven era. The establishment of the Trade and Technology Council with the EU is an indicator of the direction in which the winds are blowing. There has been even more marked progress with the US on this front, as indeed with the other two Quad partners.

A different dimension is the contribution we can make to the stability and security of the global commons, especially in the Indo-Pacific. At the same time, India is a partner of value in forums like BRICS and the Shanghai Cooperation Organization (SCO). Our independent stance always leaves open participation in any endeavour at conflict mitigation or resolution. The combination of Covid support, digital delivery and development projects has also created a deeper constituency in the Global South. It is not lost on the developing world that we commenced our G20 presidency with the Voice of the Global South Summit. Nor, for that matter, that we championed the membership of the AU in the G20.

The last decade has also established convincingly that Indian development initiatives are truly demand-driven and do not conceal a hidden agenda. Certainly, India's ability to straddle the big fissures that global politics is currently grappling with is part of its overall standing in the world.

DECODING MODI-ERA DIPLOMACY

We have till now focussed on how India has dealt with the world differently and the extent to which this, in turn, has shaped global views about India. Our appreciation, however, would be incomplete if we do not give adequate attention to the change in the very understanding of what foreign policy is all about. It may look as a shift in emphasis but is very much more than that.

Foreign policy is now seen as a direct instrument to accelerate national development and modernization. The flow of technology, capital and best practices are the ensuing focal points. Wooing the world is expressed in encouraging investors, especially by making it easier to do business. Interactions with them are as frequent as those with technology-providers and high achievers in different domains. AatmaNirbhar Bharat Abhiyan and Make in India provide an overall framework that facilitate such exercises, supported by initiatives like Production-Linked Incentive (PLI) on manufacturing or Gati Shakti in infrastructure.

The quest for technology and best practices is even visible in the PM's itinerary abroad, whether it related to a battery storage facility in the US, river cleaning in South Korea, bullet trains in Japan, skill development in Singapore, or railway stations in Germany. As this mindset was applied outwards, it also witnessed the export of projects, products and services that spoke of India's improved abilities. This includes a range of infrastructure, connectivity and public facilities that extend from South Asia to Africa and Latin America and, not least, a steady increase in defence exports to a growing list of nations.

The aggregate result is a developing perception of India as a partner of growing consequence. This has helped exports and market access abroad, with beneficial consequences at home. When a PM personally engages with all his ambassadors in that regard, we really know that India is changing.

In many ways, the operational culture of foreign-policy decision-making has adjusted to the new era. Central to that endeavour is a conscious effort to overcome silos by tighter coordination, more intensive strategizing and stronger feedback. Whether it is global trade negotiations, national security situations or multilateral concerns of development, the emphasis is on collective deliberations and decision-making. Starting as it does from ministers and secretaries, this has had a natural impact on the bureaucracy at large.

The same outlook is also demonstrated in respect of important partners and key issues. We see this now in respect of a multi-ministerial interaction with Singapore, the Trade and Technology Council format with the EU and the 2+2 Ministerial Dialogues in Defence and External Affairs with key nations. Behind that process was also a deliberative exercise that sought to prioritize, maximize and intensify India's international relationships. It could be the attention given to leadership-level exchanges, including to the chief guest for the Republic Day, and how they fit in with the larger game plan. Where feedback was concerned, the national-level Pro-Active Governance and Timely Implementation (PRAGATI) exercise was customized for the objectives of foreign policy. Drilling deep down to specifics enabled delays, roadblocks and policy obstacles to be identified and addressed. As a result, many development projects abroad began witnessing more efficient execution.

The systemic improvements came into full play during Covid, whether it was in the Vande Bharat Mission or the Vaccine Maitri initiative. They were demonstrated during evacuation exercises as well, ranging from Yemen and Nepal to Afghanistan, Ukraine and Sudan.

From 2014, there has also been a strong conviction that India should be more active in shaping the global agenda. Obviously, some issues of particular priority for India itself, like terrorism and tax evasion, did not get the attention they deserved in the councils of the world. There were others like maritime security on which India could make a crucial contribution. In due course, when an important debate like the one on connectivity unfolded, the strong confidence level of the Modi government allowed it to take the lead. When it came to climate challenges, India, till 2014, was widely perceived as a reluctant participant. Since then, it has emerged as a credible champion of both climate action and climate justice by becoming an exemplar on renewables and advocate of resourcing.

There was also a belief that we were mostly responding to the initiatives of others rather than putting forward our own thinking. However, whether it was at the UN, G20 Summits or COP meetings, the flow of ideas turned into more structured proposals, like the ISA and the CDRI. The creativity continues, recent examples being One Sun One World One Grid (OSOWOG), Lifestyle for Environment (LiFE) and the International Year of Millets (2023). To take the agenda forward, there was an openness to explore new partners and collaborations where required. The Quad, the I2U2 and the SCO are relevant examples. As confidence grew in our ability to contribute to global solutions, it took diverse forms, a collective one like the development agenda for Africa as well as a unilateral one like the Vaccine Maitri. By dint of application and imagination, the early thoughts about making our presence felt more strongly have now become reality.

While addressing practical challenges to India's progress, much thought has also been given to branding India in a manner reflecting the rise of a civilizational state. The truth is that two centuries of colonialism had skewed the global discourse so drastically in favour of the West that the heritage, culture and traditions of the rest of the world were relegated to the sidelines. Part of the responsibility for that predicament also rests with the leadership of developing societies. They subscribed to equating modernity and advancement with emulating the West. For reasons both ideological and political, many of them often ran down their own past.

As a result, the imperative for cultural rebalancing to accompany its economic and political facets has only grown with times. Prime Minister Modi has led from the front in this regard. His initiative in 2015 to globally celebrate yoga has been phenomenally successful. The propagation of our medical and wellness practices has also gained traction. When it comes to environment, the advocacy of lifestyle changes is being widely welcomed. Even food habits are relevant in this regard, reflected in the Indian endeavour to lead greater cultivation and consumption of millets, our ancient grains. Some of this is expressed through the optics of how the leadership carries itself and expresses its views.

A large part of the challenge that still needs more effective redressal is in the deeper concepts and entrenched assumptions of contemporary international relations. That is still work in progress but hopefully one that will see improvements in the coming years.

Yet another notable feature of the Modi-era diplomacy has been its people-centric approach. There were multiple drivers for this greater emphasis on the human factor. One, of course, was the external reflection of a domestic campaign to improve development indices and extend social welfare. Supporting Indians abroad is a natural extrapolation of this approach.

Another is the understanding that India needed to prepare for the requirements of the knowledge economy. It was essential to envisage a global workplace, not just a trading place. And that meant working out the requisite institutional arrangements and practices rather than leaving our citizens at the mercy of the vagaries of the mobility industry.

Then, there was greater consciousness about the importance and contribution of Indians abroad, be they students, professionals or those more settled. Their welfare was envisaged as an obligation that should be addressed with utmost seriousness. And finally, there was a sense of a changing India itself. A rising power should not leave its people abroad to face adversity on their own. Such detachment not only reflects badly on our standing but could also undermine the faith with which Indians could proceed abroad.

Instituting robust welfare measures applicable beyond our borders, extricating our citizens from crisis situations and organizing repatriations as they happened during the Covid pandemic are all steps in that direction. Indeed, the transformation begins right at home with radical reforms in the ease of issuing passports. This was paralleled by initiatives to facilitate mobility while ensuring that Indians were not treated in a discriminatory manner. Concluding Migration and Mobility Partnership Agreements (MMPAs) with countries ranging from Australia to Germany are the policy reflections of this concern.

DELIVERING ON PARTNERSHIPS

The progress report of the last decade is an encouraging one. Stronger expressions of diplomatic energies and activities have clearly raised India's profile in global councils. Prime Minister Modi, in particular, is perceived as a global figure who, while advancing his national interest, has a broader vision and a commitment to collective good. When it comes to the complex challenges that inevitably arise in world affairs, India is no longer seen as ducking the tough decisions.

The regional perception in the Subcontinent started to change from 2014. Understandably, this has not been a linear path, but overall, there is appreciation for the enormous strides that connectivity, cooperation and contacts have made. The extended neighbourhood also appreciates India's stronger sense of purpose as well as high-level visits happening after such long gaps. Where the major powers are concerned, they, too, have seen India prepared to engage more confidently and independently, perhaps in its engagement with multiple partners on defence, technology and energy or, indeed, standing its ground firmly when it comes to protecting its national interests from external pressures.

There is a global dimension to India's progress, which is no less important. In myriad ways, we have been active on a range of international issues that actually shape our contemporary era. Whether it is debt relief, global minimum tax or fairer market access, India has been a powerful voice in global conversations. When it comes to terrorism, India's own counter-actions and collaboration in restricting terror financing and listing of sanctioned terrorists have contributed to greater international awareness. We not only took the debate on maritime security to the UNSC but are participating in concrete initiatives across the Indo-Pacific, including hosting a key fusion centre.

One subject on which India made a decisive difference was connectivity. By taking a comprehensive and clear-cut view of the principles underpinning it, its policymakers were able to shape the debate in favour of greater transparency and better viability. But what has affected global perception most profoundly has been the Indian stance during the Covid pandemic. By providing vaccines to a 100 partners and medicines and materials to 150 nations, India demonstrated an altogether different level of global responsibility. The accrued goodwill has clearly helped define its profile at a time when the world is in transition.

In international cooperation, a lot depends on the willingness to walk the talk. For decades, we were known for partnering with other nations in their development efforts, mostly through training and exchanges but also, on occasion, through projects. In the last decade, this development has been significantly scaled up. There has been a visible expansion in lines of credit, grant assistance, capability building, infrastructure and economic projects as well as human resources enhancement.

But more than this scale, what has really changed is the effectiveness of delivery. Monitored continuously and supervised strongly, long-pending projects were brought to successful conclusion and new ones undertaken with greater professionalism. Connectivity, socio-economic facilities, logistics and energy in our immediate neighbourhood have been particular beneficiaries. Post-earthquake projects in Nepal and infrastructure in Mauritius are prominent examples of the enhanced quality of delivery. Despite the Covid challenges, India was also able to keep most of its commitments made to African nations as part of the India-Africa Forum Summit (IAFS).

During this period, the footprint of India's international partnerships has also expanded perceptibly. It now ranges from renewable energy in the Pacific to community projects in the

Caribbean. It could be the refinery in Mongolia, the Metro Express in Mauritius, a textile factory in Kenya or water supply in Tanzania, many India-supported endeavours have been game-changers for the partner countries.

A more vigorous India has been able to forge new relationships that recognize its growing value. An obvious example is the Quad, which has facilitated other Indo-Pacific engagements in domains like technology, supply chains, education, maritime security, etc. When it came to Eurasia, India's inclusion in the SCO in 2017 underlined its salience to that grouping's agenda. During this period, membership of export control regimes like Missile Technology Control Regime, Australia Group and Wassenaar Arrangement were as significant as plurilateral initiatives led by India, especially on sustainability. These memberships also spoke of a larger phenomenon of India's rise and the response of the world to it. That all 54 African states attended the IAFS Summit, that all 10 ASEAN leaders were present at the 2018 Republic Day and that India engaged 27 EU countries in Porto in 2021 and that 125 nations participated in the Voice of Global South Summit in 2023 are illustrations of where it stands today.

Often, that proposition is tested through elections to international organizations, and by and large, India has come through successfully. Indeed, the growing demand for our participation in different forums, engagement in various formats and presence on multiple occasions are reflective of our global stock.

FINDING OUR OWN SOLUTIONS

As we come out of Covid, like every other country, India is also assessing its costs, evaluating its experiences and drawing its lessons. What can be said with some degree of confidence is that we have weathered the storm better than many others. Strong fundamentals and considered policies ensure that India stays very much on course to becoming a leading power in the future. While much of that is dependent on continuously enhancing capabilities, it is equally essential that India's vision of its prospects remain confident. After all, we have struggled with decades of downsizing, hyphenation, non-involvement and risk aversion.

The pathway for the future is built on a mindset of fierce independence, though the challenge is to refresh it for contemporary times. Our ability to express this outlook has naturally changed with our strengths. Today, we have many more resources and instruments at our command to achieve national goals abroad. But even capabilities and aspirations produce results only when filtered through an accurate understanding of the world in which we live.

A crucial aspect of diplomacy, therefore, is a comprehensive landscape analysis, which captures the contradictions and nuances so essential to make policy choices. At the highest level, it centres on multipolarity and rebalancing while taking into account the contradictions between major nations. Drilling down region by region has meant a more granular appreciation of the issues involved. In all of this, there is the overarching reality of globalization, the ideologies of which can often mislead us through simplistic propositions. As we are increasingly discovering, one truth mainly works for one street.

The quest to develop capacities clearly benefits from domestic reform and modernization initiatives. This linkage was dumbed down to the assertion that 8 per cent growth was the best foreign policy! The reality, however, is that growth gained without transforming the foundations and framework had in-built limitations. This decade has consequently been a much more comprehensive effort that departed from established mantras. It also sought to avoid the pitfalls that were presented by a less strategic understanding of globalization. India's decision not to accede to the RCEP agreement in 2019 was significant in that respect. One important indication of the changed approach was in its very conceptualization. For the first time, Indian policymakers started framing the rise of India in terms of an era that is called the *Amrit Kaal*. By doing so, they articulate a thinking that is more long-term, comprehensive and transformational. And the fact is that the achievements of the last decade justify such a view point.

There is no shortage of indices that would point to the progress of recent years. And these do not in any way deny the magnitude of challenges that still confront India. But among them, perhaps it is worth focussing on those that are directly relevant to India's rise in the international system. A starting point is the steep decline in poverty, notable not only because it is among the more extreme problems facing India but also as it represents a wider drag on society. Equally important is the Indian middle class, which is expected to double during the *Amrit Kaal*, that is, by 2047. The world is surely assessing these developments, both from contribution and consumption perspectives. As it studies the quality of India's human resources, it would also note major expansion of universities, medical and nursing colleges and engineering and technical skills. Indeed, there is a change underway in the approaches to education and skill development that are designed to make them more world-friendly. The transformation in infrastructure is also underway, reflected in expansion of highways, railways, airports and digital networks. India is no longer seen as just limited to services. Even at home, energetic digital delivery has revolutionized governance and helped prepare the ground for deeper participation in a range of domains.

By raising the definition of basic amenities and, more importantly, delivering on them, India is rapidly changing the quality of life of one-sixth of the world. Depending on the country concerned, it is perceived by them as an innovator, producer, contributor or exemplar. Each one of these attributes make it a more attractive partner in international relations.

Developing the boldness and fortitude to advance one's prospects is almost as hard as growing actual capabilities. Learning to compete at increasingly higher levels does require confident leadership and systemic changes. As stakes get higher, it is also necessary to outthink competitors and outlast mindgames. Each phase in a power's rise has different benchmarks and changing peer groups. Adjusting our ambitions and calculations constantly will never be easy. In India's case, we have steadily outgrown the hyphenation with Pakistan and are being increasingly perceived as sui generis.

A part of the challenge is also to strike the right understandings on the optimal terms with the most appropriate partners. How to get the give-and-take right is crucial. These could be in a field of commerce and investment or indeed in domains like technology and connectivity. There are always opportunities to leverage if a nation plays to its strengths. Similarly, it has additional possibilities that could emerge from global demands of reliable supply, trusted data or critical technologies.

That said, we cannot be oblivious either to structural obstacles created by a world order devised more than 75 years ago. The heart of the matter is that in those crucial years, India was either present nominally on the high table or not there at all. Especially because of what happened to it in 1947, India consequently operates in a world where the dice is often loaded against it. Indeed, its rise in the last seven decades is really a story of changing the terms of engagement with the world, many of which were particularly adverse when it started this journey.

The problem is not one that can be quantified economically; it is even more that of assumptions and narratives. The world order consists of institutions and practices that are often closely interlocked. They determine what is politically correct and what is not. And because its key players have not only built an architecture to serve their purpose but still retain the influence to promote it, a power like India will have to swim upstream for a long time to come. Among the most formidable currents it has to navigate are the challenges emanating from 'freezing the moment'. This is a widely practised stratagem by hegemonic powers that seek to make permanent the advantageous elements of a landscape.

At its broadest level, this is visible in the manner in which the outcomes of 1945 are utilized to define an international hierarchy. The trick obviously is to imbue a particular moment with enormous significance and, thereafter, derive continuous benefit from it. Arguments to make the world more contemporary are rebutted by conflating them with challenging the original outcome in question.

This, however, is but one example of the larger tussle to maintain or change the world as we know it today. There are many more, some limited in scope and others more sweeping. They help to create and maintain frameworks, operate and defend structures and, crucially, establish and advance narratives. And they succeed to a great degree because global behaviour is shaped so much by muscle memory. We are all not just creatures of habits but followers of norms and believers of storylines.

A combination of these factors conceals the vested interests that underpin the arrangements of the day. It could be the UN and its working, nuclear non-proliferation, the selective focus on human rights, the equally calculated balancing of realpolitik and values, as well as the utilization of Cold War imagery. Particular moments also serve to define the 'other' sharply, such as after the 9/11 attack. So does the evocation of past conflicts, especially the last World War. For all these reasons, attempts to reshape global debates and concepts meet with the fiercest resistance. That is something India must expect and counter.

As a rising power, India encounters freezing the moment in different formats. It can come up against institutions and practices that do not give it its due. That is why it is such a strong proponent of reformed multilateralism. It can shape its approach to other powers, sometimes to our detriment. This requires confident thinking to create more up-to-date terms of engagement. On occasion, impactful moments can lead to such strong perceptions that it puts pressure on policy to adjust. To a considerable degree, that is the case with Pakistan after the 26/11 Mumbai terror attack. The Indian public clearly saw the governmental response as weak-kneed and pushed for a change.

There could even be situations when we will want to move on rapidly beyond an action. That was certainly the case of the Vajpayee government in reaching out to key partners soon after the 1998 nuclear tests. It is sometimes the fate of nations to also inherit the concepts and assumptions of others. The global understanding of India's place and influence is a relevant example, one very much shaped by other powers. It is only in recent years that we have managed to break out, first of the post-Partition hyphenation and then from the Indian Ocean box. The reaction to an Indo-Pacific presence is, therefore, only to be expected. One facet of a transformational decade has been to overcome this natural inclination to be a prisoner of our own history.

The difficulties of the past need not always be an encumbrance. The creativity of political leaderships is sometimes demonstrated by an ability to make it an asset in a changed context. In recent years, our nation has seen a renewed interest in Netaji Subhas Chandra Bose and the Indian National Army, as well as in those who resisted British colonialism in an earlier era. The great tribal leader Birsa Munda and the revolutionary Alluri Sitarama Raju are two such cases. While such figures may not have been entirely successful in achieving their immediate objectives, their longer-term impact as inspirational icons is very apparent today. Imageries from history are, in fact, extremely powerful in articulating aspirations for the future.

Indeed, when we look back at our own record over the last seven decades, it is still specific events like the conflicts of 1962, 1965, 1971 and 1999 that stand out as milestones. As India goes about its endeavour to ascend the international hierarchy, it must play well this game of using narratives and experiences to establish practices and habits as well.

The messaging out of New Delhi has also been far more energetic on key issues. *Vasudhaiva Kutumbakam* (the world is one family) conveys a commitment to international cooperation; 'Reformed Multilateralism' underlines the urgency of addressing the effectiveness of the UN; 'A World Free of Terror' underlines a determination to combat this long-standing threat; 'Digital for Development' speaks of how effective it has been as a governance tool; 'Mother of Democracy' is a reminder that our pluralistic and consultative traditions go back deep in history; and 'One World One Health' is an assertion of the need for timely, effective and non-discriminatory responses to global health challenges.

Developing our own lexicon, concepts, mechanisms and ideas and socializing them in world politics is also a testimony to India's continued rise. Their unfolding underlines the reality of India's vigorous participation in global platforms.

Within India, there will always be lively arguments about the balance between continuity and change in our foreign policy. That is only to be expected and, perhaps, in some ways, is even contributory to the emergence of new ideas. Normally, when it comes to diplomacy, analysis focusses on how we see the world and all its complications. Sometimes, it is useful to invert that and reflect on how the world, on its part, could be visualizing India and the opportunities there.

India's rise is a relentless exercise where the sensible only pause to take stock, never to declare victory. Without neglecting the past, it works best when our eyes are fixed firmly on the horizons and we read the international situation right as well as fashion our strategies and tactics accordingly. But to do all this and more, it is essential that Bharat is true to itself, its interests and its ambitions.

6.

MAKING FRIENDS, INFLUENCING PEOPLE

Why India Must Create a Global Constituency

In its quest to become a leading power, India has to successfully navigate the two big contradictions of our times, even while steadily enhancing its comprehensive national power. One is the East–West divide that has been sharpened by the Ukraine conflict. The other is the North–South gap that has been aggravated by Covid, debt, climate change as well as food and energy insecurity. This is on top of the natural compulsion of a rising power to maximize its friends and minimize its problems. India's search for ideal positioning in the global arena may be an unceasing effort. But those with larger ambitions must definitely develop reliable partners and assured sources of support. Their endeavour is also to shape the landscape rather than just operate in it.

The days when India could stir itself episodically while allowing processes to make their own progress are now behind us. Our interests are only expanding with time, and so must our activities and profile. The task before us is to lay the foundations in the *Amrit Kaal* for India to not only be a developed nation but also a leading power. That is why *Sabka Saath, Sabka Vikas* (working with all for the progress of all) is as relevant in foreign policy as in the domestic one. After all, diplomacy is all about making friends and influencing people. And the scope for a country that has a natural inclination to treat the world as a family (*Vasudhaiva Kutumbakam*) is immense in this regard.

In India, the term 'Rama–Lakshmana' is popularly used as an expression for describing closeness between siblings. But transpose this to the domain of global politics and reflect on its implications. The fact is that every Rama needs a Lakshmana, someone trustworthy and vigilant who will share both successes and sorrows. At crucial moments, he provided courage, counselled composure and steadied his principal. When the demon Viradh kidnapped Sita in Dandakaranya forest, it was Lakshmana who exhorted a shaken Rama to take swift counter-action. When Rama vented his frustration after Ravana's more successful abduction, it was again his brother who narrated how others dealt with misfortune through patience and fortitude. Thereafter, as Rama lost his cool with the seagod Varuna, who would not allow him to cross into Lanka, it was Lakshmana who persuaded him not to intimidate the god more than necessary. How to build close and reliable partnerships is the perennial task of diplomacy.

Every nation, however large or powerful, needs such sources of support. They may have a situational salience but the fact is that once established, such relationships have multiple ways of making themselves valuable. This is obviously a far cry from the normally transactional nature of international relations. It requires generosity, care, consideration and, sometimes, even affection. There is even some place for sentiment in world affairs, illustrated by that adage of blood being thicker than water. The solidarity of shared experiences is no weak bond either. India opened its heart through Vaccine Maitri, it was a gesture that will stand it in good stead for a long time. Indeed, as it rises up the global hierarchy of power, the requirement for reliable friends will grow, not lessen. The broader the footprint and greater the interests, the more is the importance of Lakshmanas.

The unstinted devotion of another player may be a relative rarity in real life, but significant enterprises in global history generally require assembling a larger coalition of support. This is particularly so when the nature and outcome of endeavours are open-ended. As activities are taking place far away from one's zone of familiarity, the value of associates goes up commensurately. This is further enhanced if they bring a particular skill or contribution to the collective effort. When confronting a larger or unusual opponent, the need for allies and well-wishers is still more keenly felt. We have seen this even in modern history, whether we think back to the World Wars, the Gulf War, Afghanistan or even ongoing situations. In the case of Rama, he was utterly at a loss to even guess how and where his abducted wife could have been taken. He finally tracked her through the multiple contributions of well-wishers and allies of various kinds. It does not always take a combat situation for this to be realized. In the competitive world of international politics, each friend who stands up in a difficult situation is one to be prized.

The coalition of *vanaras* that set out in every direction to gather intelligence is an equally powerful example of such sentiment. It was the force under Prince Angada, which had gone south, that learnt of Sita being in the gardens of Lanka. Without the army of monkeys, the bears and the eagles, Rama perhaps could not have got his bearings right. The need to be situationally aware when making important decisions is evident.

Often, some challenges may be beyond purely national capabilities and the contribution that well-wishers can make could be invaluable. Sampati's extraordinary sight is an analogy for accessing vital information about competitors and adversaries. And when the time came to cross the oceans, it was Nala, the bridge-building son of Vishwakarma, who provided the technology solution. Varuna went against his very nature in promising not to wash over the bridge that Nala built. This was the result of coercion by Rama, who in his anger, had threatened to dry up the seas if he was not allowed to cross.

Making friends and influencing people does involve a range of motivating factors, from incentives and flattery to assistance and threats. For most nations, this is an exceptionally patient and arduous task and may not be as easy as it seems. Generally speaking, it requires an astute identification of its components and accommodation among competing interests. On exceptional occasions, there could even be difficult choices made for larger good. At the heart of one such case is the most debated action of Lord Rama in the epic. In an ongoing battle between the two sibling monkey chieftains, Vali and Sugriva, Rama intervened to kill the former. It was, of course, Vali's destiny to meet his end by divine hands and his own personal conduct was clearly not above reproach.

But the episode and its consequences offer important insights into undertaking larger operations. Viewed from a power perspective, Rama favoured the lesser entity, the younger brother Sugriva, who was earlier ousted from his position. Common sense indicates that the weaker side is always more welcoming of intervention and even more inclined to tie its fortunes on a lasting basis. Having gained the services of Sugriva, it was farseeing of Rama to maintain the unity of the *vanara*s by taking Vali's son, Angada, under his personal protection. Inspiring his allies to act with alacrity was no easy task either. Predictably, Sugriva went back to a good life in Kishkinda after assuming the throne, and it required Lakshmana's anger to remind him of his obligations.

The entire period when the *vanara* sena (army) is sent in multiple directions is also an experience of strategic patience for Rama and Lakshmana. The coalition must not just assemble but be given time to do its work, often at the speed of its less efficient components. Sometimes, partners may not be able to deliver in time. That was the case for Rama later on with Pratardana, the king of Kashi, whose promised legions did not arrive in time to join the battle in Lanka. But it is to Rama's credit that he publicly acknowledged their intent. In life, there is always a next time and diplomacy must never foreclose possibilities.

THE PAST AND THE FUTURE

As it goes about its business of rising in the international order, India has to bear in mind that the world is continuously changing, as indeed are its ties with various players. In the early years after Independence, we sought to build a relationship with the West while creating our decisional space. At the same time, constituencies in the developing world were nurtured by building on the obvious empathy of post-colonialism. Cooperation with the Socialist bloc was explored, with tangible outcomes in the economic and security spheres. As the pressures of the Cold War grew and Sino-US rapprochement unfolded, it compelled India to double down on its Soviet relationship. A large part of its difficulties with the West emanated from the preference that the latter showed for a military-ruled Pakistan.

It was, therefore, natural that the end of the Cold War would lead to readjustments on India's part and of the world towards India. These processes have gained steady momentum in the quarter of the century that has passed. Their consolidation has been facilitated by the fact that in the last decade, New Delhi has shed much of the ideological baggage of the past. The US, in particular, is seen much more as part of the solution than of the problem. The diplomatic challenges now are one of advancing new relationships while retaining earlier ones. And, within that overall mix, assigning the appropriate weightage to specific ones, so that India gets the optimal results in a world that is under transformation.

Analysing India's ties with the five permanent members of the UNSC is a good place to start an assessment of both its record and its prospects. Those with the US and China are addressed in further chapters.

The UK: A Contemporary Compact

More than any other relationship, India's ties with the UK carry the burden of a complex past. The scars of that period are both material and psychological. The challenge now is to make history work for the future of the relationship, where comforts and convergences overcome frictions and fissures.

Interestingly, it began as a symbiotic relationship in the immediate aftermath of India's independence. Current generations will probably be astonished at the extent of influence that the UK wielded in India for the next two decades. In fact, an Indian leadership anxious to stay out of the Cold War and keep the US at bay actually perceived the UK as its best foil. So much so that its radical segment even overcame initial reservations about joining the Commonwealth, believing that a British association would shield them from American pressure.

The recent success of the movie *RRR* is a reminder of how strongly feelings about the colonial era resonate with the Indian public even today. It is quite natural that there are sensitivities and wariness in the India–UK relationship that derive from this period. The partitioning of India may have left its own deep impact thereafter, but the subsequent India–Pakistan hyphenation clearly gave it even further life. Starting from 1947, when Pakistan attacked Jammu & Kashmir, the UK was perceived in New Delhi as being partial to Pakistan. This view, which grew further from the workings of the UNSC, was aggravated by the position that the UK took in the 1965 and 1971 conflicts. Britain's Cold War compulsions, the withdrawal from East of Suez and accession to the EU gradually eroded the proximity of the initial years. When it came to developments in Afghanistan after 2001, it did not escape New Delhi's notice that Great Britain was the strongest advocate of dealing with the military leadership in Rawalpindi.

From the Indian perspective, whether it was the exercise of the nuclear option, a security concern like Afghanistan or the politics of the Indian subcontinent, British diplomacy was understandably viewed with suspicion. Moreover, as it gradually came into its own, the desire to put the past behind was also commensurately stronger in Indian politics. Weakening bonds between the elites as a result of deeper democratization of India accelerated the process. By the time Brexit arrived, the case for setting new terms of engagement was apparent.

While the past continues to cast its shadow, the present is not without its own complications. British politics is often driven by vote-bank considerations, though not to the extreme extent of Canada. And this has given space for secessionist forces targeting

India to operate from its soil and misuse its freedoms. Ideological hostility in influential quarters against the current dispensation in India has also added to irritants. Some are visibly so resentful of changes in India that they do not wish to understand the reality. When the UK claims to have a special bond with India, its impact is all the more.

However, there is also a parallel reality of the two nations cooperating in a range of domains. This long-standing duality is one of the characteristics of the ties; whether the UK would follow the US to comprehensively reset it is the major question. Till now, the UK has lagged behind, but there is growing consciousness of the distance that this has created with India. Making adjustments requires introspection on a range of concerns, from political sensitivities and security issues to export controls and mobility. That this is no longer the India of the past should be evident by now. Whether it is replacing British-era legal codes, expressing its cultural beliefs or asserting the symbolism of Netaji, times are surely changing. Because of the close past association, it is particularly incumbent on the UK to appreciate the nature of this transformation.

On the other hand, it is also essential that Indians approach the future of this partnership more clinically. They must recognize that the UK has served as an effective gateway for Indian businesses in Europe and that it hosts a successful diaspora. Its global influence may not be the same, but it is still very real in parts of the world. In certain domains, British technology and capabilities are clearly world-class. From an Indian viewpoint, there is a case for building further on the convergence that the two countries may currently have. That answer, once both countries put their mind to it, veers in a positive direction. This is reflected in their agreed 2030 Roadmap, among others.

Connecting the two countries and peoples can be pursued through different avenues, including closer political contacts, deeper economic and financial exchanges, greater skills and education flows, stronger research and innovation partnerships, and, of course, by nurturing the living bridge. Underlying this exercise is how we look at the world and grapple with issues that both nations confront every day.

The UK is a very different polity in the aftermath of Brexit. And some of these changes are precisely those that can provide impetus to a more contemporary partnership. Greater national control has allowed the UK to contemplate an Enhanced Trade Partnership with India. An agreement on a migration and mobility partnership helps to match demand, demographics and talent. The UK's Integrated Review locates it as a Euro-Atlantic actor, but with an increasing stake in the Indo-Pacific. That makes a compelling argument for a stronger understanding with India.

From India's viewpoint, there are many UKs that we seek to engage simultaneously: the Global Britain, the Atlantic UK, the post-European one, the City of London, the diaspora one, the innovation and education UK, and, of course, the strategic one. The internal balance among them has clearly shifted as a result of Brexit and the global aspect is now much more at the forefront. While refreshing their ties, India and the UK cannot ignore the issues carried forward from their history. But their conversation in the future will necessarily be different. In the final analysis, the true test of a transition to a new era will be in the ability to work together both on issues of the Indian subcontinent and the larger global stage.

Russia: A Steady Partnership

The story with Russia (erstwhile USSR) has been very different. A power that was suspicious of the Indian national movement, often to the point of being downright hostile, developed increasing shared interests as post-Independence diplomacy took root. This picked up after 1953–54, especially once Pakistan joined US-led alliance systems. Many political parties in our country also viewed the USSR as a progressive force. For an India increasingly worried about the Western arming of its neighbour, the relationship was both an insurance policy and an active contributor to our national strengths. It grew to a level where Russia's role, then as the USSR, was critical to a strategic inflection point in the Indian subcontinent in 1971.

The resulting goodwill, combined with a continuing sensitivity to India's interests, has kept these ties steady despite global tumult. Even the break-up of the USSR had limited impact, with the two nations re-discovering their mutual priority within a decade.

Today, it is this Indian relationship with Russia that is most on the global radar. In terms of significance, it compares in many respects to that with the US and China. Its economic content may be less, but for India, it has enormous strategic and security relevance. The unintended consequences of an unforeseen conflict, however, have paradoxically hastened some possibilities long under discussion. As a result, Russia could well emerge as a primary supplier of resources at the very time that India ramps up its economic growth and expands such needs.

The irony today about the partnership is that it is the subject of attention not because it has changed but because it has not. In fact, ties between Russia and India have been among the steadiest of the major relationships in the world after the Second World War. Each country has seen ups and downs in its ties with many other partners. Yet, for a variety of reasons, both have managed to insulate their own relationship from the volatility of global events. It appears that the logic of geopolitics combined with the mutuality of benefits have provided an exceptionally strong ballast to their ties.

If relations have been stable, this is not to say that either nation has remained static as a polity or even as a society. In the last quarter of a century, India has grown to emerge as the fifth largest economy, a nuclear weapon power, a technology centre, a reservoir of global talent and an active shaper of international debates. Its interests and influence have grown well beyond the Subcontinent.

Russia has, meanwhile, defined itself more nationally, with the accompanying changes in orientation and priorities. Its inherent character as a Eurasian power and its global status make it salient to the world order. Russia has also demonstrated an ability to influence outcomes across regions and issues. Its importance in domains like energy, resources and technology remains noteworthy.

The last three decades have seen the autonomous evolution of both Russia and India. They may have forged partnerships with others that may not always be convergent. Their own bilateral balance and equation have also developed with time. Yet, there appears to be a continued intersection of interests built on a legacy of goodwill that shapes their thinking about each other. What has made a difference is that they have taken great care even in a changing world not to act in a manner that adversely affects the core interests of the other. Preserving that is obviously crucial.

Though coming from different histories and geographies, India and Russia conceptually share a commitment to a multipolar world and have gravitated towards its establishment as a global modus vivendi. Their understanding of that may not be exactly the same when applied across geographies. Precisely because Russia is a Eurasian power, it is essential for India that it appreciates a multipolar world must have a multipolar Asia at its core. The operating principle of such a world is the legitimate pursuit of partnerships without seeking exclusivity. Two nations that have such a strong sense of independence should have less difficulty in appreciating the intent of the other. While Russia has stakes in the larger direction of global change, it is also a polity that has deep interests in the current international architecture. An important aspect of the future of our ties is the extent to which this accommodates India's rise.

Given the history of their ties, Indians would have expectations of Russian support, including on the reform of the UNSC. The Ukraine conflict has also led Russia to reassess its traditional focus westwards. Its consequential shift towards Asia is already visible on the economic front. For India, that will broaden an engagement that, till now, was almost exclusively reliant on the triad of military, nuclear and space cooperation.

In the coming years, the focus with Russia can be expected to shift, capturing its Asian facets more and more. The outlines of that have started to emerge. It could be connectivity like the International North–South Transport Corridor or the Chennai–Vladivostok maritime route and greater Indian involvement in the Russian Far East, or perhaps closer collaboration in Central Asia and the Arctic. All in all, India–Russia ties are poised for evolution even as they maintain their trajectory.

In very different ways, the British and Russian relationships evoke emotions with the Indian public. But policy, while not impervious to sentiment, is finally driven by empirical facts and a cost–benefit analysis. As India takes stock of a transforming landscape and seeks to chart its way forward, adjustments are only to the expected.

France: The Third Way

In contrast to the UK and Russia, France is a relatively newer diplomatic discovery, one whose colonial past has receded more in public consciousness. The minimal overhang of history offers it opportunities, just as its focus encourages growth of select domains.

For two decades now, this relationship has been steadily advancing, free from surprises and shifts triggered by external factors. The two nations not only share values and beliefs but put considerable emphasis on building national capabilities. Both of them navigated the Cold War era trying to maximize their strategic space. In modern times, they have developed strong convergences that go back to the 1950s. Since then, succeeding generations of French platforms and equipment have been an integral part of the Indian military force. India, therefore, has good reasons to see it as a major partner for its national security.

France was also an important influence in the development of India's strategic thinking, especially its nuclear-force posture. Indeed, the very concept of credible minimum deterrence was derived from the learnings of the French experience. Not just that, after the 1998 nuclear tests, this nation was the first nuclear power to show an understanding of our strategic compulsions. So, it was no surprise that PM Atal Bihari Vajpayee made Paris his first bilateral stop after the nuclear tests. Along with President Jacques Chirac, he launched the strategic partnership between our two countries that still serves us well till today. French support played an important role in India getting an exemption from the

Nuclear Suppliers Group (NSG) in 2008 to resume international cooperation in civil nuclear energy.

In the UNSC and other international forums, where competing and complex sets of interests affect choices, France has been a consistent partner. Our synergies have enabled us, for example, to be more effective in mobilizing UN action against terrorism and terrorist groups. France has also been a forthright supporter of India's case for permanent membership of the UNSC.

In the past few years, the uncertainties and disequilibrium of a world in transition have encouraged a stronger sense of common strategic purpose. Among the current priorities, one is to cooperate more closely in the Indo-Pacific, where India is in the middle and France present at its bookends. It is revealing that the two nations have entered into trilaterals with Australia and the UAE recently.

For India, in recent years, ties with France fit the challenge of 'right-sizing' its crucial partners. A nation that espouses the Third Way also holds an intuitive appeal to an independent-minded India. Its autonomy and self-reliance resonate strongly, as does its reticence on bringing in larger concerns. Once the two nations consciously decided to make this a foundation, their collaboration grew steadily over multiple regimes. As a result, in the pursuit of its larger aspirations, India has found in France another significant player committed to multipolarity.

However, while the long-standing insistence by both India and France to maintain their decisional freedom may produce convergences, each will have its own perspective. After all, they are located in very different geographies that will naturally decide both priorities and interests.

Like every other relationship, this one, too, will require assiduous tending. What should give most cause for optimism is that they have actually set out a perspective of cooperation for Horizon 2047.

The P-3 examples of the UK, Russia and France may be contrasting, but they do bring out the intrinsic value of the relationships. The fact is that permanent members of the UNSC have an importance much beyond that body. Nurturing these ties is, therefore, all the more important as India's interests unfold across the world.

RESETTING WITH THE WEST

Since international relations is simultaneously a collective and national activity, it is perhaps worthwhile to assess India's approach to the West as a whole. Understandably, some of that remains coloured by the experience of colonialism. That said, it is also a fact that this era has facilitated elite bonding to a considerable degree.

The one Western country that could have escaped the colonial taint was the US. It, however, blotted its copybook in India by strongly aligning with the Pakistani military and, thereafter, with China. These negatives were nevertheless set off against the substantive economic, technological and societal linkages that were built up after India's independence. Interestingly, even the political frictions were sometimes mitigated by circumstances. India may not have always been treated as a friend but was not regarded as a foe either.

The very same nations that evoked anxiety through their geopolitics were the ones that stepped forward after the 1962 conflict with China. Their contribution to infrastructure creation and agricultural self-sufficiency also cannot be underestimated. Our stance towards the Western bloc as a whole was influenced by the totality of these experiences and considerations.

Looking back, it is telling that for the first few decades, India's preferred partners in the Anglosphere were the UK and Canada. Indeed, much of its early international forays took place in tandem with them, the mediations on Korea and Vietnam being prominent examples. The US was, of course, an overwhelming presence, but one long regarded with suspicion due to our ideological proclivities as much as strategic calculations.

A measurement of the distance that India's foreign policy has travelled over 75 years is also in changed attitudes in this respect. The more we got beyond the romanticism of the early years and viewed the world through the lens of hard realities, the greater was the merit that was discovered in partners hitherto kept at a distance. This was accelerated when India started looking eastwards and developing an Indo-Pacific agenda. As a result, it is now the US and Australia that are assessed as having critical value, including at the Quad. If there is a pointer here, it is that the alignment of geopolitical outlook is so central to the development of ties. Indo-Pacific strategies now offer a contemporary pathway in that regard.

Challenges, however, are not with just individual nations. India's relationship with the West as a whole needs an objective evaluation. In many ways, this group is a natural partner because its members share the attributes of a pluralistic society, democratic polity and market economy. Yet, this very commonness can also create its own frictions. The continuing hegemonism visible in many quarters in the West leads to an excessive advocacy of their particular practices and convictions. Often, it is lost on them that others have different traditions, practices and yardsticks, and that the West itself would not necessarily come out well if they were evaluated objectively and publicly. Moreover, these attitudes do not stop at advocacy and extend to promoting an actionable agenda as well. That comes into conflict with post-colonial polities like India, which are reasserting their identities and standing their ground.

There are developmental frictions as well, as those more advanced seek to protect their leads. This is evident in the domains of trade, climate, patents and cross-border transactions, among others. At the heart of the contestation with the West is the tension between those who have dominated for long and others who now seek to challenge. The promotion of a rules-based order is regularly advocated, just as respect for the UN Charter is frequently invoked. But for all the talk, it is still largely Western nations that shape the agenda and define the norms. A fairer and less selective application of rules in various domains is, therefore, very much part of rebalancing. If global conversations have become more animated of late, much of it emanates from the courage to call out what is unacceptable. But for all these differences, the fact remains that those Asian nations have progressed fastest who have done so in partnership with the West.

For India, there are lessons to be learnt from how East and Southeast Asian nations leveraged geopolitics to accelerate national development. This is particularly relevant in our contemporary era of polarization. After all, no relationship is conducted without context, and the immediate one must inform India's choices even more than the distant.

In the discourses of Delhi, the term 'strategic autonomy' is usually defined as keeping a distance from the West, especially the US. The irony is that this has led us instead to develop deep dependencies elsewhere. The same logic applied in the case of non-alignment too. As we now move into a capable and confident era, it is important that our outlook is determined more by our interests and less by our insecurities.

Going by common sense, Indians must ask themselves which geographies give better access to their products and talents. As a long-term trend, there is also a fit between Western demand and Indian demographics that will help shape the global knowledge economy. Political choices, therefore, should not be divorced from those of economics, sociology or culture. There may be a process of subtle contestation between India and a world largely shaped by the West. Some of that may also show up in hedging, a phenomenon well established in the political domain. But here too, there are good reasons to be discerning and deliberate, rather than allow an attitude to become a strategy. India may be non-West but must realize that there is little profit in being anti-West.

Certainly, a calculation to broaden partners and ensure maximum benefits is an obvious one. But increasingly, in a tech-driven world, not all choices can be straddled or sidestepped. This is particularly so in respect of the digital domain and critical and emerging technologies. And while engaged in that exercise, the global scenario itself must also be clinically assessed from our perspective. Convergences and contradictions can be systemic in certain domains.

Developing affinities with the West will definitely pay well in the era of the knowledge economy. It is, therefore, crucial that we approach the larger issue as much with our heads as with our hearts. Eventually, new compacts will come into being that could more accurately reflect rebalancing and multipolarity.

The attention that the Modi government has devoted to building ties with Europe is a significant departure from the passivity of the preceding decades. Earlier, Indian diplomacy mostly concentrated on larger states, especially the UK, France and Germany. This continues to a certain degree, but there is now a more sustained focus on the EU as a collective body, and also sub-regions and smaller states. Regular India–EU summits have done much to change the atmosphere, leading to the resumption of FTA negotiations.

For India, Germany is clearly the account where there is visible space for further growth. Till now, much of that country's attention has been on other parts of Asia. That could well change somewhat in the light of new strategic circumstances. Indeed, it is the progress with the India–Germany relationship which could make the difference with that of the EU as a whole.

Among the sub-regions, the Nordic engagement has been particularly prominent, delivering results in the political and economic domains. The Mediterranean one, including Italy and Greece, has been less collective but still enthusiastic and impactful. It could acquire a new significance in the context of IMEC. The MMPA with Portugal was particularly timely in catalysing the rest of the EU.

Reinforcing relations with Central and Eastern Europe remains a work in progress, and different formats are being explored. Indian energies have also been expended in the Baltic and the Caucasus, including through the opening of embassies.

Handling the East–West contradiction is today one of the major challenges for Indian diplomacy. But the East is not a simple proposition for India. After the first decade of Independence, that has never been India's preference. Its relationship with Russia has been qualitatively different from its ties with China. It is clearly not helpful for India if the two are perceived to be in the same basket. From time to time, efforts have been made to advance such an analysis and India, on its part, has refused to be drawn in. There has been no competitive element at all in its relationship with Russia. On the contrary, it is the continuous consideration that the two countries have extended to each other that has been the foundation of their partnership. Where China is concerned, it is a very different story, in part due to the unresolved boundary question. Therefore, India's geopolitical posture will not be amenable to the extrapolation of the Indo-Pacific into Europe, and it is essential that we get the West to understand this logic of strategy.

While countries are naturally impelled by their national interest, it is also true that this positioning can help to mitigate global frictions when the time comes. This has been already evident in the workings of the G20 and some other international platforms. Indeed, it could even be asserted that calming the global discourse and stabilizing the global economy is in itself a contribution to common good.

THE AFRICAN SOLIDARITY

When PM Modi announced at the New Delhi G20 Summit the membership of the AU in that body, it was a very special moment for India–Africa ties. A year before, he had made that commitment in Bali and, thereafter, took it up personally and seriously with other G20 leaders. To many African countries, it was natural that India should step forward and advance their cause.

Yet, the fact remains that the story of India–Africa relations is a relatively uncommented one. It is often forgotten that there is a really long history of contacts, whether fostered by the dhow or the caravan. The period of Western colonialism added its own texture, creating the beginnings of an Indian diaspora in that continent. The subsequent independence struggles have generated a unique solidarity that is still on display in global forums.

As with many other regions, what was a steady but unremarkable relationship got a quantum jump due to PM Modi's personal interest. Perhaps this also reflected the extensive contacts that his home state of Gujarat had with this region. A clear approach to cooperation with the continent was articulated by him in July 2018 in an address to the Ugandan Parliament. Its essence was that India would respond to Africa's priorities, demands and needs rather than unilaterally propose an agenda. Since 2014, there have been 34 outgoing visits by the Indian president, vice president and PM to Africa, and more than a hundred incoming ones at the same level. The IAFS of 2015 laid out particularly ambitious targets for cooperation.

A decade later, despite the interruption by Covid, much of that was agreed upon has been delivered in terms of projects, capabilities, training and exchanges. Apart from practical collaboration, the solidarity with Africa is best expressed by how strongly India has pushed for its membership of the G20.

To date, India has done about 200 projects in Africa, with 65 more under execution and 81 in the works. Many of these projects were the first of their kind in Africa. Some are truly iconic in nature such as the Tema–Mpakadan Railway and Presidential Palace in Ghana, National Assembly building in Gambia, the Rivatex textile factory in Kenya, the Metro Express project in Mauritius and the Mahatma Gandhi International Convention Centre in Niger.

The narrative in other related domains has also been encouraging. More than 40,000 scholarships have been extended since the last IAFS meeting. A pan-Africa e-network launched a decade ago is supplemented by the e-VidyaBharti and e-ArogyaBharti initiatives on distant education and health respectively. We are today Africa's fourth-largest trade partner and fifth-largest investor. India's contribution of vaccines, medicines and equipment was particularly crucial during the Covid pandemic. The discussion is increasingly now on digital delivery, green growth and affordable health as the three themes of future development collaboration.

THE BRIDGES NOT TOO FAR

While Africa has been the main focus of lines of credit and grant assistance, India's growing footprint in Latin America is also worth noting. From being perceived as a faraway destination, that continent is gaining salience as a supplier of energy, natural resources and food. Its expanding middle class are natural customers for Indian products in pharmaceuticals and vehicles. The Indian IT industry is also firmly entrenched in the Latin American market. If the overall trade turnover is growing so rapidly, then the seriousness of our presence cannot be ignored. Currently, India is among the top five trade partners of both Brazil and Argentina. Indian investments are growing apace in diverse sectors, matching the strengthening political collaboration. In the task of making friends and influencing people, Latin America is no longer a bridge too far.

The example of Pacific Islands is a reflection of how much India's reach has extended in the last decade. But it is equally a reminder of what awaits it: a more intensified engagement with regions that are not proximate. Within this period, India has undertaken three summit-level meetings with Pacific Island countries, the most recent being in 2023 in Papua New Guinea. While the warmth of that reception got public attention, what is also important to appreciate is a development agenda that is demand-driven. Much of it focussed on the acute health priorities of the Pacific region. Indian commitments included a super-speciality hospital in Fiji, Jaipur Foot camps, dialysis units and sea ambulances in all member states and centres for supply of cost-effective pharmaceuticals. The digital deficit was also sought to be bridged by creating an IT hub in Papua New Guinea. A warehouse to host geo-spatial data sets was launched, alongside a centre for sustainable coastal and ocean research. Ongoing endeavours at solarization and community skill-building will also be taken forward.

Many Pacific nations were vocally appreciative of Indian assistance during the Covid pandemic, and all of them clearly saw merit in its climate-action initiatives. That Indian calculations have started to focus on a region where there were previously only tenuous contacts obviously speaks of an expanding horizon. But it also underlines how integrated global politics has now become and the importance of extending one's hand generously.

In a different quarter of the world, a similar story has begun to unfold in respect of the Caribbean Community, where there is a significant diaspora as well. Here again, a long-standing but low-key relationship is being energized through development projects, larger investments, enhanced trade and focussed capacity building. Enabling this through a politically-led framework is also beginning to yield results. The Covid pandemic provided an opportunity for India to display solidarity in a manner that will resonate for long.

NEIGHBOURHOOD: TRULY FIRST

Even as it spreads its wings, a rising India must remain focussed on its immediate neighbourhood and the extended one. The current decade has seen a radical improvement in India's linkages as a result of the Neighbourhood First policy. Whether it is rail, road, air or waterway connectivity; supply of energy; restoration of heritage; construction of housing; or expansion of capacities, India has demonstrated the value of its friendship. Neighbours are increasingly realizing that India can be a source of prosperity for them as well. In difficult times, especially during Covid, their well-being was greatly enhanced by contributions from India. Those who faced serious balance of payments crisis, like Sri Lanka, could also turn to India for support. As a result, the sense of regional togetherness has grown steadily.

That has also been the case with the regions a little more extended from India. ASEAN has discovered in India a firm advocate of its centrality and cohesion. The agenda of cooperation has widened to cover connectivity, development assistance, research and education, as well as security. The Gulf has seen a degree of attention that has been missing for the last four decades. The stresses of the Covid period have only intensified this growing closeness. The levels of investment, trade and strategic collaboration have improved markedly.

With Central Asia, too, the template of comprehensive engagement announced in 2022 has opened up possibilities in a wide range of domains. Indian capacities and partners are being explored with a much greater sense of enthusiasm.

As for the island neighbours of the Indian Ocean, they have seen India come through in both difficult and routine times.

The overall picture that emerges is now of an India that is more engaged, more responsible, more contributive and, therefore, more reliable.

GLOBAL SOUTH AND GLOBAL GOOD

As it ascends the international hierarchy, India speaks not just for itself but for a larger Global South constituency as well. The last few years have been particularly tough on developing countries. The impact of Covid was much harder, whether in terms of health accessibility or affordability. That they were then subjected to travel restraints added insult to injury. Already fragile economies reeled under the weight of lockdowns and disruptions, made worse by growing debt and declining trade. The knock-on effects of the Ukraine conflict have added to the woes, especially when it comes to 3F prices. In many regions, terrorism has been endemic along with its economic costs. Developing societies are also more vulnerable to extreme climate events that we are witnessing with greater frequency. Whether it is the 2030 Agenda or climate commitments, there is growing concern about the ability to sustain progress.

In all of this, India is widely perceived to be an exemplar in many areas. Developing countries also expect a nation like India to articulate their concerns in forums where they may not be present. For India, this is both a moral responsibility as well as an expression of global strategy. After all, the re-balancing process will extend beyond its current beneficiaries, and India is well served by investing deeply in the Global South.

There are also occasions when friends are won and opinions influenced by doing greater good. Some of it again may be directly relevant to national interest. But there is more expected of India as its capabilities grow. In recent years, we have been effective in providing succour in situations ranging from the Türkiye and Nepal earthquakes and Yemen civil war to mudslides in Sri Lanka and floods in Mozambique. The Covid period too saw intensification in international collaboration, be it the Vaccine Maitri for 100 partners, supply of medicines or equipment to 150 countries, or indeed the deployment of Indian personnel in the Maldives, Mauritius, Madagascar, Seychelles, Comoros and Kuwait.

Beyond emergency situations, however, India can help make the world safer and more secure by contributing to the well-being of the global commons. This could take the form of the Indo-Pacific Oceans Initiative (IPOI) that India announced at the East Asia Summit in 2019. This has since gathered momentum with a growing list of partnering nations. It could be the Indo-Pacific Partnership for Maritime Domain Awareness (IPMDA), which will focus on challenges like illegal, unreported and unregulated (IUU) fishing. Or indeed the Quad itself, which has taken on responsibilities ranging from collaborative connectivity and pandemic response to emerging and critical technologies. There are also practical examples of demonstrating climate action in which India has played a crucial role. The same spirit drives India's championing of the International Year of Millets. This could have substantial implications for food security and greener agriculture, especially for Africa.

Many elements of the logic that drives India's engagement with Africa also apply to its larger approach to the Global South. There is a broad message of empathy and solidarity, but their expressions could be specific to the region or the country involved. It is visible in multilateral forums through platforms like the G-77, Non-Aligned Movement or the L.69 Group. With Small Island Developing States, this is evident in development projects, renewable energy spread and disaster resilience efforts.

At a time when much of the world has fallen back to a nationalism of an earlier era, enlightened Indian interests dictate that it puts even greater emphasis on internationalism. This is made easier by the fact that in Indian tradition, there has never been tension between the two. The presidency of the G20 provides just the right platform for this message to be driven home.

It is not just that important bilateral relations have started to get the attention that they long deserved. There are also more innovative group engagements at various levels. In the immediate and extended neighbourhood, we can see that in the East Asia

Summit platforms, Bay of Bengal Initiative for Multi-Sectoral Technical and Economic Cooperation (BIMSTEC), Indian Ocean Rim Association (IORA), Gulf Cooperation Council (GCC) and a Central Asia collective engagement. Beyond that, there are the IAFS, the Arab League dialogue, the SCO, the Pacific Islands Forum, the Caribbean Community (CARICOM) and Community of Latin American and Caribbean States (CELAC). Dealings with Europe have acquired a new intensity, not just with the EU but also with constituent members like the Nordic countries or the Slavkov format. The Commonwealth remains a long-standing commitment while the G20 has evolved into a growing priority. All of these are backed up by a plethora of ad hoc arrangements, like the BRICS, RIC, IBSA, Quad, I2U2 and multiple trilaterals. In addition, there are some key bilaterals and certain specific regions that will determine the smoothness of India's rise.

India has now entered a new phase of a multi-vector engagement that seeks to maximize outcomes and benefits. Its results have heightened its profile and changed its image. As a consequence, it is today perceived as a source of ideas, a champion of causes, a driver of initiatives and an advocate of consensus. No country or region is now seen as irrelevant to India's global calculus. Each of these examples highlights the importance of making friends and influencing people. This generous, intensive and enlightened engagement with the world is key to Bharat's journey towards becoming a leading power.

7.

QUAD: A GROUPING FORETOLD

When Common Good Requires Fresh Thinking

The importance of the Indo-Pacific as a theatre and the Quad as a diplomatic platform is increasingly being recognized. Some may be interested in their novelty; others may think of them as real global change that is underway. Understandably, they have been the subject of debate and, in some quarters, even of polemics. Both subjects predate the Covid pandemic but have been shaped by it. We intuitively know that it has taken considerable diplomatic energy and determination to realize them.

With its meetings raised to a summit level, the Quad is no longer a bureaucratic mechanism but, instead, a gathering key to national interests. As we contemplate how this came about so rapidly, the more perceptive would appreciate that these were developments just waiting to happen. Indeed, this is a tale of a grouping foretold. But even for that to happen, it required global trends to intersect with strategic clarity and bold leadership. A steady course was equally important as the understandable resistance to a break from the past also unfolded.

After Lord Rama was sent into a forest exile on the eve of his coronation, he thereafter met up with his half-brother Bharata, in whose favour that decision was made. Their meeting (known famously as Bharata Milap) is, of course, a favourite subject for artistic and cultural depiction in the ages since. The hunter-king Guha, on whose lands this encounter takes place, observed the gathering of the four brothers (as the twins Lakshmana and Shatrugana were also there). He marvelled that despite each having their own interests and perspectives, they displayed very visible affection towards each other. It was not that there were no differences or tensions amongst them. Lakshmana, in particular, was deeply aggrieved at the invoking of the boons by Bharata's mother Kaikeyi and that continued to influence his outlook.

But once they come together, the distrust that would be natural in other circumstances was dissipated by their innate bonding. They realized, too, that their collective solidarity had a larger purpose because it resonated throughout the kingdom and allowed them to render their expected service. The ability of those who share values and beliefs to come together for greater good should, therefore, never be underestimated. Particularly once they have learnt to accommodate differences and appreciate a larger purpose, the groundwork is laid for a lasting convergence.

If we are now to consider the campaign underway to recover Queen Sita, Lord Rama brought together a diverse group of players to advance a shared objective. Naturally, the other side made all efforts to sow dissension among this differentiated group. In this particular case, Ravana sent the sorcerer Suka to create discord between monkeys and men. However, Suka failed to achieve his objective, as his insinuations that men do not treat other creatures fairly was strongly rebutted by the monkeys. In fact, his efforts end up counterproductively, bringing into open the conflict of interests of monkeys and demons in the forests that they inhabit together.

Ravana made another attempt with the monkey-prince Angada, invoking what he claimed was a deep friendship with his father Vali. He sought to exploit what would normally be a grudge, since Lord Rama had killed Angada's father. This too failed, as much a result of self-awareness on the prince's part as of the mutual confidence that was steadily encouraged by Rama. In its own way, the Ramayana is also a tale of the power of comfort and convergence as it is of the importance of global good.

THE CHANGING BIG PICTURE

In many ways, I bear personal testimony to the evolution of the Quad. This goes back to 2005–06 as witness to the early efforts to develop it that were particularly driven by Japan. After the 2007 effort, many of us shared the disappointment of an aborted venture. It was, however, typical of an era of ambivalence. A decade later, we were now in a position to both assess the changed geopolitical landscape and learn from the lessons of the past. A meeting at the Foreign Secretary's level in New York in 2017 was a signal that our leaderships had decided to give a new life to an old idea. The difference was also that Quad members now had greater clarity about global deficits and a stronger resolve to contribute. This was probably true of all but most marked in the case of India.

By 2019, the consensus was developing that the time had come to raise the group to a political level. I now had the privilege of participating as the EAM. The 2020 meeting of the Quad foreign ministers in Japan was particularly significant, taking place as it did in the midst of Covid. Just when the professional pessimists were beginning to pronounce on its prospects again, the logic of strategy asserted itself in 2021. The shared desire to ensure a safer global commons and strengthen Indo-Pacific stability was appreciated at the highest levels of the four governments. The practice of holding summits of Quad leaders took off, developing rapidly in the coming years. Clearly, the Quad has now come of age.

In the bigger picture, the Quad certainly represents an example of the direction in which the world is currently moving. But to see only the outcome and remain oblivious to the reasons that drove it would be to assume that major developments happen out of the blue, which, of course, they don't.

The truth is that a large part of the explanation lies in the corrections that Indian foreign policy made after the Cold War. The changes in its strategic calculations allowed three major relationships, those with the US, Japan and Australia, to unfold more naturally and fully. This journey was not without its issues, India's own nuclear posture and economic positions, as well as the priority given by the others to Pakistan among them. When events unfolded, additional incentives for relationship-building appeared. Concern for regional stability and cooperation on global issues acquired greater salience. The last three decades also brought out the importance of values in international relations. The convergence of these major relationships on the critical challenges of our time was inevitable. And it is the resulting fusion that we now know as the Quad.

Those who ponder about the changes in the Indo-Pacific geography might find it instructive to compare them to developments in Europe three decades ago. It is something of a paradox that even though Asia has been more dynamic than Europe, its regional architecture is far more conservative. Part of the explanation lies in the fact that Europe was very much at the heart of the Cold War and felt its termination more directly. The fall of the Berlin Wall opened up the ground for strategic experimentation that has led to the expanded EU as we know it now.

In contrast, there was no such seminal development in Asia. On the contrary, this was an era of steady economic progress and an accompanying political stasis. Moreover, the region had a much vaster expanse with greater diversity and a less collective persona than Europe. In fact, there were distinct sub-regions, such as Northeast Asia, Southeast Asia, the Indian subcontinent and Oceania, each with their particular characteristics and history.

Prosperity also unfolded at a differential pace, both between and within these sub-regions. Till recently, they did not perceive an overarching scenario that required a shared response. To the extent that when they needed an agreed meeting point, it was provided by ASEAN-driven platforms. Most importantly, the deep underpinning to the larger stability provided by a pervasive presence of American power has helped to keep the theatre steady till now. It is the revisiting of many of these assumptions and attitudes now that has started to shape the emergence of the Indo-Pacific.

To begin with, there is the reality of the repositioning of the US. Some of it may be reflected in its changed resources and commitments, but there is also the relative growth of competitors and the increasing complexity of challenges. Both the landscape and the tasking demand a response that cannot be the same as before. Call it 'America First' or a foreign policy for the middle class, there is widespread recognition of a new era. Where the differences lie within the US are in respect of the vision, attitude and strategy. These are not just divergent but very consequential in their impact on the rest of the world.

The US is undeniably the premier power of our times and will remain so. Indeed, such is its centrality to the current order that be it an ally, a competitor, the agnostic or the undecided, none of us can really be indifferent to its posture. There are different ways by which the US is coming to terms with its constraints and its challenges. And, as we have all seen since 2008, that has not exactly followed a predictable path. Some of the US's answers lie in reprioritizing; some in a more mobile and affordable footprint; and some perhaps in more tools of influence. Building a technology and financial edge has long worked for it and maintaining that against stiffer competition will be another national response. Where the US, as an entrenched power, is understandably struggling is in respect of new manifestations of exerting influence and wielding power. As an open society, it is not easy to deal with rivals with command polities. It not only has inherent vulnerabilities but also structural constraints while practising these contemporary forms of competition.

But what is important to recognize is that in its own unique way, the American polity is going through a serious introspection.

That could well result in a different method of engaging the world. Among its policy changes are a greater emphasis on burden sharing and openness to partners beyond established relationships. Its search for global solutions leads it to contemplate a new form of plurilateralism.

The second big driver of the changes we see around us is, of course, the growth of Chinese power. There are three autonomous aspects to this phenomenon that need considered analysis. The first is the enormous expansion of Chinese capabilities in virtually every field. The second is a projection pattern that changed beginning with 2009 and, more vigorously, after 2012. The third, and this was particularly apparent during the pandemic, is China's deep relevance to the global economy. These trends obviously cannot be viewed in isolation and must also be seen in terms of their implications for others. They have propelled global economic and strategic rebalancing, that too in a radical manner.

The US, as the dominant power of the day, is the most affected on both scores. Equally, the changes have had an influence on the rules and practices of the current order, management of the global commons and on the nature of world politics itself. None of that is surprising given that the combined import of these developments has been multiplied by their focussed leveraging for strategic purposes. That seamlessness exhibited abroad by China is a reflection of both a tightly integrated worldview and its domestic outlook.

So, let us be clear that this is not just about the rise of simply another power, however major. We have entered a new phase in international relations and the full impact of China's re-emergence will be felt more than those of major powers before it. And naturally, the reverberations are strongest in its immediate vicinity.

These developments centring on the US and China are largely responsible for the concept of the Indo-Pacific taking root so rapidly. They have fundamentally shaken the old order but not yet created a new one. The region has come to grudgingly appreciate that it can neither be insulated from their relationship nor indeed indifferent to what it portends for global goods. What this has in common with a very dissimilar situation in Europe a generation ago is that sharp geopolitical changes are redefining the very contours of the landscape. In Europe, it happened when American power was at its peak, encouraging a generosity that overcame the cautions of that continent's history. In the Indo-Pacific, it is a very different story, where it is the relative limitations of American abilities that has triggered a rethinking on the part of all parties.

Both, in their own ways, have encouraged a greater sense of collectivism. It was also inevitable that such a significant transformation in the relative weight, influence and behaviour of players should lead to a re-imagining of the arena itself. The irony is that those who are projected as taking the lead are actually coming to terms with a scenario that the fortunes of others have helped create.

THE CONSEQUENCES OF ACT EAST

There is more than adequate evidence of how integrated economic and cultural activities have been between the Indian and the Pacific oceans in history. By its very nature, the maritime domain supersedes artificial barriers and manmade lines. Whether it is trade or faith, mobility or practices, monuments or relationships, we know that the energies of its community traversed the waters over the ages with great comfort.

Assigning labels and restricting activities is a relatively modern phenomenon. In this particular case, the sharp differentiation within the Indo-Pacific was very much the result of the 1945 outcomes. In fact, it has a specific American signature to it that is highlighted by the milestones of its preoccupations in the Far East. Among them are the Second World War itself, the revolution in China, the Korean War, the revival of Japan and the Vietnam War.

As a result, it was quickly forgotten that much of what happened in that theatre was actually driven by forces residing in the Indian Ocean. To that extent, there is again a similarity to the Europe of the previous era. The interests of one great power distort the entire landscape and create concepts for its convenience. But here, too, the wheel of history has started to turn, and the old normal is reasserting itself.

The Indo-Pacific debate has, on occasion, been marked by charges of Cold War thinking. In fact, the truth is the very opposite. That is not surprising given that such rhetoric comes from the very quarters who seek to freeze the advantages of 1945. The Indo-Pacific suggests integration and plurality; its denial means division and dominance. And criticism is really meant to advance classic Cold War goals of constraining freedom of choice and exerting pressure to conform. In fact, to see the Indo-Pacific in binary terms when the interests of many are involved is a dead giveaway. The Indian Ocean may have been relegated to being a strategic backwater for seven decades after the Second World War. But today, it is not only a critical global lifeline but one smoothly fusing into the waters of the Pacific. The actions of the major powers active in the Indo-Pacific speak volumes of their integrated vision. So, if we judge nations by what they do rather than what they preach, the picture is quite clear.

At the end of the day, the compulsions of interdependence and interpenetration have triumphed over outdated definitions. Concerns about the well-being of the global commons were also a factor. Contemporary challenges required like-minded nations to work together, especially once the US acknowledged the difficulties of going alone. The Indo-Pacific, in that sense, represents the reality of globalization as much as it does the results of rebalancing.

A significant contribution to the change in landscape has been made by India's Act East policy. Three decades ago, India adopted a more open economic model that helped forge closer ties with the ASEAN and Northeast Asia. In due course, this opening acquired other dimensions, including those of connectivity, security, education and societal exchanges. The domains of activity may be different, but starting from the 1990s, India's ties with ASEAN, Japan, South Korea and China have developed far greater substance and, consequently, higher priority. Australia was a subsequent happening, but political and security convergences allowed this relationship to play catch-up.

What began for India as a solution for an economic crisis has finally ended up as a strategic correction. Today, India trades with, travels to and interacts with the East much more than it has done since its independence. Here, too, there is a falling back to history as there is a long tradition of Indian maritime activity and presence, going all the way up to the Fujian coast of China. Those who have been to the temples of Angkor Wat, Borobudur or My Son will certainly attest to these linkages.

As we consider the emerging Indo-Pacific, its policy consequences obviously drive the strategic debate. From India's perspective, its embedding in ASEAN-led structures over decades has created a regular and comfortable interface with all the players. In fact, as India's vistas kept broadening eastwards, economic stakes were supplemented by political and security relationships with those partners that nursed common interests. It could be a global forum like the G-20 or a regional one like the IORA, all of them provided additional opportunities for greater socialization. Even otherwise, those with a similar outlook and shared values tend to congregate together. But when the entire region grapples with new issues and different capacities, then those inclinations become stronger.

At the heart of the Quad, however, is a level of comfort generated by a marked improvement in multiple sets of relationships. This is enhanced by a stronger sense of common purpose in the face of regional and global challenges. Obviously, the collective ease is based on shared interests and some similar characteristics. But all of this also happened because the resistance to reforming international organizations and limitations of regional ones compelled a search for practical solutions. They, in essence, made the case for the Quad.

A TALE OF THREE TIES

The origins of the Quad actually go back to the coordination among the same four countries who responded to the 2004 tsunami in the Indian Ocean. Subsequent conversations led to a diplomatic gathering of their representatives in 2007. This did not progress further as none of the participants were really prepared to invest sufficient political capital in the initiative at that point of time.

The natural question, therefore, is what changed between 2007 and 2017 when the Quad, now in a more serious incarnation, assembled in New York. The current Quad did not come out of nowhere. It was an accumulated product of multiple developments, among them the complementary capabilities of key players, a more integrated arena and a greater openness to look beyond orthodox constructs.

But the real shift was in the enormous progress that some of the relevant bilateral ties had made in this very decade. The other three nations already had strong relationships with each other, though these too deepened discernibly in this period. What they did not have in 2007 was the degree of convergence and cooperation with India, which they had attained by 2017. Equally important was a leadership in our country that did not subject its national interests to the test of ideological preference.

This was particularly notable in regard to ties between India and the US. Those with Japan followed some distance behind. There was admittedly a greater time lag with Australia, since ties with India warmed up only after the 2014 political changes. It is in the story of these changed relationships that we must seek the explanation for the rapid development of the Quad. In the case of Japan and Australia, the relationship that India had was much thinner both in content and scope. Where the US was concerned, there were some sectoral strengths in an overall substantive but differentiated engagement. But even these had their limitations.

In the last decade, India's systemic interface with its Quad partners expanded very significantly. It extended across many more domains and enabled a full spectrum engagement with them. Naturally, the challenges and opportunities were different in each case. But as they gained traction, lessons and experiences from one were helpful to the advancement of the others.

The Rediscovery of America

Let us start with the US. The current phase of ties with India can be traced back to President Bill Clinton's visit in 2000. The background may have been of the effective management of the political consequences of the 1998 nuclear tests. But the driver was more a coming together in a globalizing world. It is essential that this starting point be duly recognized because it confirms that India and the US upgraded their engagement seeing an intrinsic value in doing so. This was the era of the dotcom revolution and H1B visa. American dominance was quite pronounced globally and there was really no 'balance of power' argument that was driving the changes. It was, in fact, the improving prosperity, expanding talent and a larger global exposure of India that made it a better partner in American eyes.

In many ways, this was a natural progression of the relationship once the constraints of the Cold War era receded. Suggesting, as some do, that these ties do not have their own merit and must necessarily be directed against others is a mind game being played to discredit both the relationship and the Quad. This is all the more contestable, given how those making such charges have leveraged their own relationship with the US so enthusiastically in the past when it suited them. Obviously, when a judgement is proffered by a party with a stake in the outcome, it must be seen for what it is.

Progress in India–US ties accelerated during the Bush administration, which correctly identified the nuclear impediment as a major obstacle to serious cooperation. By this time, both sides wanted a more normal relationship, freed from the encumbrances of the past. Therefore, they proceeded determinedly in that direction, successfully addressing the domestic political challenges to that process. This was also a moment when authoritative US studies focussed more strongly on the global relevance of India's human resources. Pretty much across the board, cooperative trends gathered momentum in a positive atmosphere. It was visible in defence, civil aviation, science and technology, trade and mobility.

The successful conclusion of the India–US nuclear deal widened the pathway to greater shared endeavours. That five successive American presidents, who were so different from each other, have been united in their pursuit of better ties with India has been a real game-changer. This consistency holds true at the Indian end as well. As a result, a relationship that was earlier notable for its argumentation and distancing has undergone a sea change.

There are many ways of capturing the transformation that has been underway for more than a decade. Trade is one obvious indicator, and it has expanded fivefold in the last 15 years. Investment is much harder to accurately define in national terms, but it has clearly multiplied in this period. The flow of talent is relevant because technology forms such a key element of the ties. The H category of visas, which enabled techies to move between the two countries, almost doubled in the last decade-and-a-half. So, too, has the number of students from India.

In some domains, this progress can be expressed through decisions and agreements. That a country that bought no American defence platforms from 1965 for four decades should now operate C-130, C-17 and P-8 aircraft, as well as Apache, Chinook and MH-60R helicopters, is not a mean achievement. Indeed, the security dimension of the relationship should be judged by more than defence trade. Policy exchanges and military exercises also testify to this shift, as do the multiple agreements that promote closer coordination. The mechanisms and dialogues today span a very wide range of subjects, from counter-terrorism and cyber security to climate action and energy, from space cooperation and health to education and homeland security.

What has changed further is that while the focus till 2014 was to remove obstacles to cooperation, the endeavour after that has been to ambitiously realize its expanding potential. Prime Minister Modi's 2023 State visit to the US, in that sense, marks a new phase of ties. The expanding agenda of cooperation and its growing relevance to key global debates underlines how far the relationship has now come. While important in themselves, the understanding on transfer of technology for jet engines and the collaborative steps in the semiconductor domain hold a symbolism far beyond. American business is beginning to overcome its long-standing scepticism about India, just as its military is learning to work with a non-alliance culture. Its strategic community is displaying a better understanding of India's value as its technology sector appreciates the significance of closer collaboration. Truly, the relationship has now moved into a higher orbit.

Although the ties have undergone a profound change, some of the divergences of the past need to be borne in mind to navigate the future in a better way. A large part of the contradiction between the interests of the two nations arose from the traditional American approach to the Indian subcontinent. The interest in hyphenating India and Pakistan and seeking to influence their bilateral dealings has been an entrenched attitude. The deliberate permissiveness with regard to Pakistan's nuclear programme in the 1980–90s was its most extreme manifestation. The US presence in Afghanistan also created new factors of regional dependency that were not in harmony with its India relationship.

Moreover, the global outlook of the US was often on a different wavelength from the security and economic interests of India. Even on the nuclear account, the 2005 understanding did not always set to rest more doctrinaire American advocacy in that domain. It was also natural that the worldview, policies and diplomacy of two partners, one developed and the other still developing, would differ on a range of socio-economic issues. Nor was it unexpected that a dominant prescriptive polity should rub against a sensitive sovereignty-conscious society.

Indeed, some of these very traits combined to create challenges for the relationship in 2013–14. But structural changes underway, along with policy optimism, came together to ensure that ties returned to their upward trajectory and stayed that way. It is not that the two nations do not have differences; what has changed is the willingness to nevertheless find common ground and pursue mutual advantage. Indeed, it has been an example of how an open-minded appreciation of contemporary changes has refashioned a pre-existing relationship.

The breadth and intensity of cooperation over the last decade has been truly impressive. It is, of course, driven by much more frequent engagement at the leadership level, and by more comfortable conversations. This is supported at the cabinet and sub-cabinet levels through regular interactions on a wider scale. New mechanisms and dialogues have sprung up in every field of activity. Foundational agreements, contemporary frameworks and a larger volume of activity are all part of the change. And wherever that is quantifiable, trade, investments, students, visas, exchanges, the numbers tell their own story.

What started as an evolutionary exercise with a limited objective has not only mushroomed rapidly but is now developing increasingly higher levels of ambition. From the bilateral and regional agendas, ties have matured to cover a broader canvas and a more complex agenda. That the two nations are partnering each other in quadrilateral and trilateral groupings is a statement of how far their relations have come.

It is particularly notable that this growth enjoys strong societal support. There is, of course, the Indian diaspora factor in the US and the Congressional support. Because so much of the relationship is driven by so many constituencies of civil society, it can also be effervescent at times. Today, the strength of the bilateral ties encourages the two nations to work together beyond the narrower confines of their national interest.

Even as this unfolds, India and the US will also have to recognize that they approach the world from different vantage points, histories, culture and levels of development. From an Indian perspective, the US as a global power can, on occasion, have interests that are in contradiction with its own. Nor may it always share our priorities and perspectives. This naturally will be mirror imaged on the American side as well, especially as India's influence and footprint expands. It is, therefore, all the more important that strong levels of comfort are established at this juncture. Because willy-nilly, the two countries will have much more to do with each other in the times to come.

Rising with the Sun

The two decades that witnessed such significant developments in respect of the US also saw steady progress with Japan. Challenges for India on this account were, however, very different. Unlike the US, Japan did not have a pronounced history of leaning towards Pakistan during the Cold War. It was, of course, given to some degree of hyphenation like much of the Western world.

But for reasons rooted in history and culture, there was always a partiality in Japanese politics towards India. Respect for an ancient civilization was widely shared, and the immediate post-War period actually witnessed political warmth between the leaderships. Indian policies conveyed their sympathy for Japan's predicament, and the dissenting voice of Justice Radhabinod Pal at the Tokyo Tribunal was subtly appreciated.

On its part, Japan supported India's socio-economic goals through substantial levels of Official Development Assistance (ODA). Within the Western camp, on a range of issues, it was among the friendlier voices. The paradox of the relationship, in fact, was that the very lack of problems also limited policy attention.

As with many other states, India–Japan ties also felt the implications of what befell India during this period. Economically, a traditionally broad presence of Japanese companies failed to strike deep roots in the absence of a welcoming environment. They gravitated instead to Southeast Asia and, thereafter, to China, lowering India steadily in terms of Japanese priorities. Even when economic reforms were introduced in 1991, the Japanese business community responded with great caution, expressed in a demand that the enabling environment should come up to their expectations.

The thinness of the interface was not limited only to business, it also extended to the supportive activities that Japan normally encouraged. Whether it was education, culture or travel, the two nations continued to remain distant, even if pleasantly. The political domain was not helpful in this period either. There were already the compulsions of the Cold War that pulled the two countries in opposing directions. India's defeat in 1962 in the border conflict with China had obviously damaged its standing as well, and its economic struggles thereafter strengthened a negative stereotype.

Sometimes, situations get worse before getting better. This happened in the instant case when India's nuclear tests in 1998 shook the ties out of their complacency. It is understandable, given its history, that Japan should react strongly to that development. What was, however, perplexing to the Indian side was its sweeping disregard of the security compulsions of the other party. This was aggravated by the fact that Japan had not hesitated to ensure its own security through a treaty arrangement with a nuclear power. Relations really took a dip when Japanese policymakers of that period decided to lead the charge against India in international forums.

The resulting freeze in the relationship ended up providing an opportunity for both nations to introspect on its value. And from that exercise emerged a new phase of our bilateral ties. Just as President Clinton's visit marked the breakthrough in one relationship, that of PM Yoshiro Mori did in the other. And interestingly, while President George W. Bush took it to a higher level in regard to the US, PM Shinzo Abe did so even more personally in respect of Japan. His famous 'The Confluence of Two Seas' speech to the Indian Parliament in 2007 was not only a turning point for the bilateral relationship but an early vision of what emerged as the Indo-Pacific. The context for that unfolding is also worth recalling.

A decade-and-a-half ago, Japan, too, was contemplating an increasingly uncertain external environment that required it to contemplate greater responsibilities. Given its complex history, this naturally was accompanied by an involved domestic debate. A society with a broader agenda and taking a greater interest in world affairs will understandably look for more partners. India, no longer distanced by the Cold War, offered obvious attraction. Some of this was a regional convergence, some a shared quest for better UN representation and some a natural empathy of democratic societies. So here, too, the bilateral wheels began to move on their own logic. As they gathered greater traction, vistas of cooperation also opened up.

Between India and Japan now, the political messaging is strong, underlined by a practice of annual summits since 2006. Despite changes in administrations on both ends, the pace of cooperation has not slackened. As in the case of the US, this continuity is the strongest proof of structural change. The official description of the relationship has continuously grown, titled most recently in 2014 as a Special Strategic and Global Partnership. Trade may have remained limited despite a Comprehensive Economic Partnership Agreement (CEPA) in 2011, but Japanese investments in India have expanded both in sectors and volume. Japan ranks fifth as a source of investment and more ambitious goals were set during PM Fumio Kishida's visit in 2022.

The economic partnership as a whole has intensified, whether we consider currency swaps or development assistance. In fact, the ODA has more than doubled in the last decade itself, with disbursement touching ¥328 billion in 2021–22. Its implementation record has been impressive, boasting so far of six metro rails in key Indian cities and a number of other major connectivity projects. What has also changed is a Japanese inclination to shape a more conducive infrastructure, expressed in its support for industrial and freight corridors. There are ongoing dialogues now in energy, space, steel, textile, start-up funding, digital skills and healthcare, among others.

The high-speed rail project from Mumbai to Ahmedabad stands out as the flagship initiative. Given its ripple impact, it can even be envisaged as the third technology revolution, following upon that of the Maruti-Suzuki car and the Delhi Metro. Similarly, while the ODA cooperation is a long-standing one, the Act East Forum established in 2017 specifically targets improved connectivity for India's Northeast.

But it is those familiar with the intricacies of Japanese society who are more likely to appreciate the progress with India. The yardsticks for that are examples of cooperation in domains of particular sensitivity. The 2016 agreement to cooperate on civil nuclear energy is an even more telling illustration of the growing comfort. No less significant are the series of understandings in the domain of defence and security. The 2014 agreement on defence cooperation was followed by those on equipment transfers and information protection in 2015, naval cooperation in 2018 and reciprocal supplies and services in 2020. Policy exchanges in defence have been supported by staff talks between services as well as bilateral and plurilateral military exercises. As with the US, India holds 2+2 ministerial meetings with Japan since 2019. Again, the bilateral comfort is beginning to be transposed on a wider canvas, starting predictably with the US and Australia.

Building a New Mateship

The relationship that has developed most visibly in recent times is that with Australia. Indeed, within a short space of time, it has narrowed the gap that stood out in comparison to the other two Quad members. As in the case of the US and Japan, the 1998 nuclear tests did impact ties and the road to recovery was also not an easy one. But the Australian relationship also carried its own unique challenges. It says something about India's priorities that the first prime ministerial visit took two full decades after independence, that of Indira Gandhi in 1968.

In many ways, Australia tended to be the most distant of the Anglosphere partners. It displayed the attitude of the US to issues east of India and the approach of the UK to concerns on the west. On the other hand, the Commonwealth framework ensured that there were steady exchanges in a large number of domains, including defence, commerce, training and education. What was a substantial but not high-profile relationship also took a marked dip in 1998. Australia took the lead in calling for a special session of the Conference on Disarmament and co-sponsored a resolution in the United Nations General Assembly (UNGA) condemning India's nuclear tests. More significantly, it suspended defence cooperation and froze official contacts. The story was, in many ways, very similar to that of Japan.

It took a year for the two sides to step back from the confrontational posture. The visit of Deputy PM Tim Fisher in 1999 could be credited as the beginning of the thaw. In a sense, Australia was ahead of Japan in repairing its ties, evidenced in the visits of Foreign Minister Alexander Downer and PM John Howard in March and July 2000 respectively. The return to normalcy progressed steadily and was accelerated somewhat by the tail winds of the 2005 nuclear deal. But the reality nevertheless was that neither nation devoted the political attention to the other which was required to take ties to a higher level.

Certainly, on the Indian side, there was a continued perception that Australia had neither de-hyphenated its subcontinental relationships nor emerged from a general disinterest about the region. So, for almost a decade more, the progress of ties was left largely to civil society and market forces. It took the two-way visits of PMs Tony Abbott and Narendra Modi in 2014 to open the gates for cooperation that was so long delayed.

That ties developed so rapidly once political leadership came into play only underlines the extent of the structural convergence. The ambitions that guide this exercise are best explained by *An India Economic Strategy to 2035 Report* released by the Australian side and the *Australia Economic Strategy* issued by India. A trade of $20 billion plus and investments around $25 billion stand to benefit with a free trade arrangement whose initial phase has commenced. Australia is a major educational destination for Indian students, who now number in excess of 100,000. The Indian community, the second most rapidly growing one, is a source of strength for both societies.

But it is really in the realm of politics and strategy that the transformation has been most evident. Much of the growing convergence has been driven by concerns about the region's stability, prosperity and security. The deficit in global goods has sought to be addressed by India and Australia working together bilaterally as well as in larger forums. This reflects their shared concerns about respect for international law and a rules-based order. The two countries may have long interacted in ASEAN-led forums, the Commonwealth, IORA, etc. But stronger leadership bonding and more open exchanges have brought out the mutual benefits of closer cooperation and coordination. Australia has been an early and vigorous supporter of India's IPOI. In fact, the big change has been the realization that a stronger bilateral relationship today allows the two nations to contribute much more effectively at a regional and a global level.

The new intensity in the interactions has been on display at the highest level, despite multiple changes at the Australian end. It is notable that their Comprehensive Strategic Partnership covers an annual meeting of PMs, a foreign minister's dialogue, a 2+2 ministerial mechanism, a trade ministerial commission, an education council, an energy dialogue and sectoral working groups. Clearly, the days of attention deficit are now over for good. Recent agreements range from maritime collaboration, defence science exchanges and mutual logistics support to cooperation in cyber-enabled critical technology, critical and strategic minerals, water resources management, migration and mobility, vocational education and training, as well as public administration and governance.

Some milestones do bring out the interactive dynamic between the bilateral and the regional facets of the relationship. Greater political confidence and deeper defence cooperation, for example, contributed to Australia joining Exercise Malabar. A better understanding on the space applications front led to the Australian support for the temporary Telemetry Tracking and Command Centre for the Gaganyaan Mission. A shared concern about trade reliability and economic volatility encouraged a partnership on the Supply Chain Resilience Initiative (SCRI), along with Japan. The conclusion of the Economic Cooperation and Trade Agreement (ECTA) in 2022 was not just a trade deal; it was an expression of systemic confidence as well. It also says a lot that Australian universities have been the first to take advantage of India's New Education Policy to set up establishments in the country.

As with US and Japan, a change in leadership reaffirmed in the Tokyo Quad Summit that cooperation was now proofed strongly in respect of political developments. Indeed, the enthusiasm of each successive government more than matched those of its predecessors.

INTENTIONS OVERCOME HESITATIONS

In assessing the Indo-Pacific, there are also dimensions that are autonomous of such bilateral matters, as indeed of the Quad. Prominent among them is the IPOI, announced by PM Modi in 2019 at the East Asia Summit. This is envisaged as an open, non-treaty-based, inclusive platform for cooperation in the region. Structure-light and cooperation-heavy, it is intended to work in tandem with other mechanisms like the ASEAN, IORA, BIMSTEC, IOC, PIF, etc. Its seven pillars include maritime security, maritime ecology; maritime resources; capacity building and resource sharing; disaster risk reduction and management; science, technology and academic cooperation; and trade connectivity and maritime transport. So far, Australia has agreed to lead the maritime ecology pillar, Japan the connectivity one, France and Indonesia the maritime resources, Singapore the science and technology one, and the UK the maritime security pillar.

How the IPOI will develop remains to be seen. But it is certainly an example of fresh thinking on regional partnerships that has the potential to move cooperation in the Indo-Pacific forward. That ASEAN, the EU and individual nations have all tabled their own outlook, vision and approaches augurs well for the future. It is also an interesting thought that as India's global footprint steadily grows, it intersects with the interests of its Quad partners. A telling case is that of India's engagement with the Pacific Island nations. Relationships between like-minded countries tend to be naturally supportive beyond the confines of their actual interaction. And the complex challenges of the contemporary world certainly can use more effective international cooperation.

India is establishing IT labs in these Pacific Island societies and promoting solar electrification. Women solar engineers called Solar Mamas have also been trained. Apart from climate-related projects, Indian grant assistance supports community development, agricultural equipment, computers and LED bulbs for schools, dialysis machines, portable saw mills as well as construction of sea wall and coral farms. As noted elsewhere, the level of cooperation is being significantly upgraded as a consequence of the 2023 FIPIC

Summit, especially in the domains of health, education and space.

India has responded to natural calamities, including cyclones Yasa, Gita, Hola and Winston, and dispatched vaccines for Covid to Fiji and Nauru bilaterally, as also to Papua New Guinea and Solomon Islands through the COVAX initiative. There is a historical connect in particular with Fiji that can be the foundation of a modern collaboration. All these factors came together at the third FIPIC Summit that was held in Papua New Guinea in 2023.

The Quad nations are all democratic polities, market economies and pluralistic societies. Apart from that natural understanding, similarity in the structural aspects of their relationships has helped to foster the platform. In each case, there are regular bilateral meetings at the summit level, designated formally as annual in the case of Australia and Japan. All the ties now include a 2+2 defence and foreign ministers' interaction. Again, all four countries are members of ASEAN-led forums, including the East Asia Summit, the ASEAN Regional Forum (ARF) and the ASEAN Defence Ministers' Meeting. They also strongly subscribe to the centrality of ASEAN insofar as the Indo-Pacific is concerned. Between them, they are involved in multiple trilateral combinations with other partners, such as Indonesia and France.

In many ways, the ease of working together has been increased by other experiences, whether they are bilateral or more collective. That all of them offer mutual logistics support and work on white shipping obviously enables better maritime security coordination. Their shared view of United Nations Convention on the Law of the Sea (UNCLOS) 1982 as the constitution of the seas is no less relevant. Similarly, three of them (Japan, Australia and India) being members of the SCRI and the IPOI makes a difference. The working of the Quad takes into account the consequences of globalization and requirements of the global commons. There is undoubtedly a strong shared interest in the oceanic domain as all members are maritime powers. In fact, well before the revival of the Quad, some of them were conducting the Malabar Exercise among themselves. And the same convergence is also underlined in the support they expressed together in Tokyo in 2022 for the IPMDA.

But significant as this may be, any one-dimensional projection does injustice to a group that can make a serious contribution to larger welfare. It is, therefore, essential to have informed visibility of the entire Quad landscape. And it does span a growing range of issues.

Where critical and emerging technologies are concerned, the Quad adopted principles on technology design, development, governance and use in 2021. It urged that democratic values and human rights shape the design, governance and application of technologies. The adoption of the Open Radio Access Network (O-RAN) Action Plan encouraged a diverse, open and interoperable telecommunication ecosystem. This was followed by an agreement to facilitate exchanges and align closely on O-RAN testing activities. The Quad obviously has an interest in the expansive deployment of O-RAN across the Indo-Pacific.

In parallel, there have been discussions on the global semiconductor value chain. That the Quad members have come up with a common statement on technology supply chain principles says much for the importance they attach to this domain. Given the twin concerns of supply chain resilience and digital trust, it is natural that the Quad should be heavily focussed on the future of trusted collaboration. Progress in this domain will only further underline its salience in contemporary global architecture.

Climate action has been another significant area of attention. Here, too, the Quad has sought to apply itself to practical initiatives. The green shipping network between the four aspires to decarbonize the shipping value chain and to establish green corridors in the Indo-Pacific. India has a particular interest in exploring collaboration on green hydrogen and to dovetail it with its national mission. The Quad has also partnered with the CDRI in its adaptation and resilient activities. This is aimed at collectively advancing climate monitoring and disaster risk reduction in the Indo-Pacific.

Infrastructure has been a natural focus, given the widespread unease generated by strategically led connectivity initiatives. Given the nature of the challenge, much of the deliberations are on debt management and debt sustainability. The development assistance institutions are coordinating on promoting sustainable and alternative financing. There is a clear recognition that high standard infrastructure based on transparency and market viability should be promoted for the larger benefit of the region.

In the light of the pandemic, it was to only be expected that the Quad would come together in its vaccine supply endeavours. The group cooperated to expand manufacturing capacity of World Health Organization (WHO)-approved vaccines and collaborate with COVAX to track demand, as also with WHO to overcome vaccine hesitancy. On its part, India has provided more than half a million 'Made in India' vaccine doses to Cambodia and Thailand under the Quad Vaccine Partnership. Other notable areas of cooperation have been the Quad Data Satellite Portal and the STEM fellowships. The analysis on climate change risks and sustainable use of oceans and marine resources is high on the Quad agenda.

An important outcome from the Tokyo Summit in 2022 was the Humanitarian Assistance and Disaster Relief (HADR) partnership for the Indo-Pacific. This has a symbolic resonance, given the 2004 tsunami cooperation. These initial agreements have now led to the finalization of the Quad's standard operating procedures. At a time when climate events are proliferating and global responses are declining, this will fill a significant gap.

By the time the Quad leaders assembled in Hiroshima in May 2023, they were ready to jointly articulate their most comprehensive collective outlook to date. This included a detailed agenda that addressed climate action, supply chains, pandemic and health concerns, infrastructure, education, connectivity, digital capabilities, standards, R&D, cyber and space technologies and maritime domain awareness. They issued three statements of principles: on clean energy supply chains, critical and emerging technology standards, and secure software. Their global and regional perspectives, while reiterating many known positions, clearly highlighted where the convergences were strongest. As each year, indeed each meeting, widens the ambit of cooperation, it is increasingly clear that Quad is here not just to stay but to grow steadily.

An interesting feature of the evolution of the Quad, and it is still continuing, is how the comfort levels are constantly encouraging exploration of new areas. In early 2023, this was visible in domains ranging from maritime security, multilateralism, counter-terrorism and HADR. When it came to the IORA, the Quad members committed to working more intensively together, as they visibly did in the 2023 Colombo meet. The Maritime Security Working Group similarly met in the US to take more practical steps, even as the IPMDA started to take shape.

On multilateralism, the Quad supported for the first time the Inter-Governmental Negotiations (IGN) process on Security Council reforms. It agreed to address attempts to subvert the UN and international system and to take forward the 2030 Agenda for SDG without prioritizing a narrow set of goals.

A different cluster of issues illustrate the contribution that the Quad can make to keep the world and itself safer, secure and protected. On counter-terrorism, starting with policy exchanges and experience sharing, the potential for mutual benefit was rapidly explored. A working group was established even as the focus on the use of emerging and evolving technologies in terrorism sharpened. Cyber security is also evolving as a productive arena of work. Sharing model approaches, encouraging development of talent, ensuring supply chain resilience and security and networking industries are its prominent facets.

The objective of the Quad, in the words of PM Modi, is to do global good. The need for that to be a collaborative effort is self-evident. It is equally natural that nations with significant capacities and shared interests would step forward in response to the need of the day. That India should be one of them makes sense, given how much it has grown on both scores. Indeed, its presence imbues the Quad with greater credibility because it does not carry a history of alliances. But for this to happen through partnerships with the three Quad countries was not always a given.

It can unfold today because painstaking efforts were made over many years to strengthen the bilateral relationships, which are the real building blocks. But even that, by itself, was not adequate. It took considerable openness of mind in all the Quad leaderships to envisage collaboration in a more contemporary manner.

Indeed, the Quad is proof that PM Modi walked the talk in declaring his intention to overcome hesitations of history. Similarly, the other three nations took a leap of faith beyond the orthodoxies of alliances. Since 2017, practical progress has validated the relevance of this sensible approach.

If the Quad is to continue growing, we must also be cognizant of what we should not seek to do. Trying to straitjacket it, subject it to stress tests or impose congruence over convergence are all harmful, not helpful. The Quad works precisely because it is flexible and understanding, a welcome supersession of the rigidities of the Cold War era. Therefore, efforts to set expectations that are modelled on the relationship that the US had with its Western partners should be resisted. Nor should we readily accept the opposite paradigm, that of a purely transactional arrangement. Each one of the Quad partners has its own culture and tradition, but the fact is that there is a strong democratic overlap. Fortunately, the governments in question have all shown a maturity that would, hopefully, also percolate more deeply into the public discourse.

The Quad is the aggregate of the progress India has made in key relationships over two decades. It is also an assertion of going beyond traditional confines and set working habits. That it has opened up so many new vistas should only encourage us to intensify it further. This coming together for an agreed agenda powered by a shared outlook is manifestly a statement of practical goodness. It is, at the same time, a revelation how a crucial landscape, when examined by a Bharat with clearer eyes, will help find its own solutions.

❋

8.

DEALING WITH CHINA

Appreciating the Importance of Realism

There are few debates on the merits of realpolitik versus ideology that would match the conversations in India about China. Not surprisingly, it can also become one of nationalism versus internationalism, however misplaced the latter may be in this case. This starts from our early years of independence, meanders through an era of conflict, witnesses the subsequent normalization, and finally arrives at the choice between a 'Chindia' outlook and an 'India First' one. The impact of the border events in 2020 have recently revived this argument, contributing to a growing awareness of the complexity of the challenge before India. As a result, facets like trade, investment, technology and even contacts have begun to be viewed from an integrated perspective. The current state of the relationship is clearly unnatural; what its future holds seems ripe for debate.

In essence, the competing perspectives derive from the differing viewpoints set out in 1950 by PM Jawaharlal Nehru and his deputy, Sardar Vallabhbhai Patel. The latter was as hard-nosed as they come and least susceptible to protestations from neighbours that diverged from ground reality. In his estimation, India had done everything to allay China's apprehensions, but that country regarded us with suspicion and scepticism, perhaps mixed with a little hostility. Patel cautioned that for the first time after centuries, India's defence had to concentrate on two fronts simultaneously. And his view of China was that it had definite ambitions and aims that shaped its thinking about India in a less-than-friendly way.

In contrast, Nehru felt that Patel was overly suspicious and stated in a note to him on 18 November 1950 that it was inconceivable that China would 'undertake a wild adventure across the Himalayas'. Guided by a positive predisposition towards a leftist regime, he also felt that it is exceedingly unlikely that India may have to face any real military invasion from China in the foreseeable future. He appeared to take at face value the repeated references by China desiring friendship. To those who felt otherwise, he warned against losing our sense of perspective and giving way to unreasoning fears.

Each one eventually was to temper their view with some realization of the complications of a modus vivendi. The choice of words in what was an internal debate is obviously not quite diplomatic. But their gut instincts nevertheless were articulated quite clearly. One bet on a world of left-wing romanticism; the other voted for time-tested calculations about neighbours, especially big ones.

There were naturally multiple expressions of this divergence in approach, and that played out in the ensuing decades. As competition and even conflict characterized certain periods, public attitudes also started to take root accordingly. These may or may not have been shared by the governments of the day. Some displayed a consideration that was at variance with popular sentiment or even sought to shape opinion by advancing new objectives. Others were more hard-headed and would not let difficult issues be brushed under the carpet. Whatever the nuances, the defining imagery of diplomatic complacency remains the 1954 Panchsheel declaration.

If there is a common thread in the tendency to expect best-case scenarios, it is the optimism of a particular brand of Indian internationalism. One illustration of this Nehruvian approach was in the debate about permanent membership of the UNSC. Whether it was feasible to successfully assert our claim at that point of time is an issue in itself, and would we have been granted the same consideration had roles been reversed is a corollary to it. But there was not even an attempt by India to leverage this issue for national gain, either with China bilaterally or with other major powers. It appeared that the basics of diplomacy had given way to the influence of ideology. Instead, Nehru's decision in 1955 was to declare that India was not in a hurry to enter the Security Council at that time, even though it ought to be there. The first step, instead, was for China to take its rightful place. After that, the question of India could be considered separately. And no surprise, far from reciprocating Nehru's 'China First' policy, we are still waiting for that country to express support for our own similar ambitions!

A very different situation reveals how deeply this mindset was divorced from ground realities. It was November 1962 and Sela and Bomdila had fallen to the advancing Chinese forces. As the then PM sought American help, he tellingly conveyed to the US President that because of its wider implications in the global context, India did not seek more comprehensive assistance. Apparently, we gave precedence to keeping distance from the West than to the defence of the nation! It is this lack of realism that has long dogged our approach to dealing with China. And it is precisely in this domain that we now see the difference.

If the positions and protestations of China got traction with an earlier generation, the state of Indian politics indicates that it is not altogether a vestige of the past. The previous driving factor was a desire to make common cause in the international arena. It was very much propelled by non-Western solidarity and Asian togetherness, more than tinged by ideological proclivity. Since then, public opinion has hardened and the earlier inclination to be excessively trusting is not maintainable. The world, too, is more transactional, and there have been decades of experience that influence thinking in India and China about each other.

How does the contemporary Nehruvian then approach the relationship? In times of stress as we currently are, like Nehru, the inclination is to indulge in ultra-nationalist rhetoric. This is done even while being in denial of the 1962 outcomes, when not actually misportraying it as something more recent. But ideology, habits and connections die hard. So, it is apparently necessary to have a double messaging, one for the more credulous within India and another for a different audience abroad. It is the latter that encourages them to advocate the view that China prizes harmony above all, without questioning why that does not apply to its neighbours. It also leads to admiration of the Belt and Road Initiative (BRI), while overlooking its violation of India's sovereignty. There are less-than-subtle suggestions of China's unstoppability by describing its rise as a force of nature and ill-concealed sympathy for its model of economic growth and technology appropriation.

But it is the actions more than the articulation of these Chindians that are of deeper concern. By consciously underrating the China challenge, any sense of preparation in India was undermined; till the change of 2014. The neglect of the border infrastructure was paralleled by an unwillingness to accelerate industrialization and create deep strengths. Even now, 'Make in India' endeavours are attacked by them while ostensibly expressing concern at the trade imbalance with China. The combination of politics, policies and populism lowered our national guard and still continues to target our national morale. Not surprisingly, this is about as far as we can be from the traditions of realism.

In the years that have passed, the Nehru–Patel dichotomy of approaches has continued within the Indian system. It finds resonance in each era through the issues of the day, from the boundary question and border areas management to FTAs and technology issues. Not all of the debate is restricted to its bilateral format. Understandably, given the influence of the two countries, it spills over into the global arena just as easily. Issues like connectivity, debt, development and maritime claims have also become contentious. Overall, there is no question that many of them today are being approached with a higher degree of thought about their implications. The era when Indian policymakers were sanguine about the 'String of Pearls' did finally end in 2014.

But there is also a fundamental issue of defining national interests clearly, defending them vigorously and appreciating the nature of power. Asian or even developing world solidarity may have its place, but it was never enough to counter the competitive instincts of a neighbour. Indeed, it is this kernel of the 1950 debate that continues to be relevant.

Today, there are animated conversations across the world on how best to engage China. Naturally, this is even more intense in India, given our proximity as well as the border events of 2020 and thereafter. Polemical positions within India may be driven by political tactics; it is the underlying policies and actions that speak for actual thinking. The true stance of various political forces vis-à-vis China is not episodic, whatever may be the temporary posture. The realists among them hold a worldview that stresses building national capabilities, which puts key concerns like terrorism firmly on the table, calls out actions on unsustainable debt and opaque connectivity, and approaches global developments with national security foremost in mind. It is precisely this approach that will push for upgrading the boundary infrastructure, as it has after 2014. In addition, they would deploy an Indian 5G stack, understand the value of critical and emerging technologies, and, not least, seek from the turbulence of our current era better solutions for our advancement.

Indeed, the nature of the challenges we faced predicate that India's analysis continuously monitors how the rest of the world is responding. Much of what the world faces today has come out of miscalculation on the part of some powers and its intelligent usage by others. But the course of history is far from linear, and even major nations are not impervious to becoming complacent or making errors. In fact, a common failing is to seek immediate gains at the cost of larger credibility. The realist, therefore, has to objectively analyse the state of play while being sceptical about the inevitability of events and trends. It is on this score that our epics may shed some light.

In world affairs, as indeed in human relationships, parties tend to help others out of goodwill, generosity or calculation. In real life, one can often spill into the other. The trigger of the Ramayana narrative is actually an act of exceptional trust, the two boons that King Dasaratha gave to his wife Kaikeyi on the battlefield. While involved in a war between the *asura* Sambara and the king of the gods Indra, Dasaratha was rescued by her when severely wounded in a night attack. It was these promises that Kaikeyi invoked to send Rama to his exile in the jungle and demand that her own son Bharata be crowned king.

If we consider the boons to be latent capabilities that were exercised when the time came, this episode is an object lesson on injudicious sharing. In recent decades, international relations have also witnessed how countries and economies were built up, perhaps less as an act of gratitude and more as one of utility. This was especially visible in the last years of the Cold War, when it came to exercising military and other pressures through third parties. But a lack of understanding of the players involved led to long-term consequences.

The Western world found that the Islamic card that it played against the USSR came back to haunt them within a decade. And when it comes to strategic understandings, the economic benefits that China obtained became the foundation for the upturning of the global order and the contemporary competition that we witness now. India, too, carries the consequences of its own past dealings. Its strong advocacy of Chinese interests in the 1950s was obviously not repaid in kind. It is bad enough to forget that gratitude has a short shelf-life in diplomacy; it is even more so when basics of diplomatic calculation are overridden by misplaced beliefs of political solidarity.

In personal terms, vulnerabilities are often created as a result of thoughtlessness. On occasion, it could also be an emotional response to a challenge. To some degree, that could be extrapolated to explain the behaviour of nation-states as well. But a more credible explanation can be found in the mindset of strategic complacency that polities and rulers often display.

A telling example is the case of the key antagonist, the demon-king Ravana of Lanka. In that era, exceptional figures performed the most exacting penance that could be rewarded by their wishes being granted by the Gods. In this case, Ravana was given the boon of invincibility by the creator Brahma. But in his arrogance, he invoked it only against what he saw as likely threats, *devas* and *gandharvas*, *asuras* and *kinnaras*, *nagas* and *rakshasas*, all creatures other than men. He left out humankind because he could not even envisage that such puny beings could be threatening. And it was for that reason that Lord Vishnu took a human form, that of Lord Rama, to kill Ravana.

The issue here is the threat that was overlooked, which thereby created a window of vulnerability. There is another lesson, too, from Ravana's behavioural characteristics and that, paradoxically, is the attitude of those who feel wronged by history. He is badgered by his advisers to regain their dominant status in Lanka, a land that was once ruled by his maternal grandfather Sumali. Ravana consequently begins by displacing his elder brother Kuber, who comes from a different stock. But it then becomes an endless quest, powered by a sense of entitlement and absence of restraint. There are important learnings here for entrenched and rising powers alike, both in charting a path and in managing their ambitions. Total security will always be a fruitless quest.

A different example presents itself much earlier in the epic, when Bharata and accompanying sages try to persuade Rama to return to Ayodhya after the death of King Dasaratha. The sage Jabali makes a particularly impassioned appeal, underlining that the promise that Rama made to his father was no longer binding after the latter's demise. This provokes Rama's anger and he questions how trust would be maintained if vows were so lightly discarded. The sages appreciate his stance while confessing that they had to make their best effort to bring him back. The point eventually is about credibility, not just as a personal virtue but as a larger systemic underpinning. If states do not honour agreements and adhere to obligations, they must weigh any tactical gains against the larger damage that they have done to their reputation.

A MULTIDIMENSIONAL CHALLENGE

The Galwan clash between China and India in June 2020 saw the first fatalities on their border in 45 years. It was not just the underpinning of peace and tranquillity that was shattered as a result. Working assumptions about their relationship built up over four decades were now suddenly questionable. China's disregard for established agreements, which led to this turn of events, also has its own further implications. But even as India gears up to take on a new level of concerns on its northern borders, there are cascading questions posed by China's posture. Together, these immediate developments and long-term concerns create a multidimensional challenge to Indian foreign policy.

Among the many issues that India has to address in its endeavour to ascend in the world order, the relationship with China undoubtedly presents the most complex problem. On the one hand, the parallel but differential rise of the two polities constitutes the core of global re-balancing. Willy-nilly, the two countries have ended up creating greater space in the international architecture. Together, they are drivers of what was touted in more optimistic days as heralding an 'Asian century'. At one time, there was even talk of concluding a bilateral FTA, a discussion that was set to rest only after 2013. On some aspects of the development debate, they find themselves on the same side.

Yet, an intractable boundary dispute and different politico-economic models have created a competitive narrative in this very period. That they are immediate neighbours has added to the intricacy of their ties. A common periphery and balance of power have also contributed to a sense of rivalry. It is also a reality that China's reach and influence has extended significantly during this period. A lack of appreciation of this aspect 15 years ago has added to our vulnerability in the Indian Ocean.

From the Indian perspective, the answers are in a combination of realms, many of them centring on building our national strengths and upgrading our infrastructure. But there is also a conceptual transformation underway in the diplomatic approach. The global landscape today offers many more opportunities for

India to leverage, once it goes back to the realist tradition.

The serious debate about the future of this relationship today dwells on how to establish the most advantageous modus vivendi. Because it is an immediate neighbour, China's rapid growth has been particularly impactful, both on the balance with India as well as its presence in their common and near periphery. Moreover, for various reasons, China has not given the same regard to India's rise as the rest of the world. In their ties, the present is very much shaped by the past, whether we speak of the ground situation, national power or even sentiment. And the past is not without its share of problems.

At the same time, their cumulative effect on the established world order is creating greater openings for its change. The fact is that neither can wish the other away and both clearly have the ability to run the long race. Even otherwise, they had to take the rest of the world into consideration when it came to calculations about each other. Perhaps, this is more so in the current global scenario. If and how they come to terms seriously will not only shape the prospects of the two countries but that of the continent, and perhaps even the world now.

Most Indians are familiar with the modern history of our bilateral ties. Perhaps not everyone may know every nuance of how it evolved. But generally, people have a sense of the ups and downs of this relationship. The first decade of the 1950s can only be described as one of Indian naiveté. On multiple issues, Indian foreign policy took up China's cause to an extent that it impacted its own relationship with the West. What is important to note is that this criticism, whether on bilateral or global issues, is not a retrospective one but offered even as events were then unfolding.

After the 1962 border conflict, India and China exchanged ambassadors only in 1976, a decision taken by the Indira Gandhi government. It then took till 1988 for the first Indian prime ministerial visit to China after 1954, that of Rajiv Gandhi. And indeed, the re-building of our ties was actually a very painstaking endeavour. This, if you think about it, is something of a paradox. Because, do remember that India was among the early nations to actually recognize the People's Republic of China (PRC). However, the quality of our ties in many ways was determined by the border conflict and the three distant decades thereafter.

It took a conscious effort on the part of both nations to orchestrate a recovery and restore a sense of normalcy. As a result, for the next many years, interactions and exchanges grew steadily in many areas. China became one of our largest trading partners; a very significant source of investment, even of technology; a participant in projects and infrastructure building; and a substantial destination for tourism and education. As for the border areas, a detailed and practical set of understandings and agreements focussed on their management, even as negotiations were conducted on the resolution of the boundary dispute.

The advancement of India–China ties since 1988 was obviously predicated on ensuring that peace and tranquillity in the border areas would be maintained and that the Line of Actual Control (LAC) observed and respected by both sides. For this reason, it was agreed in 1993 that no activities of either side shall overstep the LAC; that the two sides shall keep military forces along the LAC to a level compatible with good relations; and that prior notification for military exercises near the LAC would be given.

In 1996, these commitments were not only reaffirmed but further developed through additional provisions. It was decided that the two sides would reduce or limit the number of army, border defence and paramilitary forces along the LAC and exchange data accordingly. More importantly, it was explicitly recognized that large-scale military exercises involving more than one division (15,000 troops) would not be held in close proximity to the LAC. If that were to be conducted, the strategic direction of the main force involved shall not be towards the other side. The 1996 agreement also provided for prior notification if exercises involving more than one brigade (5,000 troops) were to take place. This would include date of completion of the exercise and de-induction of the troops involved.

At the same time, the 1993 agreement to jointly check and determine segments of the LAC with differing perceptions was upgraded to a shared objective of speeding up the process of clarification and confirmation of the LAC. Not just that, there were subsequently detailed understandings in 2005 and 2013 on handling situations of friction, if they were to arise.

In the years that passed, we obviously did not make significant progress on arriving at a common understanding of the alignment of the LAC in the India–China border areas. The appointment of Special Representatives (SRs) in 2003 did intensify the engagement, not just on the boundary question but on the larger relationship as well. A specific mechanism was also established in 2012 to address issues pertaining to the border areas. But all the while, there was also increasing construction of border infrastructure and depth-area logistics on the Chinese side. In contrast, the belief then in India was that our own border areas were best left undeveloped. This turned out to be a serious misjudgement that has cost us dearly.

Since 2014, there have been better efforts by India to reduce this very considerable infrastructure gap that had developed over three decades. Greater commitments raised the budget to four times the previous level. A better road-building record, which doubled construction and tripled tunnelling, was also indicative of improvement. Nevertheless, the infrastructure differential remains significant and, as we have seen in 2020, consequential. It, therefore, takes considerable operational ingenuity to make up for the lapses of the previous decades.

For all the differences and disagreements India and China may have had on the boundary, the central fact was that border areas remained fundamentally peaceful between 1975 and 2020. That is why the events in Galwan have so profoundly disturbed the relationship. They signalled a disregard for commitments about minimizing troop levels, informing about their deployment and movement, and respecting the status quo. The combination of these steps heightened the associated risks of breaching peace and tranquillity, with the results that we all know well by now. The impact this has had on both public and political opinions in India has been profound.

Significantly, India has never received a credible explanation for the change in China's stance nor convincing reasons for massing of troops in the border areas. It is a different matter that our own forces have responded appropriately and held their own in challenging circumstances. The issue before us is what the Chinese posture signals, how it evolves and what implications it may have for the future of our ties.

Even before 2020, the India–China relationship witnessed decisions and events that reflected the duality of coexistence and competition. We saw trade grow dramatically, though its one-sided nature made it increasingly controversial. In sectors like power and telecommunications, Chinese companies successfully obtained access to India and built impressive market shares. The number of Indian students in China grew, as indeed did Indian tourists who visited there.

In the global arena, India and China made common cause on some developmental and economic issues, notably in climate change (UNFCCC) and trade (WTO). Our membership of plurilateral groups like BRICS and RIC was also a meeting point.

Yet, when it came to interests and aspirations, many of the divergences were also apparent. China started the practice of issuing stapled visas for residents of Jammu & Kashmir and Arunachal Pradesh. Their reluctance to deal with India's military command in the northern sector led to the freezing of exchanges for some time. Water-marking of Chinese passports covered Indian provinces within their boundaries in an attempt to assert claims. Border area frictions continued to grow as China's infrastructure steadily advanced.

In India, these multiple realities naturally fed an increasingly animated debate. There was a powerful lobby that not only advocated deepening ties but even exempting China from the limited security scrutiny that was then in place. To some, such expanded cooperation was a compensation for the improvement in India–US ties that was then taking place. This perhaps was buttressed by a natural proclivity to build on a Nehruvian outlook to China, as much as to the world. Discussions on the boundary question were, therefore, publicly projected far more positively than the actual progress justified. And as trade expanded, active proponents in its favour came into their own.

Yet, the systemic response remained much more cognizant of hard realities, seeking to put in place filters of various kinds, pushing back on boundary-related issues and increasingly highlighting the trade deficit. The last was effective insofar as the commitment to an FTA was finally abandoned.

As both India and China moved into a more confident era, their *inter se* relationship also witnessed additional issues of difference. This was visible in 2013 when the China–Pakistan Economic Corridor (CPEC) was first announced. Frictions in border areas continued to grow, though they remained below a certain threshold till 2020. China's blocking of UN listing of Pakistani terrorists involved in attacks on India became a matter of growing controversy. As the CPEC advanced, becoming part of the BRI, the violation of Indian sovereignty was deemed unacceptable. China's opposition to Indian membership of the NSG created another problem, hardly mitigated by its undermining of any efforts towards UN reform. And when it came to trade, promises of better market access looked less and less credible in the absence of delivery.

As the aggregate consequences of these developments began to be felt, the two nations sought at the SCO Summit in Astana in 2017 to limit damage by not allowing differences to become disputes. At the same time, they tried to explore the factors of stability in the relationship. Subsequent summits in Wuhan and Mamallapuram were largely in that direction. But far from mitigating differences, they have ended up witnessing a relationship under exceptional stress as a result of the events of 2020.

LESSONS FROM THE PAST

Given the gravity of its state now, it is natural that those who study the relationship will be particularly concerned where our ties are heading. It is hard to offer a definitive answer at this point in time. Whether it is our immediate concerns or more distant prospects, the fact is that the development of our ties can only be based on mutuality. Indeed, the three mutuals, mutual respect, mutual sensitivity and mutual interests, are its determining factors. There are discussions underway through various mechanisms on disengagement at the border areas. Many of the close-up deployments of the two sides in frictional areas have been resolved on the basis of equal and mutual security. But any that remain and the larger issue of de-escalation will continue to cast their shadow on bilateral cooperation.

It is untenable to suggest that there can be a return to 'business as usual' for the larger relationship when the situation in the border areas is far from normal. Looking beyond, when a neighbour prepares, trains and exhorts, it is wise to focus on the capability rather than the professed intent, especially in a culture where public rhetoric is taken seriously. At the minimum, therefore, whatever engagement is feasible has to be undertaken with eyes extremely wide open.

In that context, the Indian side has to draw lessons even from the near past when it comes to handling China. To begin with, the public characterization of our ties is important. By describing it as a 'strategic partnership' in 2005, there was conceptual confusion about its real nature. Clearly, this description sat ill with unresolved boundary differences, growing transgressions and competitive neighbourhood activities. In fact, what it led to was the very complacency that made India underestimate the implications of Chinese-built ports in Hambantota and Gwadar.

Similarly, ritualistic reaffirmations of territorial integrity could not continue in a one-sided way. A balance has therefore been introduced. The neglect of the border infrastructure also spoke of a casual attitude towards the boundary dispute till 2014. Even more concerning was the underplaying of Sino-Pakistani cooperation in Pakistan-occupied Kashmir (PoK), until the current Indian government took a firm stand in 2017 on the BRI. Despite that, there are some from the old order who still advocate softening our stance.

On the economic side, it would appear astounding to many now that an FTA with China could even be contemplated. In such an atmosphere, informed scrutiny of activities within our country was not easy. The collapse of the Quad in 2007 in face of China's objections sent its own message, making its revival a decade later that much harder. The very term 'Chindia' that was in vogue a decade earlier, with all its Nehruvian connotations, underlines why the loss of strategic clarity can be so damaging.

Given how severely developments since 2020 have eroded confidence and trust, it is obvious that stabilizing ties is the first order of the day. How to embark on that endeavour is best captured by certain propositions that reflect both experience and expectations. To begin with, agreements already reached, such as those of 1993 and 1996, must be adhered to in their entirety, in letter as much as in spirit. Cherry-picking individual provisions are hardly likely to advance the objective of finding common ground.

Where the border areas are concerned, the LAC must be strictly observed and respected; any attempt to unilaterally change the status quo cannot be countenanced. We cannot be in denial that peace and tranquillity in the border areas is the foundational basis for development of relations in other domains. If they are disturbed, so inevitably will the rest of the relationship. This is quite apart from the issue of progress in the boundary negotiations that are being separately held. Attempts to conflate one for the other will inevitably be seen through; it will never obfuscate the problems created by the developments of 2020.

While both nations are committed to a multipolar world, there should be an acceptance that a multipolar Asia is one of its essential constituents. Obviously, each nation will have its own interests, concerns and priorities, but sensitivity to them has to be shown by both sides. At the end of the day, relationships between major states are reciprocal in nature. As rising powers, each will have their own set of aspirations and their pursuit too cannot be ignored. There will always be divergences and differences but their management is essential to our ties. And finally, civilizational states like India and China must always take the long view. Departures from these axioms, as we witnessed in 2020, have serious implications.

For a variety of reasons, it is common for the Chinese to speak today of 'international relations in the new era'. There is much that this terminology signifies, as is often the case with them. Whether we agree or not, what is undeniable is that the world order has now entered a very different phase from how it was envisaged after 1945. Without exaggeration, the rise of China is the most profound change in global politics since that of the US and the USSR after the Second World War. It has not just implications and lessons but significant policy consequences, especially for neighbours. India, therefore, would also do well to regard its own relationship with China as also having entered a new era. If there were any doubts on this score, the changed Chinese posture in the border areas has demonstrated that graphically. India is historically used to thinking of a Chinese presence to its north. For the last two decades, China is also rapidly growing as a maritime power, and we will also have to anticipate activities in the south.

Since there is so much flux underway, this might also be an opportune moment to reflect on how China and India have approached each other traditionally and whether there are indeed takeaways for the Indian side.

Looking back at seven decades of engagement, it would be fair to state that India has essentially taken a bilateral approach in respect of outstanding issues with China. There are many reasons for this, including a sense of Asian solidarity and a suspicion of third-party interests that emanated from other experiences. Brief exceptions to this are mostly in circumstances when PM Nehru was compelled to turn to the US and UK after Bomdila fell to the People's Liberation Army (PLA) in 1962. To some extent, the post-1971 relationship with the USSR also encouraged India to look at its relationship with China in the larger global context. But these were not lasting, and after 1988, India reverted to the earlier tradition of engagement without leveraging. Underlying this narrow view was also a belief that problems between the two countries were resolvable in the near term.

On its part, India has been remarkably consistent and steady in its approach to the resolution of differences, including on the boundary question. As a result, Indians have generally been less contextualized in their approach and do not readily correlate the relationship with developments in larger world politics. There was neither an inclination to practise balance of power nor indeed an appetite for using opportunities presented by international developments. Nehru's own excessive caution in 1962 was one illustration of this belief. In fact, Indian policy in the past has exhibited such a degree of self-restraint that it led inadvertently to the expectation that others can have influence, if not a veto, over its choices. That era, too, ended in 2014.

The Chinese approach to India has been quite contrasting. While there have undoubtedly been sentiments of Asian commonness expressed from time to time, these have not obfuscated time-tested approaches to dealing with neighbours. So much so that Pakistan's membership of Western military alliances was overlooked by China in the 1950–60s as part of a balancing strategy. A decade later, this was taken to higher levels through nuclear and missile collaboration that specifically targeted India. When it comes to bilateral negotiations, China has focussed on differentials rather than on maintaining the logic of its positions. There have been radical shifts in its stance, especially in regard to its claims and priorities on the boundary question.

Overall, it can be asserted that in keeping with its fundamental world view, contemporary China has treated its relationship with India as a subset of a larger engagement with the world. Modulations accordingly reflect not just the bilateral dynamic but the global situation as a whole.

It is worthwhile to dwell for a moment here on the relevance of the West in the unfolding of India–China relations. This is often the subject of Chinese polemics, and Indians then tend to go on the defensive. There is no question that given its dominance, the West has been very much a factor of calculations for both parties. But the record shows that it is actually China that has been more active in bringing it into play.

For two decades after the PRC was founded, India's ties with the West were relatively much better, though there were issues of divergence. Indeed, China itself was key among them, especially between India and the US during the Nehru–Krishna Menon period. It was, therefore, something of an irony that as ties worsened over the border dispute, China's portrayal of India's relationship with the West started to change. When we finally did turn to the West, it was actually only as Chinese forces overwhelmed Indian defences in November 1962. Yet within a decade, it was China that made a sharp about-turn through its rapprochement with the US, reflected in the visits of Henry Kissinger and Richard Nixon. The resulting China–Pakistan–US triangle, thereafter, posed a serious challenge that could be answered only through the Indo-Soviet Treaty of 1971.

It is noteworthy that in pursuance of its interests, China had no hesitation in establishing global coordination with the Western bloc. There was a time when it even publicly advocated the formation of a 'single line' of nations in the same latitude (China, the US, Japan and Europe) to counter the USSR and its friends. Vietnam was kept in check through direct pressure and India, more indirectly, through Pakistan. This was the history that was sought to be put behind when India and China came to terms pragmatically in 1988.

But it is still one worth recalling for many reasons. To start with, China had built up enough constituencies of support in the West to insulate its economic cooperation from whatever political differences may crop up from time to time. This allowed it to reap economic and technological rewards while still engaging in political disputation. India must, therefore, fall neither for a simplistic description of national contradictions nor assume a zero-sum game between China and the West. Then, for all the homilies that are now handed out about the evil intentions of the West, Indians would do well to remember the advocacy of a China–US G2 last decade. Given inconstancy of policies, these are tendencies that must never be entirely disregarded. After all, a little more than a decade ago, China was making common cause with the US on

South Asia. In contrast to China's swing from one extreme to the other, India has maintained a stable and evolutionary approach to the West.

How, when and to what extent India should engage the West is its national prerogative. The expectation that we must conform to the ups and downs of another nation's policy is unrealistic and unjustified. And, of course, previous events have demonstrated that when they so wish, India and China can keep their ties on a positive trajectory and insulated from other relationships. Expressing anxieties about the West should not become a cover to constrain the legitimate interests and choices of the other party. Therefore, when such arguments are advanced, the best response is to place a mirror in the room!

PREPARING FOR A DIFFICULT ERA

India and China are quite distinct in their persona and behaviour, even though they are neighbours. As it is not a command polity, public opinion plays a much greater role in India's perception of its external relationships. It is not only more quickly exercised but when that happens, also slower to forget. Factors like faith and values have a relevance that is not readily appreciated by those who do not share them. Moreover, reactions are less determined by cost–benefit analysis, and perceptions tend to be more permanent. The interplay of internal politics with foreign policy can also be complicated in a democratic and pluralistic society like India. We may be seeing public reversals in the traditional stance of political players who embraced China earlier on matters ranging from security to economics. But transient politics should not let us hide the deeper truths. Insofar as border areas are concerned, the outcomes of 1962 and continuous neglect of the infrastructure have to be effectively addressed through determined responses. And that is exactly the exercise underway.

When it comes to the border, India stands significantly disadvantaged by the topography. The nature of the terrain makes the boundary far harder to secure from the south than from the north. This is further compounded by the outcome of the 1962 war. In many sectors, China vastly benefited by the 38,000 sq. km. territory that it gained during the conflict. In fact, even recent developments like the bridge building across Pangong Tso and establishment of border villages take place in areas whose control passed into their hands 60 years ago. And the infrastructure neglect till 2014 compounded this predicament.

India, therefore, needs to factor in these legacy complications while refashioning a response for a more difficult era. Some of that is to step up its efforts on the ground, some to explore effective technology options. Given the manifest commitment to defend its interests, an optimal combination will always emerge to be continually refreshed. All of that has come into sharper focus for a government that is fully seized of the magnitude of the challenges before it.

The second issue is that of comprehensive national power. Naturally, there are outcomes that reflect the lack of purpose on the Indian side till 2014. Technology and tactics can offer some compensations on their own score. India is, therefore, compelled to imaginatively address the problem of dealing with a powerful adversary. Policymakers of the past may shirk their responsibility, but the record is there for all of us to see. Indeed, we have already noted a radical shift in the positioning of many who advocated a very different outlook in office.

The sensible response, of course, is to build deep strengths as rapidly as possible, where necessary, in partnership with others. The current geopolitical scenario offers more possibilities in this respect. But there must be both the full awareness and the greater determination to exploit such opportunities. Nothing is more important than securing our borders.

There are even larger developments pertaining to India's status that feed into the problems of our times. We are all aware how much Partition diminished our strategic stature. But what it also did was create the basis for a subcontinental balance of power. And even worse, the incomplete exercise of sovereignty in Jammu

& Kashmir in 1948 allowed a physical contiguity that is now a matter of deep concern. Ideological blinkers were responsible for the wilful neglect of the first principles of international relations in the past. Even open Sino-Pakistan collaboration since 1963 has consistently been underestimated, failing to prepare us for what was to come next. When the CPEC was unveiled as part of the BRI, its forthright rejection by India was second-guessed publicly by some in the country. Excuses were advanced and workarounds sought to be invented, all the while ignoring a clear message from China.

In its current state, it is natural that there will be a debate in the relationship about ways of mitigation. An issue that presents itself is whether intensive economics is an effective answer to complicated politics. There was a period when significant sections of opinion in India believed in such possibilities. When China was described as a 'strategic partner' in 2005, this was in the expectation that the optimistic view of ties would prevail.

In the last decade-and-a-half, those hopes have been belied. Economics has hardly helped in stabilizing politics and, to add insult to injury, actually become a cause of problems in itself. One part of it is the reality of global supply chains that emanate so much from China, but the other is the fact that we have made it so hard till recently to undertake manufacturing in India. Indeed, there are influential voices that still argue that this is neither the competence nor the destiny of India! The result is that market-access challenges and a mounting deficit have made trade with China increasingly problematic. This is fuelled by the contrasting shares that technology and digital businesses have in each other's markets. The irony is that those who claim to be concerned are the very parties responsible for this predicament.

Indians must realize that only a sustained effort in building domestic alternatives can rectify the situation. But there is no doubt that the Covid pandemic has heightened awareness of the risks of such massive external exposure. This has only been accentuated by the concerns emanating from the escalated friction in the border areas. 'Atmanirbhar Bharat' has now emerged as much as an expression of strategic response as of economic capability. Even though there is a strong proclivity in India to deal with China more bilaterally, some of the global debates of our times do intrude into the ties. This is particularly so in respect of domains like supply chains, technology, data and connectivity. In fact, the more global China becomes, the more these larger discussions will shape the response of its interlocutors.

Like the rest of the world, India, too, is grappling with the reality that the established economic models are unable to cater to the realities of the day. It is clear that the logic of comparative advantage does not work with respect to those who are autonomous of market forces. And obviously, the world is simply not geared to take on the challenge of unrestricted competition, when every factor of production and consumption can be leveraged.

Where India is concerned, it is only a departure from an established way of doing business that can yield results. And there are transformations underway, that of resilience and reliability when it comes to supply chains and trust and transparency when it comes to data. These offer real possibilities to build greater national capacities in various fields.

In the interim, it is essential that India is cautious about exposing its economy more substantially to unfair trade. This is not protectionism but economic self-defence. Resisting the lure of quick fixes is also necessary to build up domestic supply chains. When it comes to global competition, India's choices are best made in terms of what serves its interests well. These considerations must guide its choice of partners on connectivity initiatives and technology development as well.

The ability of India and China to cooperate in multilateral and plurilateral forums has naturally had some effect on their ties. Even now, there are some regional, developmental and political platforms that they co-inhabit. At the same time, the last decade has seen the emergence of new mechanisms dedicated to promoting the welfare of the global commons where the interests of the two neighbours diverge. It is helpful for the overall India–China relationship if the sum total of their diplomatic activities remains on the positive side of the ledger. But this is not that easy to realize given the differences on display when it comes to the expansion of the NSG, reform of the UN or the spread of the BRI.

Accommodating the rise of others while in the midst of your own cannot be easy. When it comes to strengthening multipolarity, India will obviously first evaluate how much of it applies in Asia itself. Similarly, when it comes to rebalancing, Indian choices will lean towards those options that accelerate its growth. But what should be clear is that a nation like India, which long viewed sovereign equality as a fundamental principle of international relations, will continue to do so in the times ahead.

Seen from a narrow bilateral perspective, it is not unexpected that the rise of India has been underplayed by China. Efforts to structurally shape its shared neighbourhood is naturally of deep interest to us. Prominent among that has been the BRI, one of whose corridors, we have noted, violates India's sovereignty. The maritime space is also beginning to undergo a noticeable transformation, one clearly not to India's benefit.

In all of this, the global commons has been left to the commitment of like-minded partners who share a sense of responsibility. India's interests and influence have widened eastwards at this very time. The conceptualization of the Indo-Pacific and the emergence of the Quad are examples of a contemporary response to emerging demands. They also underline the importance of not according a veto to others on sovereign choices.

When it comes to India–China relations, references are often made to it being the foundation of an Asian century. This goes back to some remarks that were made by Deng Xiaoping more than three decades ago. Events of the last few years, however, point to the converse reality that their inability to get along can jeopardize such prospects. The search for a modus vivendi, therefore, becomes a quest for multipolarity in Asia. And that, in turn, has evolved into a larger debate about exercise of choices, concerns about the global commons, respect for international law, and an engagement on the basis of sovereign equality. In its economic dimension, there is a parallel debate underway on the need for fair trade, the importance of equal opportunities, the compulsions of risk mitigation, and building resilient and reliable supply chains while promoting trust and transparency.

In the games that nations play, political romanticism and cultural pride can often become manipulative cards. Forging a united front against the West and suggesting that Asia must be for Asians are tried-and-tested tactics that appeal to the insecurity of the post-colonial world. The reality, however, is remorselessly unsentimental and much more competitive. In a globalized world, keeping others out while seeking access to their regions is unrealistic. In a strategic one, partners should be chosen on interests and not on the basis of sentiments or prejudices. A more culturally assured India would surely see the difference.

India's answers for a more balanced and stable relationship with China lie in a range of options across multiple domains. Given the developments of 2020, they obviously centre around an effective defence of the border. This was undertaken even in the midst of Covid. A fitter and more technology-enabled military is evidently the need of the day. Peace and tranquillity on the border areas clearly remain the basis for normal relations. This is far from equating it with resolving the boundary question. The reality is that even this lower bar was breached in 2020! Economically, further progress in expanding manufacturing and promoting 'atmanirbhar Bharat' is key. Internationally, building more relationships and promoting understanding of its interests will strengthen India. We must continue to compete effectively, especially in our immediate periphery.

Establishing a stable balance between India and China after 2020 is not easy. If that has to emerge, it can only become sustainable on the basis of three mutuals. The international situation could even contribute to that process, as India strives to find an optimal positioning in the East–West and North–South divides. But there has to be an acceptance of multipolarity in Asia. The last few years have been a period of serious challenge, both for the relationship and for the prospects of the continent. The continuation of tensions will have its consequences. New normals of posture will inevitably lead to new normals of strategy. Whether a long-term view of their ties will prevail is the big question.

The India–China relationship is now truly at a crossroads. The national will, policy confidence, global relationships and growing capabilities of India are on display. Choices that are made will have profound repercussions, not just for the two nations but for the entire world. Respecting the three mutuals and applying the resulting propositions to the growth of their ties may help both nations to make the right decisions. That is best done when the relationship is approached with clinical analysis, global strategy and delivery on the ground. It is only when our approach to China is steeped in realism that we will strengthen our image before the world as Bharat.

9.

RE-IMAGINING SECURITY

Adjusting Habits to Contemporary Times

Corrosion is now the new competition. In a world of constraints and risks, nations now penetrate and influence rather than directly confront each other. So, if the threats are different, our defences must be too. And that starts with greater awareness of our times. There was an era when we thought of security essentially as policing, law and order, intelligence and investigation. We would stretch it understandably to counter-insurgency, counter-terrorism and border defences. As an extreme case, our thoughts perhaps extended to military conflict. Today, however, you might want to think that through again. Life is not what it used to be; neither are its challenges.

It is not that these entrenched problems have become less; it is quite the contrary. It is that even as we remain focussed on the abnormal, the 'normal' has taken very concerning forms. Every day, all around us, activities and interactions are happening that put our polity and society at risk. Unless we wake up to how much globalization can impact our security, a day may come when we will find ourselves compromised beyond redemption. More powerful nations are struggling with their own versions of this predicament.

Our world has changed profoundly and so, too, must our sense of security. This means looking at the variables of global politics and appreciate what it really means to be in an interdependent and interpenetrative world. The 'knowledge economy' that we are now getting accustomed to can generate new metrics of power. The strongest today is increasingly defined as the smartest. And as the epics would confirm, this is not altogether unprecedented.

Knowledge is power and, in critical situations, often more than that. In a competitive world, this puts a premium on intelligence, assessments and understanding. In a battlefield situation, insights and information can be a veritable trump card. And indeed, this is exactly what we see unfolding in the Ramayana.

The battle between Lakshmana and Indrajit, Ravana's son, is considered in many ways to be the turning point before the final denouement. Its setting is preceded by a 'psy-ops', where Indrajit created a virtual Sita and killed her in the presence of the monkey army. He then sought to use the resulting confusion to complete an *asuric* sacrifice that would make him invincible. It is here that knowledge makes a difference. His uncle Vibheeshana understood exactly what he was doing and counselled Rama accordingly. Lakshmana was sent to Nikumbhila to prevent the completion of the sacrifice. After battling for three days and nights, he killed Indrajit by using the *Indrastra*.

There is also a preceding encounter with another son of Ravana, the giant Atikaya, where inside information makes a difference. Struggling to hold his end up in the duel, Lakshmana was advised by Vayu that only the *Brahmashakti* can kill this demon, which it did, much to his relief. Indeed, Rama himself was the beneficiary of his charioteer Matali's advice to use the *Brahmastra* against Ravana at the crucial moment of their battle. Clearly, informationized warfare provides not just an edge but can be a complete game-changer.

If there is an underestimated character in Ramayana, it is Ravana's younger brother Vibheeshana. Perhaps his disassociation from the parent clan, even for virtuous reasons, left a taint in the public mind. But the fact remains that at the turning points of this saga, he made a crucial contribution. This was something that Lord Rama understood and anticipated when he welcomed him into his ranks despite the reservations of his advisers. He sensed Vibheeshana's ambition to replace Ravana and, significantly, crowned him as the king of Lanka before the battle began. Apparently, regime change has a long history!

On his part, Vibheeshana provided invaluable information through a network built by his allies Anal, Sampati, Pramati and Panas. It was to him that Rama continuously turned for tactical intelligence during the course of the war. And when Rama and Lakshmana were disabled by Indrajit using the *Nagapash*, it was Vibheeshana who gained time for their recovery. Adopting from the ranks of adversaries is always a tricky situation. There are inbuilt doubts and suspicions to that process. But as Lord Rama demonstrated, it really pays off when this is not just sound judgment in the beginning but also the courage to stick to that call through trying times.

A related aspect is the power of the narrative. If assiduously built up, it becomes the basis for dominance, where even the will to resist can be weakened. Ravana is generally regarded as invincible until he was defeated by Rama. The reality, however, was a little different, and it is to Ravana's credit that he was able to create such an effective reputation. That he defeated virtually all his contemporaries was crucial in this projection. So, too, was the fact that his son Meghanada was able to vanquish the king of gods (Indra), thereby earning the sobriquet Indrajit. But it was also true that, on occasion, Ravana was bested in combat and forced to accept that outcome. Among those who defeated him was Vali, when Ravana sought to capture him in the midst of his meditations. There was also an encounter with King Kartavirya Arjuna of Mahishmati that went rather badly. They both happened to be immersing themselves in the Ganga at the same time, and Arjuna's activities interrupted Ravana in the midst of his worship. In the ensuing battle, Ravana was captured and taken back as a prisoner to Mahishmati. It finally took the intervention of his grandfather, Sage Pulastya, to secure his release. In both cases, Ravana not only beat a retreat but came to a compromise with his adversaries.

Sometimes, even great powers realize their limitations and arrive at accommodations. Expending energy on 'forever wars' or trapped in an infructuous conflict is neither prudent nor rewarding. Growing power is always accelerated by smarter calculations and course corrections. But most of all, Ravana's reputation underlines the power of narratives and how they can become a potent weapon in themselves.

UNDERSTANDING THE SECURITY CONUNDRUM

As a start, let us reflect on the changes that are not always sharply perceived, and then understand how much of our challenges really reside below the waterline. Does it really take acts of violence or spilling blood for a happening to be assessed as injurious? A lot of our security threats are gradual and corrosive, not necessarily blunt trauma. If our nation's unity and integrity is weakened and alternative loyalties created, should we remain indifferent? If sympathy, succour and support are given abroad to separatists in the name of democratic freedoms, should we display equanimity? When national development, especially critical infrastructure, is impeded, do we show indifference? When influence operations are undertaken to shape societal thinking, can we really afford to be complacent? If policy choices for an open economy lead to de-industrialization and external dependence, what does it say for our future? Strategic autonomy can only come from strategic security.

Much of the security debate now revolves around exposure, penetration and vulnerabilities. This is the new world where normal activities can so easily be transformed into malevolent intent. Raising such issues is not a case for tightening control, strengthening authority or turning our backs to the world. It is, in fact, a plea to wake up, prepare, augment, and most of all, not let our defences down.

Indian society is continually seized with the challenges of security, perhaps more than many of its contemporaries. Like the rest of the world, it faces conventional and non-conventional threats of a broad range. Law and order issues and even internal security are obviously more complex in a large, pluralistic and diverse polity. Concerns about terrorism are particularly sharp since India has experienced unrelenting violence from across its borders. Externally, the task of securing unsettled boundaries has always been an exacting one. That current generations have direct memories of multiple conflicts also shapes our thinking.

Each of these aspects naturally requires an upgraded response. But there are significant concerns as well that are embedded in our increasingly connected existence. Because they are intrinsic to the engagement with the world, there is no getting away from these problems. When it comes to security, doing more and doing better is no longer enough. India needs to do things differently and that means thinking differently. Enhancing security today requires re-imagining it.

Those who spend their lives dealing with national security perhaps appreciate more readily how much our very definition of that term has evolved. Change is driven by the impact of globalization on all societies, the penetration of technology into our daily lives and a more competitive global scenario. What, where, when and how threats emanate is as complicated to anticipate as the manner in which we need to respond, protect and counter. We are required to not only deal with a more intricate framework in which threats are assessed but do so with greater variables. Together, they ensure that the normal has become increasingly unpredictable and that the uneventful is but an exception.

At the heart of the security conundrum is the seamlessness created by the fusion of economic interdependence and technological interpenetration. They have facilitated the flow of information, ideas and ideologies in a manner previously inconceivable. There are the human aspects as well, pertaining to the extent of observance of rules and norms. We cannot be oblivious of the paradox that while our existence is more capability-driven, we are more vulnerable at the same time. The very factors that hold so much promise for growth and prosperity are also the source of anxiety in the wrong hands.

Understanding why security issues need to be approached beyond the orthodox construct springs from these particular realizations. India is a polity that not only values its engagement with the world but is actively seeking to expand it. In fact, the drivers of progress at home link us more deeply every day to a range of factors outside. The task before us is, therefore, to arrive at optimal solutions that maximize benefits while minimizing risks. The era when this could be done through physical controls is now well behind us. Instead, the requirement is to comprehend, anticipate, prepare and out-think whatever problems the nation is likely to encounter. To do that effectively, it is absolutely vital to develop an accurate and updated understanding of what the world is really about. And today, our existence is shaped by a set of trends and happenings whose externality does not in any way mitigate their deep domestic relevance.

Any objective global assessment now has to recognize the prospect of uninhibited competition among nations, especially the major ones. What that essentially means is that they have not only developed many more capabilities and influence but are also more inclined to exercise them. It is expressed through visible linking of sectors that were generally regarded as autonomous. Business, energy and finance are treated as intrinsic to strategy, as are sports, tourism, education and politics. Norms and firewalls have fallen by the wayside in that process, as have assumptions of what is fair or acceptable. Some of this transformation is structural, but it is strengthened by changes that are behavioural. Globalization and technology would reflect the former; nationalism and unilateralism the latter. The world has seen a sharp increase in risk-taking propensities. No country can remain uninvolved or unaffected, and India is no exception. The bottom line is that our external environment is now much more hazardous.

But the home front is no less challenged, since the phenomenon of borderless politics has erased that comfort too. Many of the same forces also contribute to it, but the variables stack up differently. The ability and the inclination to pronounce on, influence and direct developments in other societies are clearly on the rise. Like established globalization, borderless politics is also played to the benefit of a few. But as in that case, it also shares the advantage of being marketed as in the interest of many. Its expressions range across every medium of opinion formulation and image shaping. Through shaping narratives and argumentation, it seeks to both legitimize and de-legitimize. This may be a broader phenomenon, but that should not obfuscate its security implications. After all, it can disenchant or disturb, or on occasion, incite and encourage challenges. Indeed, motivating beliefs are often backed by a flow of accompanying resources to make them more actionable. It is, therefore, a naïve polity that does not monitor external transactions and when required, regulate them.

Significantly, Western nations are as active as non-democratic ones in this respect, whether legislatively, through intelligence or by administrative action. When India is sometimes targeted on that score, the irony is that such criticism often comes from those with more stringent monitoring practices. Like many other developments, borderless politics, too, spans a broad spectrum. At one end, there is a desire to assist fellow travellers and those with shared benefits and interests. On the other extreme are endeavours that lead to radicalization, violent extremism or even terrorism.

Then there is the securitizing of the routine. We tend to think of dangers and vulnerabilities as arising from unusual situations: a conflict, a clash, a disturbance or preparations for them. But modern life has taken us into a web of technologies, activities and instruments that can be utilized without the user or the target even being aware. Every day, in myriad ways, we are exposed to risks of different kinds. The most obvious example is that of data and the processes that help generate it. How data is harvested and AI is developed is one of the most intense areas of global contestation. It could be digital transactions and the cyber world that have become so much more salient in our daily routine or the critical infrastructure on which a society is so dependent.

In fact, the Covid experience taught us how even domains unconnected with technology can enhance our vulnerability. In a world of supply chains, shortages can emerge at sensitive moments in key areas. This may be the outcome of logistical disruption, but equally of a planned strategy. As a result, global concerns have focussed more on resilient, reliable and redundant supply chains and, in the digital world, on greater trust and transparency.

The real problem, however, is the weaponization of everything. In recent years, the world has recognized how domains like trade, finance, investment and logistics can be leveraged for strategic purposes. Indeed, market shares and sectoral dominance have been created with that very end in mind. Some nations have put forward entire initiatives that advance objectives that remain hidden until it is too late. Others have been starker, like in the application of sanctions as means of pressure.

Once the mindset of weaponization sets in, almost nothing is safe. It can be directing or withholding the flow of tourists, the supply of raw materials and components or exercising the power of a large vendor or customer. When the market economy is subjugated to non-market goals, we then realize how the normal has added to fragility. In truth, the world has long lived in a twilight zone where rules were manipulated for globalization gains. Now that the chickens are coming home to roost, we are belatedly waking up to the resulting concerns. Ironically, when strategy demands, even espousers of free-market virtues are prepared to give their principles a short shrift. Security assessments, therefore, now require a comprehension of how dependencies are created and exploited. There is also an understandable trend among polities with greater security consciousness to scrutinize investment inflows and business takeovers.

On top of all this is the now increasingly recognized power of big tech companies, whose market capitalization often exceeds the GDP of nations. This is not just about the mammoth size of the relevant enterprises. Nor is it necessary to enter a debate about the politics and ethics of their influence. As realists, we can be neither oblivious to their relevance in our daily life nor impervious to the outcomes that they can help influence. Concerns about privacy and commerce have now mutated into something much larger. We are used to State and non-State actors. But enterprises with their own mega-interests are breaking new ground in modern international relations.

The problem that society at large faces is that these enterprises seek to work on their own agenda and norms. Moreover, recent events have underlined that even strong States find it tough to fully gauge, leave alone control, enterprises of this scale. Such entities can even provide capabilities that are normally associated with governments or stake out their own line of geopolitics. Businesses betting against governments and nations is not new in itself. But the manner in which they do so has been facilitated by our way of life. We cannot be blind to these winds of change.

WAR BY OTHER MEANS

It can be justifiably argued that every society's understanding of security matures, whether spatially or otherwise. Distant threats became more real and imminent as mobility improved. Those who mastered such techniques on an impactful scale became dominant; the rest were their victims.

We, in India, of course know it as part of the Panipat syndrome and, thereafter, the colonial experience. History offers many telling examples elsewhere. The modern era, however, has taken this to a completely different level. For, in effect, globalization and technology have, between them, erased distances and, thereby, create unprecedented challenges.

The old way was to contemplate military capabilities or coercive acts that were instrumental in creating outcomes, balances and influence. Even then, human relationships and financial transactions that were more humdrum and repetitive made a crucial difference. Imperialism advanced by combining all of this effectively. But today, the latter two are more potent in the penetration of societies through the course of normal activities and in creating options, leaving it to be decided when and whether they are to be exercised.

The most underestimated concerns are, therefore, what take place as routine in daily life. From the security perspective, globalization should be assessed for the interpenetration and interdependence that it embodies. And that, in turn, underlines that distance is no longer a safeguard. After all, we have all discovered that self-radicalization can happen without leaving home. Globalization has not only brought the world to our doorstep, it has also carried the accompanying opportunities and anxieties with it. The more technology-centric our life becomes, the more serious the challenges will be.

Even as this spectrum of vulnerability widens, our expectation of what constitutes adequate protection is also expanding. National security was traditionally viewed largely in narrow military, policing and legal terms, highlighting the assumption that threats were both far away and well-defined. But neither hold true any longer. Furthermore, experiences of dependence and pressure, such as of technology and finance, as also of food or fuel, have rekindled a global debate on the merits of strategic autonomy. Bringing economic security to the heart of national security has been facilitated by the rise of China, the changed American discourse, impact of Covid, the Ukraine conflict and the Middle East violence. It has given more weight to livelihood concerns as opposed to profitability considerations.

This steady expansion of what impinges on collective comfort levels has added sharper edges to every nation's calculation. Indeed, disruption itself has become the driver for constantly evolving definitions of security. The value that partnerships and cooperative arrangements now offer as reassurance has increased in value.

Changes are not just structural; they can also be behavioural. We must recognize the inflection points of the last two decades in this context. These include the 2008 global financial crisis and changed leadership styles in many power centres. It continues all the way to the Covid pandemic and the Ukraine conflict. All in all, we are seeing heightened competition in global politics led by major powers. There is less questioning now when nations use every instrument of influence at their command to advance their interests.

In the past, such tools were visualized as a spectrum, with application of force as one extreme and the power of example as the other. There were practical options that emerged in between, and even their use was tempered by shared interests and common restraint. Perhaps these have not always worked. Whether it was the selective use of force or the application of sanctions, those who had an edge have often chosen to use it. But as a whole, the belief in globalization tended to be a discouragement to adventurism. However, as stakes rose and contradictions sharpened, major powers have displayed the mentality of 'war by other means'. What characterizes our times is a willingness to be far more muscular and unabashed in using the toolbox of influence and capability. That it also contains more tools only encourages the practice further. In fact, we are seeing that approach develop to a point of exploiting many aspects of our globalized life and its activities.

Trade was always political, but is much more so today. Market shares are being openly leveraged for political messaging, whether by buyers or sellers. Monopolies, whether of goods or technology, are being even more ruthlessly exploited. Finance is equally potent, be it the power of currencies or the desperation of debt. Connectivity has acquired a growing connotation of linkage and dependency, assisted by lack of transparency and market viability. Technology, in fact, takes it to a new level because it can be harnessed even more intrusively. As for data, this offers a unique insight into the very mindset of societies. Even the flow of tourism, when it is directed, becomes a card in the influence game. All of these are 'normal' facets of interdependence, often entered into without adequate thought or due diligence.

But competitive politics is not just an exercise in leveraging or coercion; it is equally one of inducements. As a result, projects, activities and interactions all represent avenues to promote and exercise influence. We see that across a broad swath ranging from education and business to media and entertainment. That interpenetration is now so natural and extensive makes these possibilities that much easier.

Encouraging acquiescence or engineering change is as old as politics. The modern nation-state provides the analytical construct for this to be played out as international relations. In its most extreme form, these endeavours are aimed at asserting control by subjugating others. Reality, however, rarely reaches that level. It is more often expressed as acquiring and sharpening instruments of influence. In a way, it is work continuously in progress. The more dominant nations, by definition, are more active in offense while the vast majority are focussed mainly on defence. Creating a global order is one outcome of this exercise since it establishes mechanisms that regulate behaviour and legitimize demands. Depending on the domain, standards can have great utility by making the capabilities of a few the aspirations of many.

In the evolution of societies, progress in the security world and that in everyday life have always been connected to each other. Advances in one are naturally transposed on the other, whether we speak of materials, communication, platforms or activities. What has often begun in laboratories or businesses has ended up in armouries. Equally, commercializing security inventions or discoveries has been successful over the ages. However, as the world has become more globalized, the lines separating the two are becoming fainter. Some of this reflects the more integrated nature of technology; others derive from a deliberate civil–military fusion. In some nations, in a situation where less is taken at face value, we must be aware that economic activities cannot only enhance security capabilities but can even be driven by them. Where business ends and security begins is no longer easy to distinguish.

Behaviour, too, can be shaped by setting norms and establishing etiquette. That is why rule-making and rule-observance have become so central to debates in international politics today. But the rules of the game are often inadequate to either advance interests or establish an effective defence. It becomes even more complicated when the rules are non-existent, disputed or simply disregarded. Therefore, serious polities naturally concentrate on building capabilities rather than assuming intent. India, too, must recognize clearly that the former can be insurance on the latter. The basis for assured security lies in deeper strengths, a realization that has separated the bigger powers from the rest.

This is particularly pertinent to India because our industrial and manufacturing capacities have not kept pace with the overall growth. Even as we endeavour to introduce corrections, the logic for advocating rules and norms remains generally strong. In the foreseeable future, we are more likely to be injured than to gain from their absence. Smaller nations that do not have our resilience will have no choice but to bend before a few power centres. Even between major powers, rules could prevent the instability that is in no one's interest. At the same time, there is a developing awareness that in domains like the digital one, rule-making can be used to freeze the leads of established players. Increasing capabilities, therefore, needs to be accompanied by bolder policymaking and building narratives.

Shaping opinions and conditioning thinking are integral aspects of political contestation. If the domain of information has assumed a higher profile now, it does not imply only recognition of its salience but also the availability of new tools. The anachronism of propaganda may have now yielded place to an industry driven by technology and data, but like many other practices in vogue, we should not forget that this too has its history.

Controlling the narrative is always a fight and technology has made it far more complex. Those responsible for law, order and security have to struggle with it every day. It can distort, motivate, alarm, confuse and mislead, sometimes all at the same time. But do not forget the impact of the routine: what we read, see and hear all the time. Think about it: these are also processes of acceptance or rejection at work. The forces that drive them often extend beyond nation-states and traditional definitions of power and influence. On occasion, they could root strongly for the status quo and be sensitive to departures from it. The vehement opposition from select quarters to the change in respect of Article 370 is a case to point. But they may equally make the case for radicalism, or perhaps even extremism in a more acceptable form. We see their hand at work as well when cross-border terrorism is depicted as just a more vigorous form of post-Partition differences.

In fact, the very image of nations is often moulded with an

agenda in mind. Data protectionism is an argument used to trivialize digital delivery and justify data monetization. In the same vein, the concept of 'big emitters' seeks to evade historical responsibility. Either way, entrenched elites will monitor and resist the kind of rebalancing that gives emerging societies the confidence to define their own interests.

As with standards in the material field, rising powers typically face narrative challenges from the established views of early movers. In the world of ideas, they seek to define political correctness and make that universal. Often, external interests are strongly aligned with local elite with whom there is a mutual understanding. Our own experience in recent years has revealed how good governance can be distorted as excessive state control or how anarchy and worse are justified as exercise of democratic rights. A polity that is oblivious to such practices is a society in danger.

The globalized era encouraged the promotion of an integrated broad truth, magnified by well-crafted echo chambers. The unfolding of multipolarity has, however, brought back the natural diversity of our planet. In the ensuing competition, there is always the possibility of both misunderstanding and misrepresentation. Since so much in security derives from perception, we cannot be impervious to the shaping of our image. If we expect an easy passage up the global hierarchy of power, we will be deluding ourselves. How to define norms, where to shine the spotlight, which parts of reality are picked, these are all par for the course. So, too, are the adjectives used in reporting, the free pass from fact-checking and the selectivity of judgement. But knowing full well the bias and interests, it is still a contest that we have to enter with zest and vigour. Creating and propagating our own narratives is, therefore, of great importance. Sections of the world have their views, but we should not be intimidated from having a view on those views. Swimming upstream is the karma of all rising powers.

THE ROAD AHEAD

Building adequate state capacities to deal with a more complex security matrix is a common challenge for larger nations. The very tools that allow us to render more effective services can also help to secure our people better. As with more orthodox external threats, conducting security policy in an informationized environment is the task for which we need to prepare fully. It will have its own challenges and debates, but the direction that we need to move in is difficult to dispute.

The world may have changed in many ways, but an incessant challenge that India grapples with is that of terrorism. That the dangers it poses to the international community are realized is a matter of satisfaction. But to the extent that compromises are made for political gains or regional strategy, it is a reminder of the task that remains. As a primary victim, we cannot expect that others will fight for our cause if we do not do so ourselves. Mobilizing world opinion must be accompanied by a robust defence of our own interests. In the realm of ideas, it is also important that the trap of normalizing terrorism must continue to be resisted vigorously. We must ensure a brand differentiation between two neighbours who each produce their own brand of IT graduates: one on information technology, and the other on international terrorism.

Security has many dimensions, and promoting socio-economic development is one whose worth is increasingly appreciated. As its impact is felt more deeply, challenges diminish accordingly. India is now seriously focussed on achieving its SDG targets. Precisely because the benefits are so self-evident, there are also ongoing attempts to obstruct development and delay progress. The resistance to road-building in Left Wing Extremism (LWE)-affected areas is one obvious example. But if national prospects are undermined or border area infrastructure paralysed, then it is a worry of an even greater magnitude. As the record shows, this can come in many forms and appearances, some openly negative while others take the cover of public good. While noting the centrality of these endeavours to our prospects, it is imperative that we give due priority to ensuring uninterrupted progress.

The digital domain has a special resonance when it comes to development, especially after the Covid experience. Passport issual was an early field of change, but we can now see that governance itself has undergone a transformation. Given the enormous Indian digital market, it is natural that there is a competition in harvesting the data generated. Smart networks and services in different areas are also a subject of contests. Sensitivity to protecting digital services and data is obviously not unique to India. Like many others, we, too, are evaluating the vulnerabilities enhanced by new technologies. India's endeavour is to find the optimal landing ground that addresses its multiple concerns. These include data protection for citizens, making it easier to do business, ensuring the public interest of efficient governance and safeguarding national security.

A similar sensitivity to telecommunications was a much-awaited step. It will encourage a broader effort to make our security outlook more contemporary. Health security was another important revelation from the Covid experience. Today, we may be exporters of many products and, indeed, a key producer of vaccines. But none of this should obscure the danger of a large society like India depending on others for basic needs. The attitude of states at a time of extreme stress offers lessons that we ignore at our peril. But if we get it right, it can facilitate the building of capacities that trigger their own virtuous cycle.

An active debate is underway on the nature of India's economic engagement with the world. No one seriously doubts the reality of globalization or questions the need to interact with other economies. The key issue is the terms negotiated by India. Foreign-trade liberalization should not be practised at the cost of fair competition in our own markets. And unfortunately, that is exactly what we have seen in the past. The subsidizing of production and denial of market access in other parts of the world have made it very difficult to compete. If critical production is no longer viable, then it is not a matter of trade policy but a concern of national security. Let us be clear: India can only be consequential abroad if it has adequate capacities at home. It is not our fate to be just a market for goods or a generator of data for others. A rising India will only really advance when it is an *atmanirbhar* Bharat.

India's emergence on the world stage has been an exceptionally eventful journey. And external challenges have been as formidable as the internal consolidation process. The traumatic Partition left consequences, some of which are being addressed only now. And through all this, those opposed to the re-emergence of India have done their best to make that process difficult. Terrorism, radicalism and separatism have been used on multiple occasions. We have been through difficult years but came through stronger due to the sacrifices of our people. The takeaway is the need to deter our diversity being projected as fault lines. Strengthening national sentiment, by itself, may not discourage such continuing endeavours. That we are an open society also means that there are more opportunities for mischief. Eternal vigilance, in our case, is not just the price of liberty but of national unity as well.

India's rise in the global order is not merely an ascendance on the ladder of power. It is simultaneously a transformation of a civilizational society into a modern nation-state. Securing borders and improving governance are no longer enough; they are just the foundation on which many other capabilities need to be developed. As is often the case in India, different eras will coexist, even in the domain of security. In the coming period, our concerns will gradually become more global. But we must not lack the boldness to seek some of the solutions there as well. Just as we prepare for contingencies at home, we must develop habits of cooperation abroad.

If the world carried the burden of pre-existing conditions before it was hit by the pandemic, India was no exception. The conventional narrative in that regard tends to focus on issues of finance and trade, with some social and political problems added for good measure. But a truly self-critical assessment of the last quarter century would raise deeper questions about our very understanding of reform and globalization. It is often said that in India, we make the changes we must rather than the changes we should. In other words, we react to the crisis of the moment and slip back into a default position of complacency once that appears addressed. And the truth is that this is pretty much what has happened to us since the early 1990s.

Debates on reform have focussed largely on different aspects of the economy, industry and commerce, which is perhaps natural if we recall that the triggering crisis was one of balance of payments. But the undeniable reality is that large swathes of economic, social and human activity were left untouched. Whether it was agriculture or labour, education or administration, the power of vested interests kept the impulses of further reform well at bay. Our human development indices then naturally did not improve as much as they could have, and requirements of urbanization remained as ineffectively addressed as the demands of rural growth. Not just that, the absence of progress across the social front began to tell increasingly even on the economic one.

This domestic scenario was mirrored by an external strategy that has hardly enhanced India's competitiveness. In the pursuit of globalization, we have been driven by short-term calculations and tactical gains. India imported to consume, trade and profit rather than to absorb, innovate and produce. The contrast with East Asia could not be starker. The over-leveraging of low-cost options from outside obviously eroded domestic manufacturing. Quite unconsciously, we began to perceive in the efficiencies of others a solution for our own limitations. And with that, the cause of reform remained at a level that was comfortable for the order of the day. If self-assessments remained positive, it was because they were based on benchmarking ourselves against our own past rather than vis-à-vis competitors. By the second decade of this century, these realities have caught up with us. It has led to a growing realization that globalization without a strategy is like driving without a destination. And the true yardstick for reform can only be its impact on comprehensive national power.

Policymakers across the world dealing with the impact of the pandemic are now focussed on economic and social recovery. Nations have made decisions in line with their particular circumstances, many conscious that the real challenges still lie ahead. Addressing both lives and livelihood has been an overarching concern for all.

Expectedly, this is India's primary preoccupation too at this time. The pathway to recovery, however, also has steps of resilience that reflect the pandemic experience. These could be in terms of the more direct concerns, as in the health and pharmaceutical sectors. Or they could be broader, covering domestic manufacturing, distribution and consumption. Rapidly creating a pandemic response infrastructure and meeting huge socio-economic needs during a crisis have created a new level of expectations, perhaps more than we realize. If the Indian public has shown commendable fortitude and discipline in the face of adversity, it is in no small measure due to leadership and motivation. However, it is essential to think through strategies that would hasten to put the scars of the pandemic behind us.

In a sense, a foundation for that has been laid by a set of initiatives since 2014. National campaigns addressed a wide range of challenges that were traditionally excluded from the debate on reform. They range from financial inclusion to digital delivery, both on a mass scale; from power and water for all to affordable housing; education and toilets for girls to sanitation and cleanliness; urban planning and rural incomes to accelerating infrastructure building; digitization and formalization to skills development; as well as promoting start-ups, entrepreneurship and innovation. The message was of improving human development indices, leapfrogging using digital tools, empowering the aspirational, and expanding opportunities and benefits. No less important was the fact that transformation was brought about through mobilizing and motivating society at large. By doing so, it finally put behind us the colonial mindset that the people and the government are two different entities. This commitment to societal transformation is clearly appreciated by the public at large.

We must have no illusions about the fact that the road ahead will be a long and arduous one. Looking at the horizon, there are lessons from experiences of others that India needs to imbibe, whether in terms of human resources, social infrastructure or economic capabilities. Basic amenities of power, water and housing can no longer be treated as a luxury. Nor can education, healthcare, skills and employment remain optional for some. In particular, a greater focus on technology and manufacturing is central to India's prospects. Digitization could well hold the key to the credible emergence of social welfare in a nation with stretched resources. Let us understand that in a world where trade wars and technology battles are likely to be more commonplace, de-industrialization is truly akin to unilateral disarmament. Therefore, making it easier to do business is not just an economic objective, it has enormous social and even strategic implications.

In the final analysis, it is central to the rapid strengthening of India's comprehensive national power. As far as reform is concerned, India would truly arrive when we internalize that this is an endless process with ever-widening application.

Challenges for national growth and development are not limited to socio-economic domains. Addressing governance deficits and implementation shortcomings are a major part of the solution. The problem, of course, comes in many forms and variations. They range from outdated policies and inadequate frameworks to casual implementation or even downright neglect. At the end of the day, it is as much about capabilities as it is about strategizing. If we bemoan the limitations of border infrastructure, we must ask ourselves the reasons for their current state. Quite apart from a deliberate neglect, the periphery will reflect in large measure the capabilities, or their limits, in the heartland. Leaving parts of the country underdeveloped or under-governed has its obvious risks, more so at the border. It also cannot be that we rise to special challenges, while neglecting the daily routine. Safeguarding borders, after all, is a 24x7 exercise, not only a crisis-driven response.

Our own debates in regard to national security need to recognize this value of putting in place the requisite structures and systems. Advocating sweeping solutions without laying the groundwork may be dramatic politics; it is not serious policy. On the contrary, our recent experience through the Gati Shakti initiative shows how much the national infrastructure can advance through stronger focus and integration. Breaking down silos and ensuring a more integrated governance process is just as important to national security. Underlying it is, of course, a basic willingness to fully recognize the challenges that the nation faces. By playing down issues like cross-border terrorism or competitive geopolitics, there has been a tendency to look away from the hard choices. In a more difficult world, that is going to be less possible.

Building Bharat is not a matter of falling back on our past; it is primarily about re-imagining our future.

10.

THE ROADS NOT TAKEN

Recalling Leaders, Revisiting History

It is not often that we reflect on what we inherit. But even when we do, there is an inclination to think of the choices made as the only ones possible. Obviously, that cannot always be the case. It is, therefore, useful to regularly revisit the past, especially with regard to strategic assessments. Much of what was long assumed to be the tenets of Indian foreign policy is actually the predilection of the first PM, Jawaharlal Nehru. And this was so because he comprehensively dominated the scene for two decades. But the truth is also that in the early period after Independence, there were vigorous debates even in this domain. A lot of this was driven by his peers, including those who did not share Nehru's ideological bent of mind.

Three relationships, those with Pakistan, China and the US, featured strongly in the argumentation. Overall, Nehru's critics felt that he harboured a sense of false internationalism that came at the cost of national interest. On Pakistan and also on Israel, they believed he was driven by an appeasement that was an important facet of a domestic political strategy. On China, he was perceived by them as displaying misplaced and impractical idealism that ignored the primary logic of statecraft. And where the US was concerned, his views appeared to be an extrapolation of a left-wing antipathy that was so popular in certain circles of the UK. Because these relationships are today the focus of change, it is important for the public to be more familiar with the critical viewpoints. After all, some of the roads not taken then are now being traversed.

Looking back, it is also interesting to note that diverging perspectives were not limited to a narrow group. On the contrary, they ranged from his own deputy Sardar Patel, who passed away early after Independence, to other cabinet colleagues like Dr Syama Prasad Mookerjee and Dr B.R. Ambedkar, who both quit to found their own political parties. In Parliament, criticism of foreign policy was often voiced by Opposition leaders like J.B. Kripalani, Ram Manohar Lohia, Deendayal Upadhyaya and Minoo Masani. But there were differences within Nehru's government as well, most notably on China, as ties with that country worsened. Current generations would perhaps be surprised at the salience of foreign-policy issues in driving domestic politics, both within the ruling Congress party as well as in the founding of alternatives.

One reason to go back in history is precisely because differing political viewpoints gained ground to the point of one of them (the BJP) eventually coming to power. Another is that the very issues of debate then are still the focus of challenges and opportunities now. Whether we could have created different outcomes is, therefore, not an entirely academic issue. But as Nehruvian beliefs used to be projected as a norm and others as deviations, these contestations are surely worth recognizing.

The conviction that Third World-centred solidarity would be a force strong enough to overcome any contradiction between newly emerging governments would be quixotic at best of times. But when actually practiced by a serving PM vis-à-vis an immediate neighbour, it became downright dangerous. This led to downplaying signals and actions in the 1950s that had implications for our security and well-being. We expended political capital espousing the cause of a neighbour who finally turned on us. And, at times, we even deluded ourselves that we had influence over their thinking!

To evaluate such policies, it is worthwhile to reflect on the basis for this supposed solidarity. At its heart was the conviction that there were sentiments and forces stronger than nationalism and powerful enough to overcome cultural identities. Those who hold such views tend to believe that others do so as well, especially if they belong to a similar school of thinking. It was this display of false internationalism that worried Nehru's peer group and led them to voice their concerns. The critique came with considerable variation in intensity, arguments and even the issues. Because they did not necessarily prevail at that point of time does not make their viewpoint irrelevant, especially if subsequent events demonstrated validity.

The standing of those asserting competing points of view is also material. Many of them were truly stalwarts of the independence struggle and some distinguished themselves in the Constitution-making process as well. It is also worth noting that Patel and Mookerjee directly shaped the map of India as we know it today. Obviously, we have to appreciate the compulsions of that period to also grasp the factors driving decisions. But, somewhere in all that, there are learnings from the voices of dissent as we try to find new solutions to old problems. Whether it is the standing of the leaders concerned, the intensity of their differences or the importance of the issues, there are good reasons for us to look back at their urgings with fresh eyes.

If there is a symbol of loyalty and sacrifice in India's folklore, it is the elderly eagle-king Jatayu. He was very old and virtually blind when Sita was abducted by Ravana. Yet, as the demon-king crossed his path, Jatayu gave his all to prevent evil from happening. He attacked Ravana with his talons, broke his bow with his beak and brought down his chariot. But in the combat, he was bested by the abductor, who chopped off his wings and eventually left him to bleed and die. But before he did, Rama and Lakshmana found him and learnt who was responsible for the kidnapping of Sita. On his demise, the last rites were performed by Rama, who was truly moved by the sacrifice of Jatayu.

Thereafter, it was his elder brother Sampati who made the difference. The monkey contingent under Prince Angada was beginning to despair about finding Sita. As they spoke about Jatayu's fate, Sampati who overheard them came to their assistance. He used his extraordinary eyesight to locate Sita, although she was imprisoned far away in Ravana's garden in Lanka. It was this 'over-the-horizon' visibility that then allowed Lord Rama and the monkeys to now make their plans.

In India's case, too, those with experience and wisdom had insights to offer. Some of our leaders of that era contributed to national security by challenging decisions, even at great personal cost. Their loyalty was no less than that of Jatayu. And their insights, as we now appreciate all the more, as valuable as that of Sampati. We owe it to them and to ourselves to revisit their counsel.

PATEL AND NEW INDIA

In recent years, Patel has featured more prominently in our national debates and discussions on security. Part of the reason is the change in our political circumstances that allows him to be brought back from the shadows. But equally, it is a reflection of our times when hard challenges and multiple uncertainties have highlighted the importance of leadership. More than any other figure of contemporary India, Patel symbolizes strategic clarity and decisive action in the midst of difficulties. Not just that, he is also closely associated with nation-building and systemic reform. For all these reasons, he emerges as a natural inspiration for New India.

Seventy-five years ago, both the world and India were experiencing a different kind of turbulence, one no less in its seriousness. The Second World War had just ended, comprehensively overturning the global order. New centres of dominance emerged with very different interests and outlook. Forces set into motion, many predating the conflict, eventually ended colonial rule in many parts of the globe. At home, of course, the endurance and determination of our independence struggle finally prevailed. But it did so at the cost of the partition of our country, with all its accompanying consequences.

This was the context when Patel ascended the leadership stage and took on the immediate challenges of nation-building. He was already recognized as among our pre-eminent leaders, admired for his political vision as much as for his organizational skills. On the assumption of power, he took on the most daunting responsibilities of governance, characteristically setting his personal interests aside. It is generally agreed that he was the preferred leader of his own organization, but he eventually yielded to the choice of Mahatma Gandhi in that regard. And it is this period of his national leadership that holds the most relevant lessons for us today.

In the popular mind, Patel is seen as responsible for the accession of Jammu & Kashmir, Hyderabad and Junagadh. In reality, his contribution was even greater. In fact, these examples, challenging as they were, took place on a firm foundation that he had laid through a set of high-stakes and fast-paced negotiations with many other Princely States. To those unfamiliar, it is necessary to underline that even some southern Princely States were reluctant initially to sign the Instrument of Accession. Certain British officials from the Political Department deliberately encouraged many rulers to hold out, suggesting that a 'third force' created through aggregation could be viable. As a result, each state had to be individually and painstakingly engaged. In that process, some actually went to the very brink. Those geographically more contiguous to West Pakistan were tempted by Jinnah's ostensibly generous offers. It finally took the enormous pressure exerted by Patel to ensure their accession. There were smaller principalities that were being difficult too, often instigated from behind by larger ones. It was only in early August 1947 that the tide turned decisively.

Two negotiations that continued after Independence under Patel's direct oversight were those pertaining to Junagarh and Hyderabad. Interestingly, both of them threw up the possibility of going to the UN, but Patel prevented it decisively. Because these events happened within India, we tend to think of them as politics rather than diplomacy. But as V.P. Menon has so ably chronicled, the exercise involved the toughest negotiations we can imagine. And whether it is in their objectives, strategy or tactics, they remain worthy of deep study even today.

That there were differences between Nehru and Patel on referring the invasion of Jammu & Kashmir to the UN is a well-known fact. Indeed, that was only one aspect of a larger divergence on handling the issue. This eventually saw Nehru divest Patel of the responsibility in the cabinet for Jammu & Kashmir and hand it over instead to Gopalaswami Ayyangar. On China, I have already examined how the two leaders reacted differently to its professed posture vis-à-vis India. But for all this, the discipline that the government, Parliament and politics impose ensured that much of the disagreement remained restricted to their internal correspondence. In response to Nehru's sensitivity to criticism on foreign policy, Patel gave him an assurance that he would limit the forum of expression to cabinet meetings.

Rather than focussing on what has been already highlighted, it may be worthwhile to explore some other views that are less known publicly. One relates to the difficult navigation of the Cold War era by Indian foreign policy. Significantly, on such issues, Patel was often the voice of moderation and caution. He felt that there was little to gain by excessively antagonizing Western powers, especially when India's direct interests were not at stake. The issue was not so much about specific choices and positions but more a discomfort with a larger attitude. From time to time, they found echo in positions that were also taken at that time by C. Rajagopalachari. As India–China ties worsened at the end of the 1950s, foreign policy views were asserted more independently by serving members of the Nehru cabinet. The point to appreciate is not whether they were right or wrong in their immediate stance. It is more that they came out of a stronger sense of national interest rather than an ephemeral sentiment of global solidarity.

There are two live issues right now in respect of Indian diplomacy on which Patel offered his views in his lifetime. One pertains to the US, and he obviously had a much less suspicious view than Nehru. In 1948, a year before the latter paid his first visit to that country, Patel opined that the US actually held the key to the international situation. He felt that without American cooperation, it would be difficult for India to industrialize significantly. Keeping that in mind, he made out a more India-centric case for collaboration than Nehru, whose overall assessment was more coloured by the need to create a non-aligned front. Two years later, in one of his last public appearances, Patel pointedly remarked that many people believed that India should not take American help because it would lose prestige and be perceived as joining a bloc. He felt that India was quite capable of realizing its own interest and position. In that sense, the origins of an 'India First' outlook go back many decades, though it clearly took a nationalist ideology to bring it back to life now.

The other issue pertains to the hesitation in recognizing Israel and establishing full diplomatic relations. Patel was clearly uncomfortable with the vote-bank pressures on Nehru and believed that this should not be given a determining say over the making of national policy. As with some other foreign policy issues, his thinking did not prevail, and it was not until PM Modi's 2017 visit to Israel that this issue was finally put to rest.

The quest for a more perfect union is one that is pursued by all diverse societies and federal polities. Indeed, if there is one area in which Patel left an indelible imprint, it is in national integration. As a civilization that values unity in diversity, it is vital that we nurture the bonds that bind us together. Our journey in the last 75 years has not been without its obstacles. If we have successfully surmounted them, it is, in large part, due to a national determination that emanates from the Sardar's legacy.

But there are issues left over from his era in which neglect had been rationalized to great measure over the years. Catering to vested interests or ignoring ground realities cannot serve us well. World politics is extremely competitive and others are constantly looking for weaknesses within. Our deep underlying pluralism that harmonizes so much diversity is our civilizational strength, not just a contemporary creation. We know this instinctively, though some parts of the world may struggle to understand.

An India that is true to its roots will always be strong and resilient. Our thinking is best driven by self-belief and national awareness. Sardar Patel presciently cautioned us in 1948 against submitting our positions to the interests and judgement of others. That holds true as much now as it did then.

THE MOOKERJEE ALTERNATIVE

If Sardar Vallabhbhai Patel pursued his beliefs and commitments while functioning within the government, that was not the case with his contemporary Dr Syama Prasad Mookerjee. There are many facets to his contributions that are worthy of discussion. After all, he was a notable educationist, an influential political personality, a leader in providing humanitarian relief and an ardent espouser of our culture and traditions. Above all, he was a fierce nationalist and one quintessentially Indian, who approached his nation and its prospects through that perspective.

Our focus is naturally on those activities that were critical to the direction of immediate post-Independence India. Many became the basis for a cohesive and alternative way of thinking in this country. These expressions of nationalism drove a debate over many decades about the nature of our politics and governance. They also influenced our view about development and progress, including on how best to stand on our own feet. And of course, they shaped our approach to engaging the neighbourhood particularly and the world at large. At one level, each of them may look like a different domain. But the truth is that they represented a holistic worldview, and, in real life, each was inseparable from the other.

The question that is most deeply associated with Mookerjee is that of the accession of Jammu & Kashmir and the ensuing debate about that process and its implications. His position is, of course, summed up by the famous slogan: '*Ek Desh mein do Vidhan, do pradhan, do nishan, nahi chalenge* [There cannot be two

Constitutions, two PMs and two flags in one nation].' In Parliament and outside, Mookerjee brought up concerns of balkanization and the weakening of the Indian polity as a result. He flagged the implications of contesting sovereignty, claiming competitive status and restricting the display of national symbols. These issues no longer require any further elucidation after so many years and so many experiences. We all know how damaging it has been economically, developmentally, socially and in terms of national security when Jammu & Kashmir were not fully integrated into the mainstream. When that was decisively rectified on 5 August 2019, obviously our national integration emerged that much stronger. But from a foreign-policy perspective, what is worth examining is how this issue was taken advantage of by external powers vis-à-vis India.

Such an assessment is not a retrospective view. Even in 1953, Mookerjee conveyed to PM Nehru that his handling of the Kashmir problem had neither enhanced our international prestige nor won us wide international support and sympathy. On the contrary, he felt that it had created 'complications' at home as well as abroad. He, therefore, urged Nehru to re-examine policy dispassionately rather than be carried away by 'false internationalism'. This reference to complications abroad must be noted because that is precisely what came to preoccupy Indian diplomacy for the period thereafter. As Mookerjee was to state in Parliament, India went to the Security Council on the question of aggression, not on the question of accession. How this was distorted by interested powers is a parallel that he draws in a manner similar to Patel's caution.

With the passage of time, the diplomatic consequences of the early misjudgements on Jammu & Kashmir have receded from public memory. It is possible that the gen-next is even unaware of the pressures that our country faced. Yet, this must be recalled in order to fully appreciate the significance of what was done in respect of Article 370 in 2019. The global manipulation of the Jammu & Kashmir situation is worth examining in some detail. This would explain what Mookerjee meant when he spoke of complications.

In December 1947, India referred the matter to the UN under Article 35 of the UN Charter as a threat to international peace and security created by Pakistan's support to the invaders. There is a separate debate on whether this was the best pathway that India could have chosen at that time. But there is no need to get into that discussion. What we should bear in mind is that the British-appointed Governor General had, two months earlier, accepted the Instrument of Accession in regard to Jammu & Kashmir under the relevant legal provisions. But this did not stop major world powers from taking advantage of an opening that the situation provided.

As the recent colonial power, the UK was in the lead. It was also the one with the strongest post-Partition agenda and, therefore, the most mischievous. The UK influenced the passing of a Security Council resolution calling on both India and Pakistan to refrain from any acts that would aggravate the situation. In effect, the aggressor and the victim were put on par. Declassified records indicate that there was a clear strategy in the Commonwealth Relations Office to bring in Pakistani troops and balance out India.

The next step was a move through Belgium, as the president of the Security Council, to establish a three-nation commission. In that process, India's main request that Pakistan refrain from assisting the invaders was conveniently dropped. The further sleight of hand happened when the title of the resolution itself was changed from 'Jammu & Kashmir Question' to the 'India–Pakistan Question'. Canada took over from Belgium and carried the Western agenda forward by pressing for a Pakistani military presence in place of the invaders if they withdrew. Matters reached a stage where India threatened to leave the Commonwealth in protest against such bias.

As the stakes rose higher, the US and other Western allies also got drawn deeper into the game. Intense pressures were exerted over the next few years, including the threat to withhold assistance to India. The turning point, of course, was a 1957 UK–US draft resolution that ended up being vetoed by the USSR.

India's defeat in the 1962 conflict with China saw a renewal of such efforts in the next decade. The Harriman-Sandys Mission of

1963 that sought to arbitrate on Jammu & Kashmir was the most serious of these endeavours. If they failed, it was less due to intent and more because of global circumstances and India's resistance. The illegal 1963 China–Pakistan agreement on Shaksgam Valley made it awkward for Western nations to make common cause with Pakistan beyond a point. But by 1965, Western partiality for Pakistan reasserted itself through their efforts on suppressing its responsibility for initiating the conflict.

Although this issue moved purely to the bilateral format as a result of the Shimla Agreement of 1972, attempts to interfere in Jammu & Kashmir nevertheless continued. This happened publicly during the Clinton Administration. Even the reaction of Western powers to our 1998 nuclear tests tried to link it to this issue. While the Bush Administration moderated this somewhat, there were nevertheless conversations behind closed doors. Barack Obama also brought up Kashmir during his presidential campaign and there was a debate about the US Ambassador Richard Holbrooke's remit that bears recalling.

Such diplomatic endeavours aside, what has hurt our interests more are the actual violations of sovereignty and territorial integrity by China. It began in 1963 and kept increasing through connectivity projects that later developed into the so-called CPEC. Each of these efforts has been countered and will continue to be so. But keeping all this in mind, we must appreciate that in mainstreaming Jammu & Kashmir, we have not just strengthened national integrity but also enhanced national security. And this is absolutely vital as India raises its profile on the global stage. Certainly, our Western partners today are much more understanding. But let that not cloud the fact that the real change has been in our own position that draws inspiration from Dr S.P. Mookerjee.

∽

A question closely related to the mishandling of the Jammu & Kashmir issue is that of India's misreading of Pakistan, its intent and its policies. This, too, is a long-standing issue that has cast its shadow for many decades on our well-being and security. And here, too, there has been a decisive shift in Indian thinking.

In Mookerjee's case, the matter acquired particular salience because it was the cause for his resignation from the Union Cabinet. He shared his assessment candidly with Parliament in 1950, diagnosing the prevalent attitude to Pakistan in words that still resonate with all of us. In essence, Mookerjee viewed Nehru's approach as weak, halting and inconsistent. In his reading, India's inaction or goodness has been interpreted by Pakistan as weakness. In fact, according to him, it has made the latter more and more intransigent, made India suffer all that much more and even lowered it in the estimation of its own people. On every important occasion, Mookerjee asserted that India has remained defensive and failed to expose or counteract the designs of Pakistan aimed at it. This could well be the natural thoughts of the average Indian citizen in the aftermath of the 26/11 attacks in Mumbai!

When it came to displaying strategic clarity about Pakistan, there is no question that Patel and Mookerjee stand out. Apart from the accession of Jammu & Kashmir and treatment of minorities, this was most notably on display where Mookerjee was concerned in regard to his own province of Bengal. Once the concept of partitioning India was accepted by the Congress, the key question became the future of Bengal, Punjab and Assam. Each of them had to be individually partitioned if the entire state was not to go to Pakistan on the basis of a tenuous majority. It was to this cause that Mookerjee then devoted his energies, ensuring that the metropolis of Calcutta (now Kolkata) and as much of Bengal as possible stayed with India. Obviously, this had direct implications for the fate of Assam and even of the Northeast. To that end, he convened meetings of a cross-section of society and led a public agitation that compelled a positive outcome.

Today, we cannot even contemplate the consequences of a different result, leave alone what it could have meant for the conduct of our foreign policy. Mookerjee did in the east what Patel did in the north and the west. In that sense, the India of today is very much their creation.

While there is a larger point that Mookerjee was making with reference to our approach to Pakistan, his specific analysis of the Nehru–Liaquat Pact of 1950 is also relevant even today. Let us not forget that this understanding was the precipitating factor for his resignation. He underlined that the pact tried to ignore the basic implications of an intolerant State; that the declared positions of the Pakistani government undermined any sense of minority security; and that an ultra-communal administration was giving life to these policies.

There is much that Mookerjee had warned about the treatment of minorities that came true in the decades that passed. He perceptively noted that there was a general impression that India and Pakistan have failed to protect their minorities. The fact, however, is the exact opposite. Mookerjee's view was that in some sections of the foreign press, a hostile propaganda has also been carried on. He believed that this was a libel on India and the truth, he felt, had to be made known to everyone who desire to know it. Apparently, some things have not changed in some quarters!

Mookerjee's remarks on the India–Pakistan equation are of greatest long-term relevance. He predicted much of what has gone wrong, not just in the pact but on the broader ties with Pakistan. In that process, he identified the key conceptual shortcomings very clearly, especially that India and Pakistan are made to appear equally guilty, while Pakistan was in fact the aggressor. Moreover, he pointed out that when Pakistan violated agreements, there was no remedy open to India. He, therefore, felt that there must be sanctions built into any understanding, an approach that would have served India well had it been seriously followed. Seven decades after these insights on Pakistan, it is essential that we reflect on the judgement that Mookerjee bequeathed to us.

This is all the more so as the equivalence between India and Pakistan that was so troubling even in the initial years after Independence morphed into a persistent hyphenation. For decades, India and Pakistan were uttered in the same breath and their differences made to look like a natural agenda left over from Partition. There were even periods when a military regime in our neighbouring country was held out as an example of development!

The 1971 outcome obviously changed much of this, but not as decisively as India would have hoped. Pakistan kept trying to create an artificial balance and was actively supported in that endeavour by both China and Western nations. This even went to the extent of assisting and facilitating its nuclear and missile programmes. And worse still, Pakistan increasingly resorted to cross-border terrorism to bring India to the table.

If truth be told, our own policies were not sufficiently robust to firmly discourage this approach either. Instead of confronting the cross-border nature of terrorism emanating from Pakistan, we even appeared to be open at Havana and Sharm El-Sheikh to a narrative that suggested that both India and Pakistan were victims of terrorism. This was exactly the false equivalence that Mookerjee cautioned us about in his time.

So, what is the answer? We have seen that unfold over the last decade in a variety of ways. To begin with, this means a clear position on the unacceptability of cross-border terrorism. It is obviously not in our national interest that we normalize terrorism by carrying on with the rest of the relationship as usual. That message has been sent loud and clear. Where egregious actions of cross-border terrorism are concerned, the operations at Uri and Balakot are as much a shift in our thinking as in our action.

It is also important to mobilize the international community through advocacy and awareness creation. Only then can we be successful in delegitimizing terrorism. As a result of our diligent efforts, there is widespread understanding today that this is not a threat to India alone. That the UNSC's Counter-Terrorism Committee (CTC) held a meeting at a 26/11 site in Mumbai was a statement of no small significance. It is also our endeavour to get global platforms and conferences, whether we speak of the G20, meetings like 'No Money for Terror' or bilateral and plurilateral mechanisms, to keep the spotlight strongly on such threats. The listing process created by the UNSC 1267 Sanctions Committee has its own importance. And there are no prizes for guessing which country features prominently in it!

Another domain where Mookerjee's views remain an inspiration is that of cultural diplomacy. As the president of the Maha Bodhi Society of India, Mookerjee was also the driving force in forging links with Buddhist nations, especially neighbours. He played a personal role in the return of holy relics from the UK and their display in Southeast Asia, including Myanmar. Today, those initiatives are being further developed through recent activities like the Dharma-Dhamma conferences, restoration of the Ananda Temple in Bagan, solarification of Buddhist sites in Sri Lanka and digitization of manuscripts in Mongolia's Gandan monastery. Indeed, the importance we attach to our Buddhist heritage was only underlined by the visit of G20 Development Ministers to Sarnath. Obviously, Mookerjee's cultural interests were much broader and must be assessed in terms of its relevance to the anti-colonial struggle. Our endeavours at deepening cultural rebalancing would surely resonate with his views about the salience of that domain.

DR AMBEDKAR AND 'INDIA FIRST'

Among the founding fathers of modern India, Dr B.R. Ambedkar is widely recognized as the architect of India's Constitution and the strongest voice for social justice and inclusiveness. He was different from many of his contemporaries in being exposed to American society through his educational experiences. As the first Minister of Law and Justice, he served in the cabinet of independent India for little more than four years. When he resigned in September 1951, the main reasons were his dissatisfaction on a range of issues pertaining to social reform. But interestingly, Ambedkar also shared with Parliament his 'actual anxiety and even worry' about the directions of foreign policy. In his view, few countries wished us ill at the time when we attained independence. However, within four years, he felt that we had alienated much of the world and that this was visible in the lack of support for India at the UN.

Ambedkar, on that occasion, quoted two realists in a manner that is relevant even today. One was Bismarck, with the observation that politics is not a game of realizing the ideal; it is the game of the possible. The other was George Bernard Shaw, to the effect that while good ideals are good, one must not forget that it is often dangerous to be too good! It would seem that even by 1951, important Indian leaders were already alarmed by the impracticality of our diplomatic outlook.

Among Ambedkar's specific grievances in this regard, one pertained to the handling of the US, which he articulated in 1951 in the 'Election Manifesto of the Scheduled Castes Federation' that had a section devoted to problems of foreign policy. Like Patel, who had passed away a year before, Ambedkar too was concerned about Nehru's outlook towards China. But, perhaps due to intervening events, he was now connecting it to India–US ties. In essence, Ambedkar asked why India was fighting China's battle for permanent membership of the UNSC. In his view, this championing by India had created antagonism with the US and jeopardized the prospect of getting financial and technical resources from that country.

In what we would unquestionably recognize today as a declaration of 'India First', Dr Ambedkar sharply emphasizes that India's first duty should be to herself. In his view, instead of trying to make China a member of the UNSC, India should get itself recognized instead. His characterization of the Nehruvian approach was of it being quixotic, if not suicidal. And his remedy was that India should focus on building its own strength instead of championing the interests of other Asian states. On another occasion, he expressed the same sentiments in his assertion that the keynote of our foreign policy appeared to be to solve the problems of others rather than of ourselves.

Like many of his generation, Ambedkar was obviously deeply conversant with international affairs and visibly invested in its formulation. His plea was clearly not one of turning India's back on the world but instead of making choices that would be primarily driven by our country's gains. In that sense, his endeavour was to get the balance between our national interest and international posture. And like many contemporaries, he appeared to believe that Nehru was leaning far too much in the direction of the latter at the expense of the former.

Ambedkar, too, shared the sense that India was being naïve in its unquestioning acceptance of the principles of Panchsheel. His own view was that they had no place in politics; nor did he believe that China, in its heart of hearts, differed on this matter. In a revealing parliamentary discussion in August 1954 where he laid out his viewpoint, Ambedkar also made a strong case for an interest-based diplomacy. He questioned what he termed Nehru's advocacy of 'Asia for Asiatics', suggesting that greater weight should be given to political values. It is surely not without reason that seven decades later, this debate is still very much in vogue.

MASANI'S PERSPECTIVE

There are many examples of what we may consider to be current issues actually being debated in our history. Those I have cited above give some flavour of what our past holds, if only political correctness does not stand in the way of objective exploration. Among the long-held tenets of Indian foreign policy is that of non-alignment. Even though it has a particular global context, this has sought to be made into an immutable concept. That India's capabilities now allow it to move beyond defensive options is often lost on those who treat policy debates as theological ones. But precisely because it is invoked so often, a critical viewpoint is also worth recognizing.

Few questioned the predicaments that the practice of non-alignment could create for India more graphically than M.R. Masani in 1959. And he did so, understandably, as the threat from China loomed large. Masani essentially asked whether our approach had brought us to a point where we were unable to repel effectively an attack on our own territory. Related to that, he suggested that by keeping a distance from the West, we were not even able to equip our forces adequately. But more fundamentally, he was concerned that India's capacity to recognize a dangerous neighbour had somehow got impaired. Its domestic reflection was discouraging our own people from even displaying patriotism. In effect, Masani was bringing out that non-alignment, while working in good times, was less productive in tough ones. Keeping a distance from others also meant that they too kept their own when they wished. Masani believed that non-alignment was not inconsistent with the capacity to recognize a dangerous neighbour and take measures accordingly. Significantly, much of what he said tallied with Nehru's hesitation to engage Western powers even as China advanced into India in November 1962.

As with the other examples, this debate, too, is worth revisiting because of endeavours to put India under pressure. When others extol our independence and strategic autonomy, it is not always meant for India's good. They seek instead to influence our thinking in a manner that constrains our options. In that quest, it is natural that they would use our own past against us. And how can we blame them, when such tactics succeeded as recently as 2007 when it came to the Quad? Strengthening a sense of independence or even autonomy does not necessarily mean staying at the centre or not making commitments. There is an inherent flexibility in that exercise, which somehow got lost when policy became dogmatic. Even today, tactical nimbleness and strategic creativity have a value that cannot be overstated.

At the end of the day, strategic clarity means both a sound understanding of the international environment as well a clear-eyed view of it from our national perspective. There have been shortcomings on both scores in our early periods after Independence and we paid a high price for it.

From the road taken, we must learn that national security can never take second place, least of all to the quest for prestige. In the final analysis, hard power will always score over soft power. Ideally, the two should be in lock-step, so that capabilities and influence grow side by side. But the desire for acceptance, particularly by competitors, should never become a significant driver of diplomacy. This realization from past experiences now drives India's attitude towards world politics in general and our regional concerns in particular. As always, the wisdom and foresight of our tallest leaders serve as an inspiration for building Bharat.

❋

11.

WHY BHARAT MATTERS

Grasping Our Value, Expressing Our Confidence

The successful landing of Chandrayaan-3 on the moon coincided with the BRICS Summit in South Africa. Predictably, that extraordinary achievement dominated the proceedings. Leaders of the Global South expressed pride that one of them was capable of such a feat. This is but one example of how much India is impacting the world today.

A few weeks later, the G20 Summit in New Delhi unanimously produced a substantive outcome. This diplomatic accomplishment was paralleled by the admission of the AU as a permanent member, that too at India's initiative. Here again, there was a larger resonance of these developments. In the years before, India's Vaccine Maitri effort provided health access for many small countries, otherwise forgotten in the pandemic. Three very different examples in very diverse domains have one message: that India matters to the world more and more.

A new generation of more globally aware Indians naturally debates our weight in world affairs. One way at approaching the issue is to consider why and how India matters to others. The answers are not always that simple, though they could start with the common-sense proposition that India has always mattered in some way. After all, such a large landmass with so many people and that rich a history and culture would naturally have made its impression. By its very existence, India occupies global mind-space and its growing vigour would only expand that appreciation. The questions now are really of the extent to which its revival is shaping the world order and what that portends for the future. This means choices, policies, leadership, delivery and, not least, an awareness of who we are and how we assert our collective persona.

In popular parlance, Hanuman is synonymous with devotion, perseverance and strength. The irony, of course, is that Hanuman himself does not know the full extent of his own powers. As Agastya revealed to Rama, this was the result of his antics in early youth that troubled many sages in the midst of their meditation. Hanuman was, therefore, cursed to be forgetful until divine duties require otherwise. As the epic unfolds and Hanuman takes on increasing responsibilities, his own self-awareness enhances commensurately. At key junctures, he is indeed the saviour of the situation. When Sita was abducted and a search mission was set into motion, Sugriva divided his army and sent them in all four directions under experienced leaders. Vinata, Sushena and Shatabali were tasked with leading the forces to the east, west and north respectively. But it was Hanuman, along with Angada, who was given the responsibility of going south, which was perceived as the most promising prospect. Just as Angada was giving up on the task, Hanuman exhorted him to keep faith and persevere.

As he stepped forward during various stages of the epic, his true potential was displayed for the world to see. When Lakshmana was struck down in battle and could only be revived by the medicinal plant *Vishalyakarani*, Hanuman was sent to the Dronagiri Mountain to gather it. Unable to identify the plant specifically in day time, he picked up the entire mountain and brought it for the more discerning monkey-chieftain Sushena to pick the right herb. As many other occasions testify, Hanuman is determined, innovative, outcome-oriented and self-confident.

The legend of Hanuman could well be the story of India in the last decade. The more we do, the more we believe we can do. It is this self-discovery that has made India so different in recent years and set it on a course that has major implications for the global order.

A DEMOCRACY THAT DELIVERS

India can matter by just being there, as a market place, as a contested ground, a resource or a platform. Indeed, as it did during colonial times. This breeds a survival mentality that, at best, can graduate to a transactional one. But India can also matter through the power of its ideas and actions as an engine of the global economy, a hub of innovation or a democracy that delivers. That is the course of destiny, and its ambitious path requires deep determination and strong perseverance. The debates within our society will decide which road is finally taken. As a nation, choices are becoming increasingly stark. The progress of the last decade points to hope and optimism, while the old order highlights our insecurities and underlines the divides.

Indians, of course, must be conscious that the world has a lot riding on our decisions. Those who wish us well will endeavour to cooperate. Others who see our rise less favourably will obstruct, if not do worse. Either way, we must be prepared for those who will participate in our discourse, even intervene in pursuit of their interests. As discussed earlier, it is vital that we do not open ourselves to the external shaping of our prospects. India certainly matters to its own people, and for that very reason, we must recall from history why our future must not be decided by those outside.

The place that India has long occupied in global thinking is manifest in the obsessive search for trade routes to it. They may have initially taken European explorers to the American continent. But when the explorers finally reached India by sea, even more significant consequences unfolded. Using it as an effective base, Europe was able to thereafter dominate the rest of Asia. In fact, even China's fate in the nineteenth century was very much shaped by the outcomes in India.

Not surprisingly, this centrality of India worked the other way around as well. Its independence set in motion a larger decolonization process that became the basis for the contemporary global order. Decades later, India's economic progress contributes to a rebalancing and multipolarity that is still unfolding. These may be some illustrations of an argument on why India matters. Pondering over its past importance certainly helps to gauge its future relevance.

Part of why India counts is obvious. For a start, it represents a sixth of humanity. So, its successes and shortcomings have clear global connotations. But for Partition, India, and not China, would have been the largest society in living memory. The case for India is, however, more than just one of demography. For it is among the few civilizational states that has survived the ravages of history. Such polities are distinguished by a different level of culture and heritage, with accompanying attitudes and mindset as well. They take the long view, especially in regard to global issues. Many of their goals and objectives also build on traditions that are not readily shared by contemporary peers. Simply put, there is not only a scale and history but an exceptionalism about India that makes it matter.

Societies can be relevant as a playing field for others or they can be players by themselves. The colonial era with its ruthless extractive culture presented that sharp choice in the last few centuries. You were either a victim or an assailant; there was no middle ground. However, the progress of contemporary times has provided the basis for change beyond that binary. It is not merely a platitude to state that this is now an era of greater cooperation. New activities and energies emerged from the freedom of nations to be taken forward by comparative advantage. In due course, their political importance increased in world affairs. In doing so, countries transcended their earlier predicament and became factors of influence. Large ones, in particular, regained their natural weight and salience in the calculations of others. Their choices and actions started to determine not only their own prospects but also those of others. This could be from a set of capabilities, a reservoir of resources, the quality of talent, the importance of location or even national will and leadership.

It is the entirety of this matrix that is shaping the rise of India. As our nation completes 75 years of independence, Indians should examine their prospects against a global context that has been equally transformational. The world undoubtedly offers vastly more opportunities, but that is also embedded with new responsibilities. India matters because these cannot be separated, and it counts on both scores.

While size and population are obvious indices of a nation's potential, neither is a self-fulfilling criterion by itself. Our own past history is proof of that assertion. There are others, too, whose political standing has been below par despite these attributes. And, in contrast, there are much smaller nations that have punched way above their weight. The core of global rebalancing has been the revival of China, India and some others in the Global South that have made their long-standing characteristics count more through national revival. A key factor is the pace and nature of development, including the enhancement of human resource quality.

In this respect, recent happenings are a source of hope for India. There is, after 2014, a holistic commitment to achieving social development goals through dedicated campaigns covering every segment. They include better health and immunization, reducing gender gaps, expanding educational access and coverage, promoting skills to fostering talent and innovation, making it easier to do business and creating greater employment opportunities. The resulting inclusive growth will naturally contribute to strengthening capabilities and expanding the marketplace. But just as notable will be its impact on the global workplace, and this really matters for the world.

A knowledge economy like India putting such a premium on human resources makes it imperative, for itself as much as for the world, to focus on realizing SDG targets by 2030. It is clear from the national campaigns initiated after 2014 that these 17 SDG defined by the UN are indeed among the government's key objectives.

And this has continued despite the Covid challenge. Take the Jan Dhan–Aadhaar–Mobile (JAM) trinity that has empowered millions of vulnerable by providing banking and digital services. In a similar way, the expanding health coverage demonstrates that this need not just be the prerogative of the developed. The Beti Bachao Beti Padhao scheme for girls' education also has such sweeping societal implications, and so does the Jal Jeevan Mission to bring tap water to homes, the Digital India network to bring masses online and the Ujjwala programme to replace burning firewood with cooking gas. These are examples of the ability to address long-standing challenges in a lasting manner. The aggregate impact of these campaigns is improving the socio-economic welfare of a significant proportion of humanity. Why India matters is because its record of progress would determine global success in meeting the SDG Agenda 2030.

Not all readily appreciate that it is India's political choices that have enabled democratic values to achieve a near universal status. Till we took the call, these practices were widely perceived as the prerogative of developed countries only. It, of course, was enabled by the fact that democratic traditions are deeply rooted in Indian history and culture. But this aspect was not asserted even by India in earlier years, and its modern incarnation was depicted for years as an anomaly. So much so that opinions in the West were quite comfortable recommending military rule as a better governance solution for the 'less worthy'. Our own region provided the most telling examples in that regard, with Pakistan touted for years as a preferred partner. In fact, India made a difference not just by building a modern democratic polity under testing economic conditions but by drawing on its own heritage of pluralism to do so. Unlike many other societies, India never put a premium on uniformity. On the contrary, its innate unity, which was expressed through diversity, is the real basis of its culture of confabulation.

In contrast to challenges faced by others in recent years, India's credentials have only become stronger with time. Whether it is in terms of electoral participation or broadening of political representation, the effectiveness of the democratic process is only more apparent. This is no mean achievement, given the alienation caused by globalization and the disaffection fomented by disinformation. In our case, we are seeing an increased vigour of democratic activities and debates, supported by the validation of power transfers. And we can confidently state that unlike in some other places, at least our election results are not doubted! It can, in fact, truly be said that democracy is not just doing well but better than ever before.

In an argumentative society like India, political debates often take the form of polemics. A globalized existence means that they can even spill beyond our borders. But for those who see first-hand how consistently our people expand their freedoms, it is evident that India's value has grown in the eyes of the world because it is not only a political exercise at home but also a democratic assertion of a resurgent society.

When the virtues of an open society are being rediscovered, it is not enough to be a democracy. We have surely been one for 75 years in a narrow sense and, in truth, very much longer societally. It is even more important to be a democracy that delivers. It is on this score that the last decade has been so critical. A genuine passion for good governance, combined with effective application of technology tools, has started to transform the socio-economic landscape. And the world can only marvel at the scale and intensity of the transformation.

By firmly establishing a digital backbone across the country, 800 million plus Indians received food support and half of them also received money in their bank accounts during the Covid pandemic. Think about the enormity of this effort: it is like supporting the entire European and American populations at the same time. Indeed, each one of the programmes and schemes has been carried out on a magnitude that approximates the population of a major nation. The Jan Dhan initiative is like banking the US and Mexico at one go; the Saubhagya scheme is like electrifying all of Russia; Ujjwala is equivalent to changing the cooking fuel for all of Germany; and the Awas Yojana is like housing all of Japan. Examples could be cited in other areas like clean water, health coverage and farm support. The direct benefit transfers (DBTs) from India's digitalization have also ended a long tradition of leakages. The 2 billion plus vaccinations too are a feat in themselves. Perhaps the biggest lesson is how these initiatives have helped to democratize technology and empower the masses. India matters because it not only symbolizes good governance; its digital public infrastructure has a larger relevance to the world.

Developed nations may gladly recognize such progress in a polity that they have long viewed as an underperformer. It certainly opens up new avenues of collaboration. But developing countries see it as experiences that are directly applicable to them, especially when they are executed on such a large canvas.

That India has now become a laboratory, a training ground, a driver of innovation and invention as well as a field of demonstration heightens its relevance. The Covid pandemic brought out its contribution as the pharmacy of the world. Its digital skill and start-ups are generating a steady stream of technologies and services. Its impact on business outcomes is as strong as on public delivery. In fact, key global challenges like climate action are likely to be more effectively addressed if India emerges as an exemplar. Its leapfrogging potential will make a real difference when realized. Similarly, the rapid progress of Make in India in different domains can validate how much more can be made with the world and for the world. The scale, scope and competitiveness that we can bring to bear have all the markings of an additional engine of growth. India matters both as an inspiration and as a key factor in decentralized globalization.

SIGNIFICANCE OF ITS TALENT

The last few years have seen a surge in India's self-confidence. A generation that is surer of itself naturally has higher aspirations. For talent to be translated into capabilities, it is necessary to create the mechanisms, institutions and practices. Large nations, in particular, require deep strengths. If there has been a major shortcoming in India's post-1991 performance, it has been in the inadequacy of that level of capabilities. Contentment with corporate profitability overrode any commitment to create resilient domestic supply chains. That growth was insufficiently reflected in expansion of employment spoke for itself. Reform itself was conceptualized in narrow terms to serve a limited constituency.

As the nation now shifts gears to upgrade the human resources chain as well as step up manufacturing and innovation, a new range of prospects has opened up, from established domains like chemicals and textiles to contemporary ones like electronic hardware, semiconductors and pharmaceuticals. The determined effort underway to better realize its potential can make a difference. The manufacturing of Apple products in India may be just one example, but it is surely a powerful statement. India will only matter if it makes a greater contribution to global production and reliable supply chains.

The enormity of India's human potential has long been undervalued, even within the country. Let us look at what is already a reality. There are currently 32 million Indian nationals and persons of Indian origin (PIOs) living and working abroad. The US is home to about 4.5 million, many of whom are important to technology and innovation. Twice that number, approximately 9 million, resides in the Gulf and keeps their economies going. Commonwealth societies like the UK, Canada, South Africa and Australia account for another 5 million plus. It could be larger or smaller nations, nearer or distant ones, historical emigration or recent movements. Indians matter because they are truly global.

The pervasive spread of the Indian community has been a natural accompaniment of globalization. It is obvious to associate it with skills and talents in various geographies. The million plus Indian students who are studying abroad are also going to increase in number. They and their domestic counterparts are being wooed through mobility partnerships offered by the developed economies. So, as the world moves towards higher skills and tougher demographics while India itself improves the quality of its human resources, the demand–supply fit has an increasingly powerful logic. Recent agreements with Portugal, Australia,

Austria, Germany, Japan, the UK, Italy and France are harbingers of this change. India matters because with each passing year, it will become a bigger factor in the global workplace.

In such a scenario, the obligation on India to take care of its own has grown steadily. It is not only that their presence abroad is greater but that the expectations of its people are too. We often tend to see that as a reflection of stronger national capabilities, and that is not wrong. But equally, there has to be the political will to deploy resources, especially in high-risk situations. Among the significant shifts in India's diplomatic posture is the inclination to undertake operations abroad for the welfare of its citizens. These often involve use of military assets. The most recent, of course, were Operations Ajay, Kaveri and Ganga that brought back our nationals from Israel, Sudan and Ukraine respectively. Of much greater magnitude was the Vande Bharat Mission, perhaps the largest such in history, through which its citizens abroad came home during Covid. There were many others, ranging from the Yemen conflict and Nepal earthquake to the South Sudan violence and Kabul's capture.

Together, they signify not only a more frequent activity in comparison to India's own past but also when assessed against the proclivity of other states. The generous usage of funds abroad to mitigate distress situations affirms this mindset. India matters because it is not only pulling its own weight abroad more but extending a helping hand to others while doing so.

EXPANDING STRATEGIC HORIZONS

International relations understandably assign a great importance to geography. The Indian peninsula has a visible centrality to the ocean that is named after it. That this sea space is also a particularly active arena of maritime projection makes it even more significant. There is a continental dimension to India's presence as well. Without its active participation, no trans-Asia connectivity initiative can really take off. After all, it provides the contiguous link between Southeast Asia and the Gulf. Location confers a centrality to India, quite apart from the potential global power that has risen just before it. Management of their overlapping peripheries becomes an onerous responsibility. That many of India's other immediate neighbours also share people-to-people and cultural ties adds to the complexity that policy has to address on a sustained basis. How well India leverages its geography is a considerable part of its relevance to the world. To the extent that it is able to influence the Indian Ocean and participate in the Indo-Pacific, its global stock will rise commensurately. And if its prosperity and progress serve as a lifting tide for the larger subcontinent, then this would be even more consequential.

History may be a mixed blessing for most states, but making the best of it is nevertheless still a policy compulsion. In India's case, Partition not only reduced its stature but also cut it off from proximate regions where it had long enjoyed respect and influence. In recent years, reclaiming its strategic legacy has been a major endeavour. The graduation from Look East into an Act East policy highlighted the seriousness of connectivity and security interests in Southeast Asia. It was also the first step towards defining an extended neighbourhood.

In the last eight years, a parallel effort was made in the Gulf to rebuild other long-standing associations that have been disrupted. After decades of limiting those ties to energy and emigration, India is working at creating full spectrum relationships. Stronger economic linkages are being buttressed by closer security coordination. The IMEC could be a harbinger of a new era.

A third initiative is currently underway and has its own basis, this time aimed at Central Asia. Here, overcoming the impediment of connectivity is central to dealing with a region with such visible cultural affinity. Of course, with regard to the sea space to its south, the 2015 SAGAR doctrine initiated a reach-out to islands whose future is so closely intertwined with India. Returning to history and recognizing our extended neighbourhoods is another reason why India matters.

Political constraints can not only limit the pursuit of national interest but also shrink strategic horizons. To a considerable extent,

that had happened in the case of India. As we strive to go beyond
the previous framework, it is only natural that the cultural legacies
should start to regain salience. The most obvious of these are in
respect of Southeast Asia, where centuries of exchanges produced
a rich shared heritage. These are visible even today in significant
monuments and living arts. Consequently, a new archaeological
find in My Son or a conservation project in Angkor Wat, Ta Prohm
and Bagan affirms the understandable desire to build further on
the past. Towards the East, the extent of the Indian cultural reach
goes all the way to South Korea. It is but natural that the cultural
revival of Ayodhya should strike a strong chord in that society.

Turning to the West, the expressions of our common history
may be a little different but no less a part of societal mores. An
energetic culture of trade picks up on old comfort to build new
links very quickly. There is an equally intuitive appreciation of
the cultural practices of its partners as well. The construction of a
temple in Abu Dhabi is symbolic of its time-honoured relationship
with Indian society.

The connection in the north to the Eurasian landmass
is similarly significant. The spread of Buddhism through the
continent carried its own intellectual, spiritual and aesthetic
messages. This legacy endures and the endeavour is really to ensure
it flowers again. Dedicated efforts have been made in that direction
in the last few years, once Indian policy broadened to appreciate its
necessity.

The sensitivity to nurturing India's cultural footprint over the
ages is now visible in focussed efforts to promote cooperation in
heritage conservation. It is not just the rising metrics of power
that count; it is also the accompanying cultural and intellectual
resurrection that is key to global rebalancing. India matters on that
account due to its unique contributions.

THE WORLD AS A FAMILY

If from the recesses of history there have emerged factors that
enhance India's relevance, this could be the case for more

contemporary periods as well. Here, too, the impediments were only in our own minds, conditioned by the politics of the day. Take the events of the last century. Indian contribution to both World Wars was significant, to a point of deciding the outcome in some theatres. Over a million Indians participated in the first one, serving in Europe, the Mediterranean, West Asia and Africa. The bicycle troops in Somme and the turbaned ones entering through the Jaffa Gate in Jerusalem are among the iconic images of that era. But it is only in recent years that the valour and sacrifice of these soldiers has entered public consciousness. Unburdened by agendas, PM Modi set the record straight and honoured them at memorials like Neuve Chapelle and Haifa. Our public naturally then began to take notice. Initiatives are now underway to create historical trails of the campaigns of our servicemen abroad.

This applies in equal measure to the Second World War, when as many as two-and-a-half million Indians took up arms. In this case, the contribution was notable on both sides, with the Netaji-led Indian National Army firing up the cause of freedom. It also extended to major logistical efforts. Countries like China and Russia were kept supplied through the Himalayan hump and the Persian corridor respectively. When an Indian military contingent marched through the Red Square in Moscow in June 2020, this was a reminder of India's contribution to the eventual victory. The stabilizing role that the Indian armed forces played from East and Southeast Asia to West Asia and Europe in the aftermath of the Second World War is no less notable.

It is this tradition of global service that became the foundation for the country to emerge as a leader in UN Peacekeeping Operations. From that, India has now evolved into an effective first responder in regional crisis situations. India matters because it can make a real difference to global needs.

In recent times, India has heightened its international profile and displayed greater diplomatic energies. Regions and nations that were long neglected at the leadership level have been intensively engaged. Countries in the Gulf like the UAE got a prime ministerial visit after a gap of three decades and Bahrain the first ever in 2019. Similarly, Central Asian states like Turkmenistan and Kyrgyzstan waited for two decades and a key partner like Australia even longer, for 28 years! Even neighbours Sri Lanka and Nepal hosted an Indian PM bilaterally after long breaks. These endeavours have been supported by more systemic linkages across multiple domains. On important issues at global gatherings, India's voice has been stronger and effective.

But at the end of the day, much depends on the overall posture adopted by us. When our national security is at risk, it is essential to stake out positions and back our bets. If we were serious that there is no longer tolerance for terrorism, then an Uri or a Balakot had to happen. If our northern borders are threatened by China, then Covid or no Covid, the Indian armed forces will be counter-deployed. Even otherwise, a rising India must continuously push the envelope to expand its space. The pursuit of national interest is respected the world over, even by competitors. Doing what it takes is even more critical when it comes to core interests. This may apply to the safeguarding of its territorial integrity and sovereignty, combating terrorism, pursuing its economic interests and, indeed, in responding to global challenges.

Participation in the Quad is a recent example that has certainly enhanced India's standing in the world. Similarly, its stance on the Ukraine conflict resonates strongly with much of the Global South. We speak for them on energy security, food inflation and trade disruptions. India matters when it displays confidence, independence and determination.

Owing to its very uniqueness, India is not an easily replicable model. But it does offer experiences for others who are facing similar challenges. Indeed, the more it rises, the greater is the value of its achievements. The world recognizes both the singularity and the relevance of India's progress. Put aside those who harbour political prejudices; the rest get it that a civilizational state rising again will display its own personality. It will speak and think for itself, radiating how it is rooted in its own culture. The more assured India is, the more expressive it will be. Only then can it overcome the image of being a poor cousin mired in its colonial history.

In this endeavour, India is uniquely positioned to bridge modernity and tradition. It will be more impactful by embracing its heritage, not by diminishing it. A combination of cultural beliefs and modernizing agenda helps address many current dilemmas. Its historical characteristics are a source of strength once they are approached with confidence. For example, the appreciation of pluralism is as much a derivative of long-standing social practices as of a constitutional mandate. Similarly, stronger nationalism at home coexists traditionally with enthusiastic internationalism abroad. Rising India wants to engage the world more, not less. India matters when it is more authentically India.

Given its growing political stature and economic abilities, India has to credibly address the expectations that the world has of it. And this has to begin in its immediate neighbourhood. Those who are physically and historically close to it will naturally turn to India, especially during moments of difficulties. These could be natural disasters or man-made situations, political and economic. The challenges arise, however, when expectations of India are selectively articulated. Neighbours would naturally like it to modulate its presence as per their convenience.

From the Indian perspective, it is not always easy to get the balance right. Doing too much looks intrusive; showing reticence can be taken as indifference, if not weakness. Or losing out to a competitive power. The politics of every partner is a significant variable and context often drives calculations.

The optimal Indian strategy is, therefore, to rise above the day-to-day developments and create structural linkages. For this to happen, a combination of non-reciprocal, generous and patient policies have to come together. They must connect societies at a fundamental level, facilitating infrastructure development, socio-economic initiatives and political comfort. Those ingredients of connectivity, commerce and contacts are the core of India's Neighbourhood First approach. It was equally evident in the manner in which India stepped forward to support Sri Lanka during its economic crisis. In the final analysis, regionalism can only be built if key players are prepared to go the extra mile. And

India matters because it alone has that ability in the Subcontinent.

As India's profile rises, its policymakers are also discovering that expectations of other nations are not confined to our immediate vicinity. Ever since its independence triggered global decolonization, India has carried the responsibility of speaking for a larger constituency. The Global South watches its positions and performance carefully, drawing conclusions from both. In the early days, these were centred on consolidating independence and rebuilding the economy. With the passage of time, more issues of greater complexity have come to occupy the agenda.

The Covid pandemic was the most recent of these, highlighting the challenges of accessibility and affordability of vaccines. Climate action has been a more long-standing concern, with the consistent evasion of financial commitments by the developed countries. The non-tariff barriers on trade and the various forms of protectionism using non-trade considerations are an even longer struggle. Obviously, on many of these issues, India has its own interests at play. But, as it demonstrated through the Vaccine Maitri initiative, it was willing to assist others even in the midst of its own challenges. It was this timing that much of the world recognized as a statement of solidarity. Rebuilding the world order after two centuries of colonialism will not be easy. But India matters because a large part of the Global South believes that it is there for them.

In the last decade, a long tradition of South–South cooperation has developed into something deeper. It captures domains where Indian capabilities have a direct relevance for the aspirations of Africa, Latin America and even the rest of Asia. Some of that has taken the form of development projects in energy, digital, manufacturing, education and connectivity. That has been supported by exchanges of experiences and best practices, including training. It is not just the immediate benefits of these endeavours that matter. They help create more options for the Global South, giving them the leverage to deal with the rest of the world on stronger terms.

On assuming the G20 presidency, the effort at ascertaining the views of 125 nations through the Voice of the Global South

Summit was also an initiative that spoke volumes of our mindset. Admittedly, India has an emotional connect with these nations. Whether it is the rise of Africa or the sustainable growth of least developed countries (LDCs), the resulting rebalancing is very much to India's strategic advantage.

In that context, especially since 2014, India has taken active steps to empower the Global South. Lines of credit and grant assistance have been vehicles to execute socio-economic projects of varying levels of magnitude. These range from power plants, dams and transmission lines to public buildings, housing projects, rail and road links, agricultural processing and IT centres. While many have been undertaken at a national scale, hundreds of smaller initiatives at the community level have had an equally effective impact. The creation of assets and facilities has also been supported by extensive training and imparting of best practices.

What differentiates India's endeavours is a conscious policy of responding to the priorities and needs of the partner country involved. Prime Minister Modi's articulation of the Kampala Principles of development partnership in 2018 really set our country apart. Unlike cases where such initiatives have been driven by extractive objectives, India's efforts are aimed more at ensuring self-reliance; and the partners appreciate it. India matters to the Global South because there are few others who have taken such an approach.

India also matters by displaying its own distinctive characteristics. As its capabilities and influence grow, its representatives are often asked in other parts of the world why it would not emulate the behavioural pattern of those who have risen before it. Obviously, such queries emanate from people who are unfamiliar with India's DNA.

It is essential, therefore, that India differentiates itself by highlighting its own national qualities, beliefs and traditions. The most basic of them is its inherent pluralism, one that allows its unity to be expressed in diversity. Flowing from that is its democratic ethos. This is not just a trait to be practised at home but equally one visible in consultations abroad. Adherence to laws and rules is another important point to emphasize with an international audience. As a corollary, we are not a polity given to pursuing coercive approaches or seeking one-sided gains. Indeed, the sum total of India's engagement with the global community over multiple decades, if not more, is of treating the world as a family. Nowhere is that more visible than in periods of stress, such as the tribulations of recent years.

NEW INDIA AND THE GLOBAL AGENDA

How, then, is India faring on the world stage? The world is not what it was even a few years ago. That process of rebalancing was perhaps inevitable, even though its pace and quality were outcomes of political choices. The contribution that India has made to this rebalancing has not been small. At a symbolic level, it is recognized in the establishment of the G20 as a premier global grouping. This superseded a purely Western combination of G7 that lost its primacy after the 2008 global financial crisis. But the change of power distribution has many facets and expressions. It may be visible in economic activities, trade and investment figures, technological capabilities and market shares. But it is also evident in the debates of the day, such as on climate change, terrorism, black money and taxation as well as the pandemic.

India has emerged as a more influential voice in these conversations, as it has done on the consequences of the Ukraine conflict. And then there is the question of shouldering responsibilities, including beyond its shores. The record of addressing humanitarian and disaster situations since 2014 has clearly established India's reputation as a first responder in the Indian Ocean and its littorals, and with Türkiye, even beyond. The ambit of India's activities has also increased, towards the Indo-Pacific in the East and to the Gulf and Africa in the West. What India is saying, doing and shaping is a powerful reason why it matters.

This image has been sharpened by the independence of thought and action that India has displayed during the course of its ongoing rise. Maximizing freedom of choice has historically been an Indian approach. At times, it is done by keeping a distance; sometimes, perhaps better by voicing opinions. But, on occasion, it is also served by working with others on specific issues and designated theatres. After all, why should we not take advantage of convergences with other powers to advance our objectives?

Given that India has such a broad range of interests, it can only bridge contradictions through a multi-vector approach. In other words, the nature of the partners will depend on the nature of the problem. Others will try and restrict that freedom, seeking to impose a veto on our choices. We saw that in respect of Quad. India should never succumb to such pressures or hedge for the sake of hedging. The compass of national interest will guide us unerringly if we do not get distracted by ideological reservations or hidden agendas. The cultivation of such flexibility is all the more important because India will come to acquire a more leading position in the coming decades. And bear in mind that this is not happening in isolation. Other powers, especially those of a middle plus capability and a regional dominance, also have similar aspirations. The multiplicity of power centres is an increasingly visible characteristic of our times. India matters because it is central to the emergence of multipolarity, whether in Asia or in the world.

We are also once again in times when the importance of norms and behaviour has assumed greater significance. There are few nations who would not assert their commitment to international law or respect for agreements and regimes to which they are party. But actual observance can be quite another matter. The example that has captured attention in recent times pertains to the UNCLOS 1982 and its application in the South China Sea. India took a principled approach to this matter by underlining that it supported freedom of navigation and overflight as well as unimpeded commerce, based on principles of international law as reflected in the UNCLOS. It also urged all parties to show utmost respect for the UNCLOS, which establishes the international legal order of the seas and oceans. More importantly, India led by the power of example when it accepted an arbitration verdict on its own maritime boundary dispute with Bangladesh.

Another debate that has also featured in contemporary consciousness relates to the relevance of connectivity to world politics. Here, too, India has been among the earliest to enunciate an objective and fair position. In essence, it declared that connectivity initiatives must be based on recognized international norms, good governance, rule of law, openness, transparency and equality. They must be financially responsible, avoid creating an unsustainable debt burden, balance ecological and environmental protection, transparently assess costs and have a local ownership. Connectivity projects must be pursued in a manner that respects sovereignty and territorial integrity.

While respect for international law is essential to any global order, it is also evident that following its letter but not spirit has had damaging consequences. When systems are gamed and the underlying principles skirted through semantics, clearly the world emerges the worse for it. It is no accident that in the light of recent experiences, there is a global interest in a rules-based order. This is not to be treated as a derogation of law but as going beyond it to promote norms. India matters as an advocate of a rules-based order.

Once we agree that India does matter, the issue that naturally follows is what it takes to ensure it matters more. That naturally is the focus of its national security strategy and foreign policy. The answer in such cases often begins at home. A nation that sets its house in order clearly counts for more in the global discourse. Some of that pertains to the quality of governance, some to the development of capabilities. Any progress in addressing long-standing vulnerabilities, such as in Jammu & Kashmir, is naturally welcome.

Where its periphery is concerned, stronger structural linkages expand the space for India's activities. A more integrated region offers the benefit to all but not least to the largest player. This can be best realized through highlighting the attraction of cooperation as well as the costs of alienation. The extended neighbourhoods that represent the next circle also need sustained attention. It is only if they are treated with the priority of immediate neighbours that India can widen its reach. That they are not so proximate also means a more bespoke policy. With the rest of the world, working with all the major powers gives India the most advantage.

But India's own growing footprint is also being driven by demands of engagement from the world. Given its institutional limitations, an efficient method of engagement is to develop more group interfaces. We see that happening as India interacts collectively with ASEAN, the EU, Eurasia, Africa, the Gulf, Pacific Islands, the Caribbean and the Nordic states. These are being increasingly supplemented by plurilateral groupings like the Quad, the I2U2 and BRICS. The bottom line is that India has, at last, broken out of the box that its competitors helped devise. A 360-degree engagement is one more reason why India matters.

For a country that has the history, scale and ambition of India, the games that nations play have to be developed to a higher level. Understanding and exploiting global dynamics is a critical aspect of that exercise. And this is exceptionally challenging because the world is in the midst of a fundamental transition. The reality of an unfolding multipolarity is tempered by the frictions of a more bipolar overlay. On many questions, the narrative can also be shaped by a larger set of players of varying sizes. As a consequence, India has to simultaneously pursue a range of approaches, some of which may appear contradictory on surface.

As a foundational goal, it must strive to promote greater multipolarity and stronger rebalancing. That will happen faster if it has many well-wishers who perceive India's rise as being in their strategic interest. Harnessing the calculations of others is clearly a useful tactic but one to be practised with both prudence and self-confidence. The obverse is no less important, and standing up to intimidation and pressures is part of our maturing. Not least, there has to be a reasonable expectation that a rising power will be tested. The quality of leadership and the ability to perform better on the ground is certainly helping to set India apart.

That India matters and will matter more with the passage of time can be convincingly asserted. Like so many other developments in politics and history, it must never be taken as preordained. There will always be doubters among us who cannot believe that our nation can even dare to think big. There are vested interests, too, that will masquerade as political correctness and global consensus. We have seen for too long attempts to distance us from our history, traditions and culture. At the end of the day, much will ride on our national unity and collective purpose. Being a serious global player requires ambition and strategy to be backed by initiative, perseverance and energy. Our own people and leadership must embrace their destiny to realize their aspirations. Keeping the faith and getting down to work are good ways to demonstrate it.

Why India matters should also be approached from the perspective of to whom it matters. As a larger factor in international affairs, it clearly features more prominently in the calculations of the rest of the world. At a time of global transition, this is particularly relevant to the larger states that are seeking to shape that process. Obviously, a rising India would also matter more to its competitors. Those who took India's limitations and shortcomings as a given will surely now reassess its progress and prospects. For India's neighbours, the benefits and comfort of being proximate to a generous and non-reciprocal polity are becoming increasingly apparent. For the rest of the Global South, a more powerful India is, if anything, even better.

Overall, the international community today engages India with greater enthusiasm and expectations. That is something that Indians should assess by themselves and from which they must draw conclusions. There will always be the polemicists and critics, but even for them, an India that will not bend to ideological bullying and be deflected from its course is one that they will have to take more seriously.

How does India look to the world today? It is among the few large economies with a robust recovery underway. We are fifth in the world, likely to be third by the end of the decade. It is a polity that, over the last decade, has shown the will to take tough decisions and embark on serious reforms. We are making big strides on human-centric development, digital public goods and green growth. India has stayed strong during the Covid storm and even gone out to help others. When its national security has been challenged, it has stood its ground firmly. Breaking from the past, it is showing zero-tolerance for terrorism. It is an India that knows how to take care of its people abroad as well. This New India shapes the global agenda and influences its outcomes. Now, it is perceived as the consensus-builder and voice of reason in a polarized world. At the same time, as the Voice of the Global South Summit demonstrated, others trust us to put forward their case. This is an India of ideas and initiatives, one that articulates the creativity and innovation of our youth.

A civilizational state is once again regaining its place in the comity of nations. It is doing so in a unique way, encouraging partnerships through its responsibilities, contributions and accomplishments. The world knows that this rise will unfold in consonance with its traditions and ethos. Obviously, its democratic values, pluralistic society and economic outlook will resonate more strongly. But they would be underpinned by deep-rooted beliefs and vast experience from a complex past and present. It is no coincidence that as policymaking is driven by those more grounded, long-standing challenges are addressed effectively. They may range from leaving no one behind to democratizing technology and promoting sustainability. Achievements, be they in space, health, start-ups or sports have instilled a new sense of pride, especially among the younger generation. And that is buttressed by a sharper awareness of heritage and the value we add to global progress.

It may be a society on the move but clearly one with a long view of its own prospects and that of the world. And it stands ready to set contemporary terms of engagement with others. Its outlook is deeply international and built around an age-old conviction of the world as one family. With each passing day, it is becoming clearer that India matters because it is Bharat.

✳

ACKNOWLEDGEMENTS

There are many who have contributed to this writing, be they individuals, organizations or platforms. My particular gratitude goes to those colleagues and friends who have helped me frame my thoughts on a complex set of issues and then to express them in words. My family should be appreciated for putting up with all that comes with the process of writing a book. My publisher, Rupa Publications, has been exceptionally patient in awaiting this effort, and that too deserves to be recognized.

INDEX